Mongolia

WORLD BIBLIOGRAPHICAL SERIES
General Editors:
Robert G. Neville (Executive Editor)
John J. Horton

Robert A. Myers   Ian Wallace
Hans H. Wellisch   Ralph Lee Woodward, Jr.

John J. Horton is Deputy Librarian of the University of Bradford and currently Chairman of its Academic Board of Studies in Social Sciences. He has maintained a longstanding interest in the discipline of area studies and its associated bibliographical problems, with special reference to European Studies. In particular he has published in the field of Icelandic and of Yugoslav studies, including the two relevant volumes in the World Bibliographical Series.

Robert A. Myers is Associate Professor of Anthropology in the Division of Social Sciences and Director of Study Abroad Programs at Alfred University, Alfred, New York. He has studied post-colonial island nations of the Caribbean and has spent two years in Nigeria on a Fulbright Lectureship. His interests include international public health, historical anthropology and developing societies. In addition to *Amerindians of the Lesser Antilles: a bibliography* (1981), *A Resource Guide to Dominica, 1493-1986* (1987) and numerous articles, he has compiled the World Bibliographical Series volumes on *Dominica* (1987), *Nigeria* (1989) and *Ghana* (1991).

Ian Wallace is Professor of German at the University of Bath. A graduate of Oxford in French and German, he also studied in Tübingen, Heidelberg and Lausanne before taking teaching posts at universities in the USA, Scotland and England. He specializes in contemporary German affairs, especially literature and culture, on which he has published numerous articles and books. In 1979 he founded the journal *GDR Monitor*, which he continues to edit under its new title *German Monitor*.

Hans H. Wellisch is Professor emeritus at the College of Library and Information Services, University of Maryland. He was President of the American Society of Indexers and was a member of the International Federation for Documentation. He is the author of numerous articles and several books on indexing and abstracting, and has published *The Conversion of Scripts, Indexing and Abstracting: an International Bibliography* and *Indexing from A to Z*. He also contributes frequently to *Journal of the American Society for Information Science, The Indexer* and other professional journals.

Ralph Lee Woodward, Jr. is Director of Graduate Studies at Tulane University, New Orleans, where he has been Professor of History since 1970. He is the author of *Central America, a Nation Divided*, 2nd ed. (1985), as well as several monographs and more than sixty scholarly articles on modern Latin America. He has also compiled volumes in the World Bibliographical Series on *Belize* (1980), *Nicaragua* (1983), and *El Salvador* (1988). Dr. Woodward edited the Central American section of the *Research Guide to Central America and the Caribbean* (1985) and is currently editor of the Central American history section of the *Handbook of Latin American Studies*.

VOLUME 156

Mongolia

Judith Nordby

Compiler

CLIO PRESS

OXFORD, ENGLAND · SANTA BARBARA, CALIFORNIA
DENVER, COLORADO

British Library Cataloguing in Publication Data

Mongolia. – (World bibliographical series; v.156)
I. Nordby, Judith
II. Series
016.9438

ISBN 1–85109–129–7

Clio Press Ltd.,
55 St. Thomas' Street,
Oxford OX1 1JG, England.

ABC-CLIO,
130 Cremona Drive,
Santa Barbara,
CA 93116, USA.

Designed by Bernard Crossland.
Typeset by Columns Design and Production Services Ltd, Reading, England.
Printed and bound in Great Britain by
Bookcraft (Bath) Ltd., Midsomer Norton

THE WORLD BIBLIOGRAPHICAL SERIES

This series, which is principally designed for the English speaker, will eventually cover every country (and many of the world's principal regions), each in a separate volume comprising annotated entries on works dealing with its history, geography, economy and politics; and with its people, their culture, customs, religion and social organization. Attention will also be paid to current living conditions – housing, education, newspapers, clothing, etc.– that are all too often ignored in standard bibliographies; and to those particular aspects relevant to individual countries. Each volume seeks to achieve, by use of careful selectivity and critical assessment of the literature, an expression of the country and an appreciation of its nature and national aspirations, to guide the reader towards an understanding of its importance. The keynote of the series is to provide, in a uniform format, an interpretation of each country that will express its culture, its place in the world, and the qualities and background that make it unique. The views expressed in individual volumes, however, are not necessarily those of the publisher.

VOLUMES IN THE SERIES

For
Margaret, my mother
Who believes in education.

Contents

Contents

Introduction

Mongolia is an independent nation state in northeast Asia. It occupies an area of 1525,000 sq km between latitudes 41° 25' and 52° 09' and longitudes 87° 44' and 119° 56'. It shares a border 3,485 km long with the Russian Federation and 4,673 km long with China. The average elevation of the country is 1,580 m and the highest point is 4,374 m in the Altai mountains in the southwest. Two lower ranges, the Khangai and the Khentii, cross the middle of the country and to the south of these is a broad belt of steppe grassland. The land declines to the east and south east and the grasslands merge with the semi-deserts of the Gobi. The rivers Selenge and Onon flow north and the Kherlen flows east. They are the headwaters of three major Central Asian river basins. In the northeast of Mongolia there are many fresh and saltwater lakes. The largest, Lake Khövsgöl, is navigable as is the Selenge river and the lower reaches of its tributory the Orkhon river.

The climate of Mongolia is continental. Average winter temperatures vary from −15 to −25 degrees C and average summer temperatures from 12 to 20 degrees C. However it can fall as low as −50 degrees C and reach 41 degrees C. There is an average of 250 sunny days each year and precipitation is low. Most of this falls as rain in July and August in the northern half of the country.

About nine per cent of Mongolia is covered with forests of birch, pine, cedar and larch. These are the haunts of many fur-bearing animals such as sable, beaver, marten and squirrel as well as various kinds of deer. Five kinds of domestic animals, cattle, horses, camels, sheep and goats, are herded traditionally in Mongolia and they share the grasslands with many other wild mammals. Camels, goats and yaks are bred in the Gobi, which is also home to rare wild species of sheep, camel and goat besides other rare animals such as the Gobi bear and the wild ass. The snow leopard is found in the Altai mountains. Many of the country's rare species are now protected in thirteen preserves and recently a number of wild horses, the

Przewalski's horse, which were bred in captivity in western zoos, have been released into the wild. Organized hunting of many wild animals for their fur and for tourism is permitted however.

Mongolia is also rich in geological resources. Coal is mined in many parts of the country to supply the power generating industry. Copper and molybdenum are semi-processed for export and deposits of gold and silver are also mined. Many more minerals lie waiting to be exploited beneath the soil and could benefit the economy greatly in the future. For a brief period in the early 1960s, oil was extracted at Züün Bayan in the Gobi but it was deemed less expensive to import the country's needs and the installations were closed down. In the 1990s, that decision is being reconsidered and surveys of the country's oil reserves have been undertaken recently.

The human population of Mongolia numbered approximately 2.2 million in 1992. Seventy per cent are Khalkh Mongols and other Mongols such as Buryats and Oirats account for twenty-four per cent. The remaining six per cent are Turkic-speaking peoples of whom the largest group comprises the Kazakhs who live in the west of the country. In the 1990s, however, many families of Kazakhs moved from Mongolia to Kazakhstan at the invitation of the President of Kazakhstan. The population of Mongolia in 1924 was 650,000 and there was no marked increase until the 1960s when improved lifestyle, health care and official population policies caused a rapid rise. By the 1980s seventy per cent of the population was below the age of thirty-five. Today, about half of the Mongolian population lives the semi-nomadic lifestyle of herdsmen. Of the remainder, approximately 500,000 live in the capital, Ulaanbaatar, and Darkhan and Erdenet, built in the 1960s and the 1970s, respectively, also have city status.

The present state of Mongolia dates from 1911 when Khalkh Mongols living in this region broke free of the control of the Manchu (Qing) dynasty of China and established a theocratic monarchy. The territory has, however, been the home of Mongol peoples for at least a thousand years. It was the heartland of the Mongol Empire which was founded by Chinggis Khan and lasted from 1206 to 1368. After the fall of the Empire, the united Mongol peoples split into a number of separate groups under the rule of princes who claimed descent from Chinggis Khan. By the 16th century Mongolia was the pastureland of the Khalkh Mongols while other Mongol groups occupied the lands to the east, south and west. In 1691 the Khalkh princes submitted to the Manchu rulers of China and their land remained under foreign control for 220 years.

During this period the territory was called Khalkh by the Mongols. To the Manchu government, the Chinese and the outside world it was

Outer Mongolia. To the south of the Gobi desert and east of the
Xingan mountains lay Inner Mongolia, the territory of the Chakhar,
Ordos, Tümed, Kharchin, Khorchin and several other Mongol
groups. These people had already been subjects of the Manchu
Empire for fifty years when the Khalkh submitted. The Manchu
government maintained Khalkh and Inner Mongolia as two separate
administrative regions and this is the origin of the modern division of
the Mongol nation between independent Mongolia and the Inner
Mongolian Autonomous Region (IMAR) which is a part of the
People's Republic of China.

In 1924 free Mongolia was declared a republic and called the
Mongolian People's Republic. This was the official name of the
country until February 1992 when the fourth constitution was ratified
and the name changed to Mongolia. This name has, however, been
used in the English-speaking world for many years both to refer to
the independent state and also to identify cultural Mongolia, that is
any of the territories where Mongols live. Today an estimated four
million Mongols live in China in the IMAR, the provinces of Gansu,
Ningxia, Heilongjiang and Xinjiang Autonomous Region. There are
Buryat Mongols in Siberia around Lake Baikal (Buryatia) and
Kalmyks (Oirat Mongols) on the banks of the Volga in Russia.
Tannu Tuva in Siberia, which was formerly Uriankhai and under the
jurisdiction of the Manchu government, may also be included in
cultural Mongolia although much of its indigenous population is
Turkic-speaking. In this bibliography, however, the name 'Mongolia'
will be restricted to the territory of the modern independent state.
Nevertheless, wherever they live, Mongols do share a common
heritage of history, traditions, religion (shamanism or Buddhism),
lifestyle and language. The language of the Khalkh Mongols is very
close to that spoken in Inner Mongolia. The dialects of the Buryats,
the Oirat Mongols of western Mongolia and Xinjiang and the Daur
Mongols of Heilongjiang Province are more distinct but not
incomprehensible to other Mongols.

When the Mongols first appeared in history they were a nomadic
people who lived in felt tents (ger) and tended their flocks and herds
in Mongolia alongside groups of Turkic-speaking peoples with similar
customs and a similar way of life. Temüjin, (ca. 1167-1227) the young
leader of one group of Mongols, challenged the contemporary power
structures in the region and by 1206 he had united all the 'people who
dwelt in felt tents' under his rule. He was granted the title 'Chinggis
Khan' in 1206 and he and his successors proceeded to extend the
Mongol Empire by military means until it stretched from Korea in the
east to the River Danube in the west. In the late 13th century,
however, the western parts of the Empire began to fall away as

independent khanates and the centre of power shifted from Mongolia to China. The ruling clan was installed in Khanbalic (Beijing) from whence it controlled China as the Yuan dynasty from 1271-1368. In 1368 Chinese Ming forces drove the Great Khan Togon Temür from Beijing and he fled with his court and part of the Mongol army into Mongolia.

For the next three hundred years the Mongols were a fragmented people ruled by petty princes who claimed descent from Chinggis Khan and fought one another for supremacy over the nation. The princes dreamed of reconquering China and restoring the empire to its former glory but the internal and external pressures towards disunity were strong. Other forces were in the ascendent in East Asia, first Ming China and then the Oirat Mongols of the Altai and modern Xinjiang. In the 17th century the Manchus, a Tungus-speaking people, swept down on China from the forest lands to the east of the Xingan mountains. By 1636 the Mongols living in modern Inner Mongolia were either dependent allies or conquered peoples of the Manchus. The Khalkh remained independent until 1691 and most of the Oirats were brought to submission by the middle of the 18th century. Only the Buryats of Siberia and the Kalmyks, an Oirat group who had settled on the banks of the Volga in Russia, were not subjects of the Manchu Empire.

The Mongols were allowed considerable autonomy under the Manchu government and their lifestyle and traditions were protected. Mongol princes continued to rule the people on behalf of the Emperor and under Manchu patronage, monastic Buddhism grew into a rich and powerful force, a society within Mongolian secular society. The Chinese were forbidden by law from settling in Mongol lands and intermarrying with the Mongols. The main concern of the imperial government's Mongolian policy was to prevent the Mongols from uniting and threatening the Manchu state. The loyalty of the Mongol princes was channelled towards the emperor and away from each other. Also nomadic migrations were restricted and the Mongol populations were organized in a system of banners or military districts. In this way the territories where each prince and his subjects might graze their animals was fixed and unauthorized movement outside them was forbidden.

By the late 19th century, however, East Asia was profoundly affected by contact with the nations of the West and this stimulated the growth of nationalism in Asia. In China the Qing dynasty was in decline and both the Chinese and the Mongol economies were deteriorating. Chinese farmers began to colonize Inner Mongolia and the Mongol herdsmen were pushed onto poorer pastureland on the edge of the Gobi. At the turn of the century the imperial government attempted to introduce a range of administrative, economic and social reforms in China and Inner Mongolia to modernize the state and strengthen it against the West. Mongols in all parts of the empire were fearful that their lifestyle, religion and whole identity would be submerged in the dominant culture of the Han Chinese. When the central government ordered that the reforms be implemented in Khalkh also, in 1911 the Khalkh princes and senior religious leaders declared an independent state of the Mongols of Khalkh, Inner Mongolia and other parts of the Manchu Empire.

A 'living Buddha', the Eighth Javzandamba Khutagt, was installed as Bogd Khan or 'Holy Emperor' of this state but in fact his government only had control over Khalkh and the region in the west around the town of Khovd. Tsarist Russia supported independence in Khalkh to a limited degree but was not prepared to give military or diplomatic assistance for establishing a Panmongolian state. In 1915 the Mongolian government was compelled to sign a treaty with China and Russia which stated that Mongolia was an autonomous area under Chinese suzerainty. The notion of a 'Greater Mongolia' was to remain a dream because it conflicted with Russian and Chinese interests. Nevertheless, Russia was assigned the role of ensuring that Mongolian autonomy was protected.

These were, however, chaotic times. Much of the world was at war from 1914-18; in 1917 revolution broke out in Russia followed by a bitter civil war; in China numerous warlords struggled for power. In 1919 the Bogd Khan's rule, which had alienated the Mongol princes, collapsed, the Chinese re-entered the country and the 1915 treaty ceased to have any effect. In 1920, White Russian armies seeking a base from which to attack the Bolsheviks in Siberia also occupied Mongolia. A new, younger group of Khalkh Mongols, who were neither princes nor high lamas and who wished for social reform as well as national independence, formed a political party and staged a second, successful revolution in 1921 with military aid from the Soviet Union. The Bogd Khan was restored as head of state until his death in 1924 but real power was in the hands of the Mongolian People's Party. This Party was renamed the Mongolian People's Revolutionary Party (MPRP) in 1925 and it had the strong backing of the Third Communist International (Comintern) and the Bolshevik government in Moscow.

From 1921 to 1990 Mongolia was a single-party state. Until the end of the Second World War it was recognized by no-one but the Soviet Union. It had little option but to adopt Soviet policies as models for change and development in a country whose conditions and traditions were markedly different from those of the Soviet Union. Although Soviet advice and orders were plentiful, material aid was limited and the Mongolian economy, lifestyle, education and culture changed very slowly during the first three decades of MPRP rule.

There was, however, considerable change in the system of government and the structure of society. In 1924 Mongolia's first constitution was ratified and the rule of princes was replaced by elected assemblies of herdsmen though dominated by members of the MPRP. Against the regime's most powerful opponent, the Buddhist church, the Party moved more cautiously in the 1920s. In 1928, however, under pressure of the Comintern there was a sharp swing to the left. The property of former princes and the monasteries were confiscated and herdsmens' collectives were formed. In 1932 a large-scale rebellion broke out and was only put down by military force. On Stalin's orders, the collectives were disbanded, some of the confiscated herds were returned to their former owners, and the harsh regime was softened for a brief period.

By this time, however, the Japanese had overrun Manchuria and their presence was seen as a threat to the security of the Soviet state in East Asia. On a pretext that the Mongolian Buddhist church was collaborating with the Japanese and stirring up counter-revolution, Stalin ordered that the Mongolian monasteries be closed and destroyed. This was carried out by Kh. Choibalsan, one-time hero of the 1921 revolution. From 1936 to 1939, an estimated 100,000 people were executed, imprisoned, sent to the Soviet Union or simply disappeared in one of the most violent periods in the recent history of Mongolia. At the same time, many Soviet troops moved into the country to repell the Japanese threat. The attack came in 1939 when fighting broke out at the Khalkh river on Mongolia's eastern border. Soviet and Mongolian forces defeated the Japanese and the Mongols showed their gratitude to the Soviet Union by providing very large amounts of material aid during the Second World War.

The domination of Mongolia by the Soviet Union in the 1930s and continuing into the 1940s is hardly surprising given the country's size and strategic location, its small population and political isolation. It has been taken for granted in the west that Mongolia had, by this time, become a satellite, a sixteenth republic of the Soviet Union in all but name. Yet it was not subject to Russian colonization and there was no overall Soviet takeover such as befell Mongolia's neighbour, Tannu Tuva in 1944. Mongols today condemn the brutality of Choibalsan's rule but many believe, nevertheless, that he deserves some credit for keeping Mongolia free, the only independent state in Central Asia, in fact, until the break-up of the USSR in the 1990s. As a result of Soviet pressure during the Second World War, the Allies ordered a plebiscite on the status of Mongolia, and in 1946 the entire population voted for independence from China. The Chinese nationalist leader Chiang Kai-shek was forced to give up his claim that 'Outer' Mongolia was a part of China. From this time Mongolia's independence was established in international law and a major aspiration of the revolutions of 1911 and 1921 was fulfilled. That status was confirmed in 1961 when the country was admitted to the United Nations and by 1992, 125 countries had diplomatic relations with Mongolia.

Not only did Mongolia's external relations change considerably after the Second World War but there was tremendous social and economic change. If the prewar period was largely one of destruction, then the postwar period was one of construction. In the 1950s education became compulsory and the livestock herding economy was collectivized. A new society comprising ards (herdsmen), industrial and service workers and intellectuals emerged and the ruling party gained real and lasting control over the minds, assets and manpower resources of the nation. From the 1960s investment in arable farming on virgin lands has produced wheat, potatoes and vegetables to feed a growing urban sector. In this urban sector Mongolia's industrial base was established. In Ulaanbaatar and new towns like Darkhan light industries began processing the products of the collectives and the state farms. In the 1970s and 1980s the mining and semi-processing of the country's mineral wealth took Mongolia into the age of high technology and made a considerable contribution to the country's foreign trade. The largest enterprise of this kind is the Copper and Molybdenum Combine at the new town of Erdenet which was founded as a joint venture with the Soviet Union. Hand in hand with economic development a new socialist culture began to flourish in the performing, visual and literary arts. They expressed the values of Soviet-style communism and celebrated the new socialist man and society.

Much of Mongolia's postwar development was made possible with aid from the USSR and eastern Europe. However the Soviet decision to back modernization in Mongolia was not so much a matter of disinterested concern for a backward neighbour and ally but the result of a shift in strategic forces in the region. In 1949 the Chinese Communist Party under Mao Zedong came to power in China. For a brief period in the 1950s relations between Mongolia and China were warm and friendly. Mao accepted Mongolia's independent status and provided financial aid, consumer goods and many thousands of workers to build flats, roads, bridges and factories.

At first, the Soviet Union looked favourably on Chinese aid. In the late 1950s, however, relations between China and the USSR deteriorated as the two states vied for the leadership of the communist world. The Soviet government, anxious to retain the

Introduction

loyalty of its hitherto pliant ally, backed Choibalsan's protégé, the pro-Soviet Yu. Tsedenbal, as Party and state leader and matched the Chinese aid with even larger donations. In 1962 Mongolia became a full member of the Comecon organization which promised even more assistance from the countries of eastern Europe. As the Sino-Soviet dispute deepened and Mongolia was obliged to take sides it is hardly surprising that the Mongolian government remained loyal to the USSR. This choice has determined the course of internal and external politics in Mongolia until 1986 when the Sino-Soviet dispute was finally resolved.

Yet, in spite of modernization and the diversification of the economy Mongolia did not become more self-reliant but less so. Under Comecon's coordinated planning system which operated in the 1970s and the 1980s the Mongolian economy became increasingly integrated with that of Siberia. Investment was concentrated in the central economic zone where products could be transported on the Ulaanbaatar railway into Siberia. The resources of the vast regions to the east and west and the needs of the people living there received far less attention. In fact both foreign aid and investment from Mongolian government funds were generally unbalanced in favour of projects like Erdenet which were to the benefit of the Soviet rather than the Mongolian economy. In addition, Mongolia was being tied to an economy that was stagnant and a system that ultimately proved incapable of supporting it.

The fragile state of the Soviet economy became increasingly evident in the 1980s and the Soviet President Gorbachev introduced a programme of liberalizing reforms. However these did not strengthen the Soviet economy but hastened the demise of the Soviet state and the communist system. As was customary, the Mongolian government adopted similar policies as the solutions to its own economic difficulties. While this ultimately did not solve the problems, it did give ordinary people greater freedoms of action and expression. In 1988 and 1989 democratic forces in Eastern Europe comprehended the weakness of the communist system and overthrew their communist regimes. In Mongolia a new generation of young and well-educated intellectuals likewise took advantage of a more liberal political atmosphere by challenging the Party leadership. A series of public demonstrations from December 1989 to May 1990 paved the way for democracy, multi-party elections and a commitment to a market economy.

The Mongolian population, particularly in Ulaanbaatar, was gripped with a new mood of enthusiasm that had been growing since 1988 as hopes were raised for greater political freedom and prosperity. Hand in hand with the new liberty there was a resurgence of national consciousness. Monasteries opened and Buddhism flourished once more. Artists searched for national forms. In the city as in the countryside more people donned the traditional costume and some gave up their city flats to live in the traditional ger. Mongols began to ask searching questions about their own recent and more distant past. The Party and the government were forced to restore the good name of many who had died cruelly and unlawfully in the 1930s and 1940s. Once more Chinggis Khan was openly honoured as the founder of the Mongol nation and as the man who had made it great. Long suppressed anti-Soviet feelings rose to the surface and statues of Stalin were pulled down.

The euphoria did not last long. By 1991 the privatization of state and public assets was underway and external trade was conducted in hard currency. However foreign exchange reserves were rapidly exhausted and the country was hit by high inflation. Shortages of fuel and spare parts crippled industry and transport. Thousands were thrown out of work and food was in short supply and rationed. In February 1992 a new democratic constitution was passed but the people were losing confidence in the new system and the new parties. In the elections held the following June the MPRP won a landslide victory as its candidates took seventy of the seventy-six seats in country's parliament, the Great Khural.

At the time of writing the future of Mongolia and its people is difficult to predict except to say that a return to the communist system strongly dependent on the USSR is no longer an option. The people of Mongolia now have the very difficult task of finding a political and economic system which will meet the country's unique and special needs. Whatever is finally agreed upon, it must, to some extent, accord with international systems because the goodwill of the international community is crucial to guaranteeing the continued independence of Mongolia.

About the bibliography

This bibliography has been prepared for the use of students, academics wishing to read on a subject outside their own field of expertise, and for the general reader. It is a guide to publications which, on the whole, provide reliable information about Mongolia, its people and to some extent its historical background and traditional culture. Some general works on Mongols living outside the country and on Mongolian nationalism and Panmongolism have also been included. This is because the presence of Mongols, in Inner Mongolia particularly, continue to influence the Khalkh Mongols' perceptions of independent statehood. Furthermore, Chinese policies in Inner

Mongolia are a factor in determining the attitudes of Khalkh Mongols and the Mongolian government towards China. A number of works on Mongolian culture and traditions which are based on studies in Inner Mongolia have also been included in the bibliography because the information they provide and the conclusions they draw are equally applicable to independent Mongolia. Works concerning the geography, archaeology or contemporary affairs of Mongol territories in China and Russia are generally excluded and inquirers are advised to consult the bibliographies specific to those regions.

When selecting items for citation, preference has been given to monographs written in English which are reasonably accessible through larger public or university libraries. However, it has to be said that Mongolia does not command a large body of literature in English and not all that has been published can be recommended as reliable and informative. Some of the best work on the country has appeared in periodicals or collections of articles and conference papers. This reflects not only the country's geographical isolation but also its political isolation during much of the 20th century. Furthermore, until recently Mongolia has been documented by a few devoted academics whose chief interests are in the fields of language, textual studies, pre-modern history, ethnography and religion. Many of these publications are excellent but extremely detailed and scholarly and may not meet the needs of the average user of this bibliography. A reader who does want to examine a subject in greater depth may consult the bibliographies in the final section, or those appended to many of the monographs and articles cited. Although preference has been given to works published in English some works in French or German have been included where comparable materials are not available in English.

Every effort has been made to provide the inquirer with some publications in each of the subject categories. However there are subjects, particularly in the social sciences, where basic studies are simply not available and the works that cover these best are the general country studies. *Mongolia: a country study* and its predecessor *Area handbook of Mongolia* (items no. 9 and 1 respectively), *Mongolia: politics, economics and society* by A. J. K. Sanders (item no. 11), *History of the Mongolian People's Republic* (item no. 134) and *US Joint Publications Research Service*, *East Asia: Mongolia*, (item no. 466), a series of articles from the Mongolian press in English translation, are particularly recommended. The reader will find these works cited in many sections of this bibliography. The collections of statistics included are also useful sources of information on the social sciences but readers are advised to treat them with some caution. The Mongolian government recently admitted to supplying international agencies with false data during the years when Yu. Tsedenbal was in power in order to suggest that the country's achievements in development were better than they actually were. The same is not necessarily true of statistical material published for the use of Mongolian policymakers but even these, especially the older statistics, were not always reliable either, because of the way the data was collected or the manner in which they are presented.

In this book the citations are arranged alphabetically by title within the various subject categories. Foreign names and words occurring in titles are spelled as they appear in the publication. Names of authors, editors and translators, and proper names and foreign words referred to in the annotations are spelled according to accepted systems of romanization if they derive from a language which is not written in Latin script. Chinese names and words are given in pinyin except in a few cases where it is difficult to identify the original characters of an author's name from the romanized version given in the publication concerned or, as in the case of Chiang Kai-shek, where a particular spelling in the Wade-Giles system is widely recognized. Russian is romanized according to the British Standard BS 2979: 1958. For Persian, the system used by J. A. Boyle in items no. 86 and 97 is used. The romanization of Mongolian is problematic because two scripts must be taken into account. At present the standard script used in Mongolia is the Cyrillic script which differs slightly from that used to write Russian, having two additional letters. Before 1950 the Mongolian script was used, a script which Mongols have used since the time of Chinggis Khan. The Mongols of China continue to use it and there are plans to reintroduce the Mongolian script as the standard script in Mongolia also. Whereas the spelling of Cyrillic Mongolian is standardized, this is not the case with the Mongolian script, especially for pre-revolutionary works, and scholars have established neither a standard form of romanization nor standard spellings for proper nouns. I have chosen to use the romanization system adopted by the translators of the official *History of the Mongolian People's Republic* (see item no. 134) when transliterating the personal and place names of modern Mongolia and Mongolian words written in the Cyrillic script. For names of historical personages and places which have variant spellings in the Mongolian script, I use spellings found in works of scholarship such as *Mongolia's culture and society* by S. Jagchid and P. V. Hyer. I have striven for consistency but there are some anomalies. I use the familiar spelling 'Gobi' rather than the correctly romanized *Gov'* (Cyrillic script), and prefer 'Javzandamba Khutagt' (the title of a Buddhist incarnation) as romanized from the Cyrillic script rather than the Mongolian script version 'Jebtsundamba Khutukhtu' since this line of incarnations was of considerable importance in the post-revolutionary period. I use the correctly romanized spelling 'Ulaan-baatar' rather than 'Ulan Bator', a form commonly seen in western publications but actually based on the Russian way of spelling the name of the Mongolian capital. Finally I use the spelling 'Chinggis Khan' rather than the common (and often misspelt!) *Genghis Khan* which was romanized for the benefit of speakers of French.

Acknowledgements

I am exceedingly grateful to many friends and fellow Mongolists who have made suggestions for this bibliography and allowed me pick their brains and make use of their personal libraries. I thank Lucy Walton for assistance in drawing the map and my husband Hans for help with the wordprocessing. I am also grateful to the librarians of the School of Oriental Studies, Cambridge University and the Natural History Museum for giving me access to their collections. My greatest thanks, however, must be to the University of Leeds, where most of the work was carried out.

There has long been a need for a bibliographic guide of this kind. That need is even greater now that Mongolia has flung its doors open to the world's business men, specialists and travellers, and Mongolian scholars are working more closely with those of other countries. I hope that this book will fulfill the needs of these people and also that it will encourage others to explore the life and society of a little-known state and its people. I trust that the information I have provided in this bibliography is correct, and I alone am to blame for any errors.

Abbreviations

ABPC   Asian Buddhist Peace Conference

CMEA   Council for Mutual Economic Assistance

FBIS   US Foreign Broadcasting Information Service

IMAR   Inner Mongolian Autonomous Region

IMF   International Monetary Fund

JPRS   US Joint Publications Research Service

MPP   Mongolian People's Party

MPR   Mongolian People's Republic

MPRP   Mongolian People's Revolutionary Party

Glossary of Mongolian Terms

aimag	province
ards	people, the rural population
bileg	wise saying
ger	a round tent covered with felt
khainag	a cross between a cow and a yak
khural	assembly, meeting
Khural, Great	National Assembly
khutagt	a 'Living Buddha', a reincarnated Buddhist saint
mangas	monster, often with many heads
ongon	the dwelling of a shamanist spirit in nature or an image
sum	division of local government
süm	monastery
tamga	seal
Tenger	the sky, heaven which was an object of worship of the pre-Buddhist Mongols
tögrög	unit of Mongolian currency (tughrik)
Tsam	Buddhist festival at which masked dances were performed
Yasa	the Law Code attributed to Chinggis Khan

Theses and Dissertations on Mongolia

Allsen, Thomas Theodore. 'Politics of Mongol imperialism: centralization and resource mobilization in the reign of the Grand Qan Möngke, 1251-59,' PhD thesis, University of Minnesota, 1979.

Barton, Barry George. 'The policy of the Mongolian People's Republic toward China, 1952-1973', PhD thesis, University of West Virginia, 1974.

Campi, Alicia Jean. 'The political relationship between the United States and Outer Mongolia, 1915-1927: the Kalgan consular records,' PhD thesis, Indiana University, 1988.

Ewing, Thomas Esson. 'Russian and Chinese policies in Outer Mongolia, 1911-1921,' PhD thesis, Indiana University, 1977.

Moses, Larry. 'Lamaism or Leninism?: Mongolia chooses a faith,' PhD thesis, Indiana University, 1972.

Nathanson, Alynn Joelle. 'Ch'ing policies in Khalkha Mongolia and the Chingünjav rebellion of 1756,' PhD thesis, 1983.

Rupen, Robert Arthur. 'Outer Mongolian nationalism 1900-1919,' PhD thesis, University of Washington, 1954.

Underdown, Michael Raymond. 'Mongolian nationalist movements,' PhD thesis, University of Melbourne, 1983.

The Country and Its People

1 **Area handbook for Mongolia.**
Trevor N. Dupuy, Wendell Blanchard.   Washington, DC: American
University, 1970. 502p. maps. bibliog.

A wide range of basic information on modern Mongolia, its country, people and
institutions is provided in this handbook. Its twenty chapters are arranged in four
broad sections covering geography, culture and social development; the economy;
politics and administration; justice, public security and national defence. There is a
wide choice of additional reading for each section. The book is very easy to consult
because of its detailed table of contents and index and it is an excellent first source of
reference for the postwar period, especially the 1960s. The book is updated by
Mongolia: a country study which is cited as item no. 9.

2 **The city of friendship.**
Mongolia, no. 3 (18) (1974), p. 4-23.

A collection of popular, propaganda articles on Mongolia's second largest city,
Darkhan, which was constructed in the 1960s with Soviet aid. There are features on the
people and the economic life of the city, Mongol-Soviet friendship and the nearby
Sharyn Gol coal mine which supports the city's industry. There is also a short story set
in Darkhan, 'Man and the city' by S. Erdene, a leading Mongolian writer.

3 **Information Mongolia: the comprehensive reference source of the People's
Republic of Mongolia (MPR).**
Compiled and edited by the Academy of Sciences MPR.   Oxford, New
York: Pergamon Press, 1990. 505p. maps. bibliog. (Countries of the
World Information Series).

An encyclopaedia of Mongolia arranged in ten broad subject sections and covering
history, geography, politics, economics, culture and society. The book is lavishly
illustrated with contemporary photographs and it contains many charts and statistics. It
was published after the breakdown of the communist system in 1990 but much of the

content was prepared some years earlier. Consequently the book reflects the outlook of the Mongolian government in the early 1980s although some adjustments have been made to take into account the reforms of the late 1980s. Certain chapters, such as those on history, religion and traditional culture, are highly politicized and do not convey much factual information or indeed contemporary Mongolian views. The coverage of geography is the most comprehensive available in English and the information on contemporary institutions, (pre-1990), and the statistical tables and maps are useful.

4 **The land and people of Mongolia.**
John S. Major. New York: Lippincott, 1990. 200p. maps. bibliog. (Portraits of the Nation Series).

This is a general but sound introduction to Mongolia, its population, history, customs, politics and culture and annotated suggestions for further reading are provided. The book is attractively produced in large clear type with many illustrations and is ideal for the general reader and for young people.

5 **Larson, Duke of Mongolia.**
Frans August Larson. Boston, Massachusetts: Little, Brown, 1930. 296p.

An inside view of Mongolian life and customs at the beginning of the 20th century by a Swedish missionary turned business man. He lived and worked among the Mongols for many years, became a close friend of Mongolian princes and living Buddhas, including the Eighth Javzandamba Khutagt, who ruled Mongolia from 1911-24. Larson was well travelled in both Inner and Outer (Khalkh) Mongolia and claimed to have been granted the title of *gün*, (duke).

6 **Life in the Mongolian Gobi.**
Caroline Humphrey. *Geographical Magazine*, vol. 43, (June 1971), p. 616-23.

An excellent and beautifully illustrated account of life in the semi-deserts of the Gobi written by an anthropologist for a popular audience. She places the life, society and economy of the region in their cultural and historical context and demonstrates that socialism in the Gobi is quite distinct from its counterparts in the USSR and China.

7 **Die Mongolen. (The Mongols.)**
Edited by Walther Heissig, Claudius C. Muller. Innsbruck, Austria: Pinguin Verlag; Frankfurt am Main, Germany: Umschau Verlag, 1989. 2 vols. map.

These two volumes are the catalogue of an exhibition of the history, art and culture of the Mongols which was held at the Haus der Kunst in Munich in 1989. Many of the objects on display were on loan from Mongolia and China and had not been seen previously in the west. One volume contains photographs of the exhibits in colour and in black-and-white together with notes on their materials, decoration and use, as appropriate. The other volume is a collection of articles by European scholars writing in several languages on the cultural and ethnographic prehistory and history of the Mongols.

8   **Mongolia.**
Albert Axelbank.   Tokyo; Palo Alto, California; Oxford: Kondansha
International, 1971. 138p. map. (This Beautiful World, no. 25).
A brief and attractive introduction to Mongolia for the general reader by an American
journalist who visited the country in March 1971. The main feature of the book is the
record of modern Mongolian life and culture in sixty-seven high quality coloured
photographs.

9   **Mongolia: a country study.**
Edited by Robert L. Worden, Andrea Matles Savada.   Washington, DC:
Library of Congress, 1991. 2nd ed. 320p. maps. bibliog.
This work is the successor to the *Area handbook of Mongolia* (see item no. 1) and is
the most up-to-date reference work on the country. It is arranged according to the
same format but with the main emphasis on events, trends and institutions of the 1970s
and 1980s and it provides a reliable analysis of the Mongolian state and society at the
end of the era of communist party rule. Like its predecessor it includes a range of
charts, tables, statistics, bibliographical references and an index.

10   **Mongolia and the Mongols. Volume one – 1892.**
Aleksei M. Pozdneyev.   Bloomington, Indiana: University of Indiana;
The Hague: Mouton, 1971. 531p. (Uralic and Altaic Series vol. 61).
Pozdneyev (1851-1920) was a Russian Mongolist who spent the years 1876-79 in
Mongolia with the Russian Geographical Society's expedition headed by G. N.
Potanin. In 1892 Pozdneyev was sent there again by the Russian Ministry of Foreign
Affairs to study the economy and ethnography of the country. The record of those
visits is contained in this book. Pozdneyev noted little of the poor living conditions of
many Mongols at that time, or the rumblings of dissatisfaction that eventually lead to
revolution in 1911. However he has left us a vast amount of detailed information on
the towns and monasteries and their cultural and economic life. He also includes
translations of a series of biographies of the eight incarnations of the Javzandamba
Khutagt, who were the most prestigious of the many 'Living Buddhas' of Mongolia.
See also item no. 222.

11   **Mongolia: politics, economics, society.**
Alan John Kelday Sanders.   London: Frances Pinter; Boulder,
Colorado: Lynne Reiner, 1987. 179p. map. bibliog. (Marxist Regimes
Series).
This monograph is a critical study of contemporary Mongolia under the control of the
Mongolian People's Revolutionary Party, a regime that lasted from 1921 to 1990. The
author demonstrates how the Mongolian state and society have developed since 1921
and gives special attention to the way the political and economic institutions functioned
in the mid 1980s. The book is valuable for its extensive factual content and data, much
of which has been drawn from primary and secondary sources in Russian and
Mongolian. These are listed in the bibliography which also cites materials in western
languages. Several charts and statistical tables are provided.

12 **Mongolia today.**
   Edited by Shirin Akiner. London, New York: Kegan Paul
   International in association with the Central Asia Research Forum,
   School of Oriental and African Studies, London, 1991. 237p. maps.
   bibliog.

A collection of papers, some of which were read at a conference on contemporary Mongolia held in London in 1987. Together they provide an overview of the Mongolian state and society in the late 1980s. This was a significant period when the country was on the verge of change from a socialist state controlled by a single party to a democratic one. The topics covered include political, legal and economic reforms, religion, education, applied art and the armed forces. Among the authors are British scholars and representatives of government and commercial organizations.

13 **Mongolia's culture and society.**
   Sechin Jagchid, Paul Hyer, foreword by Joseph Fletcher. Boulder,
   Colorado: Westview; Folkestone, England: Dawson, 1979. 461p. map.
   bibliog.

By describing the traditional nomadic culture, institutions and lifestyle of the Mongols, the authors of this book aim to identify this people as a distinct group in northern Asia and to record what they believe to be a disappearing lifestyle. They have drawn both on historical materials and the personal experience of Jagchid, a native Mongol. Although many of the examples are taken from Inner Mongolia the culture described underlies the socialist culture of independent Mongolia. This is a good reference work particularly for the student or the non-specialist.

14 **Mongolian heroes of the twentieth century.**
   Edited translations by Urgunge Onon, introduction by Owen
   Lattimore. New York: AMS Press, 1976. 217p. map. bibliog.

This is a collection of six biographies translated from Mongolian. The individuals concerned were all active in the revolutions of 1911 or 1921. They are Ayuush (1858-1939), Togtokh Taij (1871-1920) Damdinsüren (1871-1920), Khatanbaatar Magsarjav (1877-1927), D. Sükhbaatar (1893-1923), (an abridged version of D. Dashjamts and L. Bat-Ochir's biography referred to in item no. 125), and Kh. Choibalsan (1895-1952). Their stories provide valuable insights into the political and social history of early 20th century Mongolia.

15 **Mongolian journey.**
   Lumír Jisl, translated by Tili Gottheiner. London: Artia, Batchworth,
   1960. 144p.

An unusual collection of photographs, some coloured, taken during a visit to Mongolia by the author in 1957-58. The photographers were the author himself, Gombojav, the photographer of the Mongolian Committee of Sciences and Alois Keibl, photographer of the Czechoslovak Mongolian Archaeological Expedition. The pictures illustrate historical sites, Buddhist relics, traditional art and craft objects and traditional activities. The book was first published in German (Prague: Artia, 1960).

16 **The Mongolian People's Republic.**
Edited by G. Dashdavaa. Ulaanbaatar: Union of Mongolian
Journalists, 1981. 256p. map.

A volume of short articles on Mongolia marking the sixtieth anniversary of the
revolution of 1921. In spite of its eulogistic tone the book is a useful source of
information on the country, its society and institutions at the beginning of the 1980s.
Some statistical data is included.

17 **Mongolie: textes et photographies.** (Mongolia: text and photographs.)
Claude Arthaud, François Hébert-Stevens. Paris: Arthaud, 1958. 101p.
bibliog.

An excellent photographic record of daily life in Mongolia, particularly in winter,
during the 1950s. The practice of Buddhism, officially discouraged at this time, is
featured in some of the photographs. The text is in French.

18 **Nomads and commissars: Mongolia revisited.**
Owen Lattimore. New York: Oxford University Press, 1962. 238p.
bibliog.

The author of this book visited Mongolia in 1961 soon after the country joined the
United Nations and was opening up to the non-communist world. He describes the
people and the country's contemporary political and economic development against the
background of Mongolian history and traditions, about which he had extensive
knowledge. From what he saw in 1961 Lattimore concluded that Mongolia was a
prosperous country whose people supported the government and approved the close
relationship with the Soviet Union. Although some have condemned his conclusions as
naive, the book is still highly readable. It contains interesting insights into a developing
state and an explanation of why Mongolia opted for alliance with the Soviet Union
rather than China after the Second World War.

19 **Paralipomena Mongolica: wissenschaftliche Notizen über Land, Leute
und Lebenweise in der Mongolischen Volksrepublik.** (Paralipomena
Mongolica: scientific notes on the country, people and way of life in the
Mongolian People's Republic.)
Johannes Schubert. Berlin: Academie-Verlag, 1971. 324p. map.
bibliog. (Veröffentlichungen des Museums für Völkerkunde zu Leipzig,
Heft 19).

A compendium of information and data on Mongolia, in German, including
geography, population, minorities, social and political institutions, culture and the
economy. Among its many useful features arc a gazetteer, a wide range of Mongolian
terms with German glosses and international scientific equivalents, where appropriate,
and detailed cross-referencing to further sources of information. The bibliography
includes works in Mongolian and Russian as well as in western European languages.
Much of the information is presented in a very abbreviated format which some users
might find confusing at first. Although the book is now dated it has important
retrospective value.

20 **The People's Republic of Mongolia: general reference guide.**
Alan John Kelday Sanders. London, New York: Oxford University
Press, 1968. 232p. maps. bibliog.

Although it is dated, this collection of information and data on Mongolia in the 1960s
is of retrospective value. It is arranged in four parts dealing with the political and social
structure of Mongolia; finance, planning, industry, agriculture and communications;
trade with statistics; and a miscellaneous section of appendices which include a
gazetteer and a chronology of postrevolutionary Mongolia.

21 **The pre-revolutionary culture of Outer Mongolia.**
George A. Cheney. Bloomington, Indiana: Mongolia Society, 1968.
99p. bibliog. (Occasional Papers no. 5).

An introduction to the institutions, traditions and economic life of Mongolia in the
19th and early 20th century. The book is based on *Sovremennaya Mongoliya*
(Contemporary Mongolia) by Ivan Maiskii (1921) which is cited in this bibliography as
item no. 22.

22 **Sovremennaya Mongoliya: otchet Mongol'skoi Ekspeditsii snaryazhennoi
Irkutskoi kontoroi Vserossiiskogo Tsentral'nogo Soyuza Potrebitel'nykh
obshchestvo 'Tsentrosoyuz'.** (Contemporary Mongolia: report of the
Mongolian Expedition equipped by the Irkutsk office of the All-Russian
Central Union of Consumer Cooperatives 'Tsentrosoyuz'.)
Ivan Mikhailovich Maiskii. Irkutsk, Russia: Irkutskoe otdeleniya,
1921. 332p. maps.

Maiskii was sent to Mongolia in 1919 to investigate the economic potential of the
country for the All-Russian Central Union of Cooperative Societies. The result was a
unique, thorough and informed study of Mongolia on the eve of the 1921 revolution,
providing information on the people, institutions and economic geography. The results
of the 1918 census which record the human and domestic animal population are
included with a great deal of other social and economic data. A second edition of the
book was published in 1959 but it should be avoided because information has either
been altered or omitted for propaganda purposes. See also item no. 21.

23 **Studies on Mongolia: proceedings of the first North American conference
on Mongolian Studies.**
Edited by Henry Guenter Schwarz. Bellingham, Washington: Western
Washington University Press, 1979. 138p. maps. bibliog.

A collection of conference papers on Mongolian language, culture and history by
American scholars. A number of the articles might be of interest to students or a
general audience. The contents include research on the independence movements of
the late 19th and early 20th century, Mongol-Tibetan relations in the 17th century,
Mongolian contemporary opera and prehistoric migrations from Mongolia to North
America.

Among the Mongols.
See item no. 25.

Travellers' Accounts

24 **Across Mongolian plains: a naturalist's account of China's 'Great Northwest'.**
Roy Chapman Andrews.   New York, London: Appleton, 1921. 276p.

Andrews, a naturalist and the flamboyant leader of the American Natural History Museum's three expeditions to Central Asia, 1921-1930 (described in item no. 35), wrote this account about the preparatory trip he and his wife made to Mongolia in 1919. He travelled by car, a rare mode of transport in the region in those days, and he writes about his experiences of this and of the wildlife which he observed en route. Comments on the people and their way of life are limited.

25 **Among the Mongols.**
James Gilmour.   New York; Washington, DC; London: Praeger, 1970. Reprint. 382p. map. (Praeger Scholarly Reprints: Source Books and Studies on Inner Asia).

James Gilmour (1843-1891) was a Scottish missionary with the London Missionary Society who spent over twenty years among the Mongols of Khalkh and Inner Mongolia. As a missionary Gilmour was singularly unsuccessful but he was an entertaining writer. This book, first published in 1883, is a classic travelogue describing his travels and the life and customs of the Mongols, especially the common people, in the late 19th century. This reprinted edition is nicely illustrated with sketches and engravings from the 1883 edition. See also item no. 34 by the same author.

26   **In search of Genghis Khan.**
Tim Severin. Photographs by Paul Harris.   London; Sydney; Auckland, New Zealand; Johannesburg: Hutchinson, 1991. 276p. maps.
The account of a journey of exploration by a British travel writer who crossed Mongolia on horseback with a photographer in 1990. His aim was to travel an ancient Silk Road and the route taken by the armies of the Mongol Empire into Central Asia. The author describes relics of ancient and traditional Mongolia and evidence of democracy, then emerging in Mongolia, which he encountered on his way. With its excellent coloured photographs this book will delight a wide and popular audience.

27   **The land of Genghis Khan: a journey in Outer Mongolia.**
René Marie MacColl.   London: Oldbourne, 1963. 220p.
MacColl was a British journalist for the Daily Express and he joined the first group of western tourists to Mongolia in the summer of 1962. His account is not so much a description of the country as the experience of being a tourist there. The mutual lack of understanding between non-communist tourists and officials of Zhuulchin, the Mongolian state tourist agency, has not completely changed even today.

28   **Land of the blue sky: a portrait of modern Mongolia.**
Ivor Montagu.   London: Dobson, 1956. 191p. map. bibliog.
Western visitors were rare in Mongolia in the 1950s so this account is particularly interesting. The British author, a zoologist and a communist, went with his wife by official invitation in 1954 when industrialization and mass education were just beginning in Mongolia. His careful observations of life in and outside of the capital are the most valuable part of the book. Like many other travellers Montagu's knowledge and understanding of Mongolia's past is not extensive and therefore his judgements on that must be treated with caution. A translation of the summary of the Second Five-year plan (1953-58) is included in an appendix.

29   **The last disco in Outer Mongolia.**
Nicholas J. Middleton.   London: Sinclair-Stevenson, 1992. 222p. map. bibliog.
This is one of the most recent and authentic accounts of Mongolia and will appeal to a wide readership, young and old. The author, a geographer, experienced the restricted life of a visiting scholar in Party-controlled Mongolia in 1987. He returned in 1990, when the communist system was giving way to democracy, and was able to travel outside the capital and mix more freely with ordinary people. His account is both a travelogue and a perceptive comparison of the country under two systems. Middleton's factual information, both historical and contemporary, is generally reliable and his presentation of the country is one which those familiar with Mongolia, its life and customs, will recognize.

30   **Mongol journeys.**
Owen Lattimore.   New York: AMS Press, 1975. reprint. 284p.
Lattimore travelled widely in Inner Mongolia in the 1920s and 1930s and his book is full of fascinating details about Mongols, their ideas, customs and way of life. Of particular interest is the author's account of a visit to the shrine of Chinggis Khan which is in the Ordos region in the Yellow River bend. He and his companion, Torgny Öberg, took part in a sacrifice which was held each year at the spring equinox, and the

shrine, relics and ritual are described in detail. The book was first published in 1941 and has been reissued under various imprints since.

31 **Mongolia: in search of Marco Polo and other adventures.**
Silvio Micheli, translated from the Italian by Bruce Penman.   London:
Hollis & Carter; New York: Harcourt, Brace & World, 1967. 366p.
map.

An Italian discovers Mongolia while taking a trip by jeep and on horseback in 1959-60. He travelled from Sükhbaatar in the north, to Dundgov' *aimag* (province), in the south east. Then he turned west, returning to Sükhbaatar via the northern towns of Ulaangom and Mörön. A general audience will find his account both informative and entertaining as the author clashes frequently with his guide and falls in love with a Mongol beauty. Micheli also provides a rare eyewitness account of the now defunct Züün Bayan oil installations in Dundgov' aimag.

32 **Mongolia: unknown land.**
Jørgen Bisch, translated from the Danish by Reginald Spink.   New
York: Dutton; London: Allen & Unwin, 1963. 159p. map. bibliog.

A Danish travel writer describes Mongolia and its progress towards modernization at a time when the livestock herdsmen had just been organized into collectives. The book is intended for people who know nothing about the country and it is illustrated with many excellent colourful photographs. Of special interest is the author's account of his visit to Lake Khövsgöl in the northwest where he met reindeer herdsmen of the Tsaatan minority (see also item no. 147) who were just about to be collectivized. Bisch is more critical of the society he observed than Montagu was (see item no. 28) but like Montagu and many other travel writers on Mongolia, his descriptions of what he observed personally are of more lasting value than his speculations on the past and his analysis of contemporary society.

33 **Mongolia, the Tangut country and the solitudes of Northern Tibet being a narrative of three years travel in Eastern High Asia.**
N. M. Przewalski, translated by E. Delmar Morgan with introduction
and notes by Colonel Henry Yule.   London: Samson Low, Marston,
Searle & Rivington, 1876. 2 vols.

Przewalski, a Polish zoologist and sportsman, is remembered for his discovery of the skin and skull of a wild horse *Equus przewalski* in western Mongolia. He was sent to explore the country by the Imperial Geographical Society of St. Petersburg and the Russian Imperial War Department in 1871. His journey through Khalkh Mongolia along the Kalgan-Khiagt route is described in the first volume, and a trip from the southwest to Ikh Khüree, now Ulaanbaatar, in the second volume. Przewalski's account, together with his tables of geophysical measurements, is a landmark in the geographical description of Mongolia. He was also a careful observer of Mongolian life and customs but like many Europeans of his generation, he had a negative attitude towards the Mongols whom he considered apathetic, cowardly and immoral.

10

34 **More about the Mongols.**
James Gilmour, selected and arranged form the diaries and papers of
James Gilmour by Richard Lovett. London: Religious Tract Society,
1893. 320p.

This book complements Gilmour's earlier work 'Among the Mongols' (see item
no. 25) although it is less cohesive because it was assembled posthumously from the
author's writings. It includes an account of a journey from Kalgan in Inner Mongolia to
Khiagt on the Siberian border and a selection of essays on topics such as Khiagt,
Mongolian weather lore and camels.

35 **The new conquest of Central Asia: a narrative of explorations of the**
Central Asiatic Expeditions in Mongolia and China, 1921-1930.
Roy Chapman Andrews. New York: American Museum of Natural
History, 1932. 678p. maps. bibliog. (Natural History of Central Asia
vol. 1).

The American Museum of Natural History's Central Asiatic Expeditions, led by R. C.
Andrews, undertook pioneering studies of the geology topography, flora, fauna and
archaeology of Mongolia. This fascinating account of the daily life and work of the
expedition is intended for an intelligent but general audience. The book also provides
some useful comment on political and social conditions and of the life and customs of
Mongols in the 1920s. There are chapters by Walter Granger, Clifford H. Pope and
Nels C. Nelson and summary statements by G. M. Allen, R. C. Andrews, C. P.
Berkey, R. W. Chaney, A. W. Grabau, W. Granger, F. K. Morris, N. C. Nelson,
J. T. Nichols. H. F. Osborn, C. H. Pope, C. A. Reeds and L. E. Spock. A
bibliography, a list of detailed scientific reports and publications of the expedition and
an index are also included. A shorter account of this expedition was published as *On
the trail of ancient man* by Andrews (New York: Putnams, 1926), and many of the
expedition's scientific reports were issued in the serials *American Museum Novitates*
and *Bulletin of the Museum of Natural History*.

36 **The new Mongolia.**
Ladislaus Forbath as related by Joseph Geleta, translated from the
Hungarian by Lawrence Wolfe. London, Toronto: Heinemann, 1936.
276p.

Geleta was a Hungarian prisoner of war who escaped from Russia in 1920 and worked
for the Mongolian government until 1929. He was the architect of the People's House
where Party Congresses and the National Assembly met. He also built the first public
lavatory in Mongolia (which the Mongols shunned!) and converted the Palace of the
Bogd Khan into a museum. The book describes Geleta's years in Mongolia with rare
and interesting insights into a society in transition. It is illustrated with Geleta's own
photographs including some of senior government officials such as the Prime Minister,
B. Tserendorj.

37   **Tents in Mongolia (Yabonah): adventures and experiences among the nomads of Central Asia.**
Henning Haslund-Christensen, translated from the Swedish text by Elizabeth Sprigge, Claude Napier.   New York: Dutton; London: Kegan Paul, Trench, Trubner, 1934. 366p.

This book by a Danish traveller describes a trip from Beijing in China to Lake Khövsgöl in the north of Mongolia in 1923. The text is well illustrated with photographs, line drawings and music. Haslund-Christensen also wrote *Mongolian journey* (London: Routledge & Kegan Paul, 1949) about life in Inner Mongolia, 1936-39, and *Men and gods in Mongolia* (*Zayagan*) (New York: Dutton, 1935) on the Torgut Mongols of Xinjiang province, China. All three books provide a fascinating if sometimes romantic picture of the life and culture of the Mongols of the period.

38   **A tour in Mongolia.**
Beatrix Bulstrode (Mrs. Edward Manico Gull), with an introduction on the political aspect of that country by David Fraser.   London: Methuen; New York: F. A. Stokes, 1920. 237p. map.

The adventures of a doughty Englishwoman who travelled by camel caravan across Mongolia in 1913. She describes what she saw of the country and the life of its people with lively interest, although her interpretations of their significance are not always to be relied on. The many photographs included in the book are a valuable record of the period.

39   **Travels in Tartary, Thibet and China during the years 1844-5-6.**
Évariste Régis Huc translated from the French by W. Hazlitt.
London: National Illustrated Library, [n.d.]. 2 vols. map.

This work has been published in several English translations and is a classic travel account of 19th century Mongolia for English readers. Huc, and his companion Gabet, were Lazarist fathers who were sent by the Catholic Church to inquire into the conditions of the Buddhist peoples of Inner Asia with the ultimate intention of establishing a Christian mission. The fathers' journey took them through vast tracts of Inner Mongolia via Dolonor and the Ordos, through Kokonor, now in China's Tsinghai province, to Tibet. Huc provides meticulous descriptions of the life, economy and customs of the various groups of Mongols they met on the way.

40   **Weideplätze der Mongolen im Reich der Chalcha.** (Mongol pastures in Khalkh.)
Hermann Consten.   Berlin: Dietrich Reimer (Ernst Vohsen) A-G, 1919-20. 2 vols.

In the winter of 1913-14 Consten journeyed to Niislel Khüree, as Ulaanbaatar was called from 1911-24. He travelled by camel caravan from the west through the towns of Khovd, Uliastai and Kharkhorin (Karakorum). Writing in German, he describes the landscape, travel conditions and the settlements he passed through. He also records meetings with a number of important Mongols and Russians, and in an appendix he gives details of Russian trade turnover for the years 1899-1909. Consten's account of contemporary autonomous Mongolia is occasionally sensationalized but the book is still a good source of information on that period.

Nomads and commissars: Mongolia revisited.
See item no. 18.

Narrative of a journey through Western Mongolia, July 1872 to January 1873.
See item no. 48.

Expedition Mongolia 1990: the first Anglo-Mongolian expedition in history.
See item no. 53.

Mission to Asia.
See item no. 88.

The travels of Marco Polo.
See item no. 98.

With the Russians in Mongolia.
See item no. 129.

Hunting for dinosaurs.
See item no. 364.

A lost civilization: the Mongols rediscovered.
See item no. 461.

Tourism and Travel Guides

41 **All-Asia guide compendium.**
Hong Kong: Far Eastern Economic Review, 1991. 15th ed. 764p.
There is no standard travel guide devoted entirely to Mongolia and few of the guides to Asia include the country either. Alan Sanders has compiled the short section on Mongolia in this guide (p. 456-63). The rates quoted for hotels and currency exchange are now out of date but other details, such as what to see in and out of the capital, are useful as are the maps of the whole country and of Ulaanbaatar. The guide has also been published in three separate parts, Mongolia being in the third part, *Northeast Asia*, p. 190-97. The publication is updated frequently.

42 **Mongolia today: a traveller's guide: geography, nature, hunting, museums, monuments, customs, tourism.**
Compiled and edited by Henry Field.   Miami, Florida: Field Research Projects, 1978. 71p.
A collection of articles originally published in Mongolian by Mongolian scholars and describing matters and places of interest to the potential traveller. The topics covered include Ulaanbaatar, the museums of Ulaanbaatar and the monastery of Erdene Zuu in Övörkhangai *aimag* (province), the new town of Darkhan, environmental protection, hunting, the Great Gobi National Park and the ritual of hospitality in a Mongolian *ger* (tent).

43 **North-East Asia on a shoestring.**
Robert Storey.   Singapore: Lonely Planet Publications, 1992.
3rd edition. (Lonely Planet Series).
Like the *All-Asia guide*, (see item no. 41) this volume contains a concise chapter on Mongolia providing slightly more detail and more up-to-date information. There is also a selection of useful Mongolian phrases. The maps of the country and of Ulaanbaatar are very similar to those of the *All-Asia guide*. This publication is updated frequently.

14

44   **Wapiti hunting the Mongolian People's Republic.**
      Ben Osborne. *Journal of the Anglo-Mongolian Society*, vol. 7 no. 2
      (Dec. 1981), p. 97-104.
      The Mongolian state travel agency, Zhuulchin, will organize special trips for hunters in
      Mongolia. This article gives information on the distribution of wapiti (a variety of elk),
      details of how hunting tours are arranged, costs at the time of publication and notes on
      trophies. The second part of the article describes the activities of the Mongolian
      Hunting Association and the development of hunting for commerce and sport.

The land of Genghis Khan: a journey in Outer Mongolia.
See item no. 27.

Expedition Mongolia 1990: the first Anglo-Mongolian expedition in history.
See item no. 53.

China's Inner Mongolia.
See item no. 160.

A travel survey of China's Mongolian regions.
See item no. 171.

Gesprächsbuch der mongolisch-deutsch; Mongol German yariany devter.
(Mongol-German phrasebook.)
See item no. 195.

Geography

General

45 **Dust storms in the Mongolian People's Republic.**
Nicholas J. Middleton. *Journal of Arid Environment*, vol. 20, no. 3, (1991), p. 287-97. maps. bibliog.

Dust storms in Mongolia occur mainly in the spring and during daylight hours. This article examines the frequency and distribution of dust storms and meteorological factors relating to them.

46 **Economic-geographical sketch of the Mongolian People's Republic.**
Ivan Kharitonovich Ovdiyenko, translated from the Russian by members of the Mongolia Society William H. Dougherty, John R. Krueger, Karl H. Menges, Natalie Menges, David C. Montgomery, Larry Moses, Toby A. Paff. Bloomington, Indiana: Mongolia Society, 1965. 125p. bibliog. maps. (Occasional Papers, no. 3).

This book was first published in Russian in 1962. It is a concise economic geography of Mongolia giving basic information on the physical and political geography, demography, agriculture, industry and foreign trade, mainly in the period following the Second World War. Although the book is clearly dated it has retrospective value.

47 **Die mongolische Volksrepublik: physisch-geographische Beschreibung.**
(The Mongolian Peoples' Republic: description of physical geography.)
E. M. Murzaev. Gotha, Germany: VEB geographisch-kartographische Anstalt, 1954. 524p. maps. bibliog.

The classic physical geography of Mongolia translated into German from the Russian edition of 1951. It begins with an account of the history of geographical research in Mongolia, much of which was carried out by Russians, including the author. It also provides detailed studies of the country, its regions, population, vegetation, fauna and

16

climate. There is an extensive bibliography mainly of publications in Russian. Although some aspects of the book are dated, it is still basically reliable. It is the only detailed monograph study of Mongolian geography and the Mongolian version is a standard text in Mongolia. For a good, more recent account of the geography of Mongolia in English, see item no. 3.

48 **Narrative of a journey through Western Mongolia, July 1872 to January 1873.**
Ney Elias. *Journal of the Royal Geographical Society*, (1875), p. 108-56. map.

Elias travelled from Beijing in China to Western Mongolia in the hope of finding the site of Kharkhorin (Karakorum), the capital of the Mongol Empire, on his way to Xinjiang province, China. He failed to find the site but he did compile a good geographical description of the route he travelled. His account includes a log of the distances between the various stages of his journey, meteorological data and a table of altitudes. The relief map of his route is based on Chinese and Russian maps of the period. Of additional interest are his descriptions of the towns of Uliastai and Khovd and of Mongolian trade with Russia at the turn of the century.

49 **The wealth of mineral springs in our country.**
Sh. Tseren, O. Namnandorj. *US Joint Publications Research Service: Translations on Mongolia*, no. 130 (21 Apr. 1967), p. 19-21. (JPRS 40,714).

The Mongolian Academy of Sciences and the Central Council of Trade Unions have studied many of Mongolia's mineral springs. This brief but informative article was written for the Mongolian general public. It notes geographical and geological locations and the chemical composition of several springs with comments on their medical properties and other uses of the waters.

Information Mongolia.
See item no. 3.

Paralipomena Mongolica: wissenschaftliche Notizen über Land, Leute und Lebenweise in der Mongolischen Volksrepublik. (Paralipomena Mongolica: scientific notes on the country, people and way of life in the Mongolian People's Republic.)
See item no. 19.

Mongolia, the Tangut country and the solitudes of Northern Tibet being a narrative of three years travel in Eastern High Asia.
See item no. 33.

The new conquest of Central Asia: a narrative of explorations of the Central Asiatic expeditions in Mongolia and China, 1921-1930.
See item no. 35.

The geography of education and health in the Mongolian People's Republic.
See item no. 240.

An attempt to delimit the main economic zones of the Mongolian People's Republic.
See item no. 297.

Contributions to the geology of northern Mongolia.
See item no. 359.

The geology of Mongolia: a reconnaissance report based on the investigations of the years 1922-1923.
See item no. 362.

The Gobi-Altai earthquake. (Gobi-Altaiskoe zemletryasenie.)
See item no. 363.

Materials on the geology of the Mongolian People's Republic.
See item no. 365.

Soils of Outer Mongolia (Mongolian People's Republic).
See item no. 368.

Vertical zonality in the Southern Khangai mountains (Mongolia): result of the Polish-Mongolian Physico-Geographical Expedition.
See item no. 369.

Maps and atlases

50 **Asien/Asia/Asie.**
Frankfurt am Main, Germany: Reinhard Ryborsch, 1990.
A folding map of Asia and Australasia which includes Mongolia. It is drawn to a scale of 1:8,000,000 and shows physical features, towns, main roads, rail links and airports. *Aimag* (provincial) boundaries are not indicated.

51 **Bügd Nairamdakh Mongol Ard Uls: ündesnii atlas.** (The Mongolian
    People's Republic: national atlas.)
    Ulaanbaatar: Academy of Sciences; Moscow: Academy of Sciences, 1990. 144p.
The official, Mongolian classified atlas of the country with maps illustrating its physical geography, including satellite maps, political geography, history, demography, economy and society. There is also a collection of maps indicating the political, economic and cultural relations of Mongolia with the rest of the world. Each section has an introduction in Mongolian but the list of contents is in Mongolian and English. A gazetteer is provided.

52   **The star map of our ancestors.**
     D. Baasanjav, D. Zuukhaa.   *Mongolia*, no. 4(7) (July 1972), p. 31.
A brief description for a popular audience of a 12th century astronomical map
preserved in the Mongolian State Library with an illustration. A list of astronomical
terms in Mongolian are also included.

Information Mongolia.
See item no. 3.

**Paralipomena Mongolica: wissenschaftliche Notizen über Land, Leute und
Lebenweise in der Mongolische Volksrepublik.** (Paralipomena Mongolica:
scientific notes on the land, people and way of life in the Mongolian People's
Republic.)
See item no. 19.

History of the Mongolian People's Republic.
See item no. 134.

**Mongol ard ulsyn ugsaatny sudlal, khelnii shinjleliin atlas: etno-lingvisticheskii
atlas MNR: atlas ethnologique et linguistique de la République Populaire de
Mongolie.** (Ethnological and linguistic atlas of the Mongolian People's
Republic.)
See item no. 148.

A lost civilization: the Mongols rediscovered.
See item no. 461.

Flora and Fauna

53 **Expedition Mongolia 1990: the first Anglo-Mongolian expedition in history.**
London: Expedition Mongolia Publications, 1990. 110p.

In 1990 biologists from Bristol University, England, and the Mongolian State University investigated insects, mammals, spiders and plant life in the Gobi and Altai regions of Mongolia. This publication contains short scientific reports on their findings. It also describes how the expedition was mounted and includes much information of value to other potential visitors, field workers or the ordinary tourist going to Mongolia.

54 **The mammals of China and Mongolia.**
Glover Morrill Allen. New York: American Museum of Natural History, 1938. 2 vols. maps. bibliog. (Natural History of Central Asia vol. 21).

A systematic account of the mammals of Mongolia and China by order, family, genera and species, with data on their location, habitat, measurement, colour and previous studies. The information is based on the results of the Central Asiatic Expeditions mounted by the American Museum of Natural History in 1921-30. A detailed index and a comprehensive bibliography are also provided. Over half the study is devoted to the mammals of Mongolia.

55 **The mammals of the Mongolian People's Republic.**
D. P. Mallon. *Mammal Review*, vol. 15, no. 2 (1985), p. 71-102. maps. bibliog.

This article summarizes Mongolian, Russian and German literature on the 119 mammals of Mongolia and indicates their distribution. The author also mentions twenty-four other species which are unconfirmed or whose existence in Mongolia might be confirmed in future because they are known to exist on the borders.

56 **New sighting of Przewalski horses.**
Z. Kaszab. *Oryx*, vol. 8, no. 6 (Dec. 1966), p. 345-47.

In 1966 an expedition from the Hungarian Academy of Sciences reported a new sighting of eight Przewalski horses in southwestern Mongolia. If genuine, this is the most recent sighting of the horse in the wild but not all scholars accepted that the animals were correctly identified. In this article for a popular audience, the author describes what the members of the team saw and the locality in which it occurred.

57 **Observations on some large mammals of the Transaltai, Djungarian and Shargyn Gobi, Mongolia.**
Ya. Dash, A. Szaniawski, G. S. Child, P. Hunkeler. *La Terre et la Vie*, vol. 31 (1977), p. 587-97.

This article describes a conservation study of fauna and vegetation in the semi-desert regions of the Mongolian Gobi and Altai. The study was commissioned by the Mongolian government in 1972-74 in preparation for setting up the Great Gobi National Park in 1976. The article identifies a range of animals which were sighted by the researchers or believed to inhabit the region. These include snow leopard, wolf, Gobi bear, wild ass, wild camel, ibex, wild sheep, black gazelle and saiga antelope.

58 **Przewalski's horse - putting the wild horse back in the wild.**
Oliver A. Ryder. *Oryx* no. 22 (July 1988), p. 154-57.

Equus przewalski is the only true wild horse but it has not been sighted in the wild since 1966 (see item no. 56). There were, however, 660 specimens in seventy zoos around the world in 1988. This author discusses the breeding programme for the species and the efforts made to select a suitable site in Mongolia where the animals can be reintroduced into the wild. (A number were released in 1992.)

59 **The Przevalsky horse.**
Sándor Bökönyi, translated from the Hungarian by Lili Halápy.
London: Souvenir Press, 1974. maps. bibliog.

An informative book written in an attractive style for the general reader on the Asiatic wild horse. This is the Przewalski horse (*Equus przewalski*) and is named after the Polish traveller Col. N. M. Przewalski (see item no. 33) who found the remains of one near Khovd in the 1880s. Bökönyi describes the characteristics of the horse, its origins and its relationship to other horses. Habitat, diet and breeding in captivity are also discussed.

60 **Still living? Yeti, Sasquatch and the Neanderthal enigma.**
Myra Shackley. New York, London: Thames & Hudson, 1986.
Reprinted ed. 192p. maps. bibliog.

There have been reported sightings of hairy wildmen in Mongolia from ancient times to the present. The Mongols call them *Almas*. In this book on the phenomenon of wildmen worldwide, a British archaeologist examines evidence for the continuing existence of Neanderthal Man in Mongolia on the basis of documented reports and fieldwork. She concludes that the *Almas* do exist and that a link between them and Neanderthal Man is distinctly possible. An article on the Mongolian phenomenon was also published by the same author in *Antiquity* (vol. 56 (1982), p. 31-41). See also item no. 67 by the same author.

Flora and Fauna

61   **A survey of the birds of Mongolia.**
     Charles Vaurie. *Bulletin of the American Museum of Natural History*,
     vol. 127, no. 3 (1964) p. 105-43.

Very little information is available in English on the birds of Mongolia. This is a preliminary inventory which has been compiled on the basis of specimens collected by the American Museum of Natural History's Central Asiatic Expeditions of 1921-30 and on the results of investigations made in the 1930s by E. V. Kozlova, of the Leningrad (now St. Petersburg) Museum. The birds listed are located in five geographical zones, and the affinities of Mongolia's avifauna are discussed. Vaurie stresses that this is not a formal inventory as trinomials are not used and he does not provide the customary bibliographical information for each because sufficient information was not available at the time of writing.

62   **Systematic account of a collection of fishes from the Mongolian People's**
     Republic: with a review of the hydrobiology of the major Mongolian
     drainage basins.
     Robert A. Travers. *Bulletin British Museum (Natural History)*,
     Zoology Series, vol. 55, no. 2 (Oct. 1989), p. 173-207. bibliog.

A British zoologist has produced this pioneering study of the fishes of Mongolia. He reviews the hydrobiological history of the three drainage basins of Mongolia which are headwaters of the great rivers of Siberia, and identifies twenty-three species of fresh and saltwater aquatic fauna which he collected during a field trip to Mongolia in 1984.

63   **Wild camels of the Gobi.**
     Andrei G. Bannikov. *Wildlife*, vol. 18, no. 9 (Sept. 1976), p. 398-403.
     map.

The Polish zoologist and traveller, N. M. Przewalski first described the Mongolian wild camel (Mon. *khavtgai*) in 1873 but no specimen was photographed until the 1950s. In this article a Soviet biologist discusses the scientific study of the wild camel and describes its characteristics and behaviour for a popular audience.

64   **Wild horses and other endangered wildlife in Mongolia.**
     D. Tsevegmid, A. Dashdorj, translated by I. Montagu. *Oryx*, vol. 12,
     no. 3 (1974), p. 361-70. map. bibliog.

An article for the general reader describing the wild species of the Mongolian south and southwest, in particular, the Przewalski horse (*takh'*), wild camel (*khavtgai*), Gobi bear (*mazaalai*) and wild ass (*khulan*) with a discussion of conservation issues related to these animals.

Information Mongolia.
See item no. 3.

Across Mongolian plains: a naturalist's account of China's 'Great Northwest'.
See item no. 24.

Mongolia, the Tangut country and the solitudes of Northern Tibet being a
narrative of three years travel in Eastern High Asia.
See item no. 33.

The new conquest of Central Asia: a narrative of explorations of the Central Asiatic expeditions in Mongolia and China, 1921-1930.
See item no. 35.

Wapiti hunting in the Mongolian People's Republic.
See item no. 44.

Die mongolische Volksrepublik: physisch-geographische Beschreibung. (The Mongolian People's Republic: description of physical geography.)
See item no. 47.

Quelques données sur l'élevage du yak en République Populaire de Mongolie. (Some data on yak herding in the Mongolian People's Republic).
See item no. 326.

The Mongolian 'Red Book'.
See item no. 347.

Horse brands of the Mongolians: a system of signs in a nomadic culture.
See item no. 438.

Some notes on the role of dogs in the life of the Mongolian herdsman.
See item no. 443.

Archaeology

65 **New data on palaeolithic finds in Mongolia.**
Miklos Gabori. *Asian Perspectives* (*Hong Kong*), vol. 7, nos. 1-2
(1963), p. 105-12. map. bibliog.

Gabori took part in important archaeological expeditions under the Soviet archaeologist,
A. P. Okladnikov, in Ömnögov' *aimag* and in the Orkhon valley from 1958-61. In this
article, he identifies nineteen palaeolithic sites and surveys research on some sixty sites
discovered in Mongolia since the Second World War. Although there is a more recent
study of the Mongolian Palaeolithic in English, which is cited as item no. 67, this one is
less technical and would appeal to a more general audience.

66 **On the archaeological traces of old Turks in Mongolia.**
Edward Tryjarski. *East and West* (Rome), vol. 21, new series, nos. 1-2
(March-June 1971), p. 121-35. bibliog.

The author of this article is a Polish scholar who spent a month in 1963 taking squeezes
of Turkic inscriptions on stone stele in the Ongin, Orkhon, Selenge and Tuul river
valleys in central Mongolia. His article is a good introduction for non-specialists to the
range and distribution of archaeological relics in Mongolia. These include towns and
forts, burial mounds and slab graves, stone sculptures, pillars and inscribed stones.
Suggestions for further reading are provided and twenty-four photographs are
included.

67 **Palaeolithic archaeology in the Mongolian People's Republic.**
Myra Shackley. *Proceedings of the Prehistoric Society*, vol. 50
(Dec. 1984), p. 23-34. bibliog.

The author, a British archaeologist summarizes current knowledge of the Mongolian
Palaeolithic, commenting on sites, objects found and datings. The article is fairly
technical and the general reader might wish to consult item no. 65 or 68 in conjunction
with this one. See also item no. 60 by the same author.

68 **The Paleolithic of Mongolia.**
Aleksei Pavlovich Okladnikov. In: *Early paleolithic in South and East Asia.* Edited by Fumiko Ikawa-Smith.   The Hague: Mouton, 1978, p. 317-25. bibliog. (World Anthropology).
A brief account of research on the Mongolian stone age since the Second World War, with remarks on cultural diffusion and the search for Man's original homeland. The author is a Soviet archaeologist who has published extensively on Mongolian archaeology in Russian.

69 **Review of Mongolian archaeology.**
Frank Bessac.   *Asian Perspectives (Hong Kong),* vol. 8, no. 1 (summer 1964), p. 141-47.
In 1962 the Soviet Academy of Sciences published a collection of articles on archaeological research in Mongolia from 1889 by Mongolian and Russian scholars. The work, *Mongol'skii arkheologicheskii sbornik* 'A collection of articles on Mongolian archaeology' edited by S. V. Kiselev, is reviewed in this article and abstracts of several of the papers are included. Bronze knives of the Karasuk culture, bronze arrow heads, deer stones, the Xiongnu graves of Noyon Uul in central Mongolia, petroglyphs, Khitan settlements, iron objects, stone tortoises and inscriptions in the Onon valley are among the subjects covered.

70 **Rock 'art galleries' in Mongolia.**
D. Dorj.   *Canada-Mongolia Review,* vol. 1, no. 2 (1975), p. 49-55. bibliog.
This is a translation of an article by a Mongolian archaeologist for a popular audience, giving concise information on rock paintings and bas reliefs in Mongolia, with remarks on materials, ground and subjects.

Die Mongolen. (The Mongols.)
See item no. 7.

Mongolian journey.
See item no. 15.

Still living? Yeti, Sasquatch and the Neanderthal enigma.
See item no. 60.

Fossils from the Gobi desert.
See item no. 361.

Hunting for dinosaurs.
See item no. 364.

L'architecture mongole ancienne. (Old Mongolian architecture.)
See item no. 415.

Archaeology

Erdene-zuu, un monastère de XVI siècle en Mongolie. (Erdene Zuu: a sixteenth century monastery in Mongolia.)
See item no. 419.

Günjiin süm: the monastery of the princess.
See item no. 458.

History

General

71   **The empire of the steppes: a history of Central Asia.**
René Grousset, translated from French by Naomi Walford.   New
Brunswick, New Jersey: Rutgers University Press, 1991. Reprinted ed.
687p. maps. bibliog.

This history of Central Asia from prehistoric times to the 18th century examines the
rise and fall of a succession of nomadic empires. Many were centred on or included the
territory of modern Mongolia, for instance, the Xiongnu Empire (2nd and 1st centuries
BC), the 4th century Ruanruan, the 5th and 8th century Turkic states and the largest,
the Mongol Empire. It concludes with an account of the Oirat or Jungar empire of the
17th century. The book first appeared in French in 1939 and it has not been surpassed
for scope of information or its compelling and attractive style. Insofar as it deals with
the Mongols it has the special value of presenting Mongolian history at the centre of a
nomadic, Inner Asian tradition and not as peripheral to Chinese history.

72   **Essays in Mongolian studies.**
Sechin Jagchid.   Provo, Utah: Brigham Young University, 1988. 348p.
maps. bibliog. (David M. Kennedy Centre for International Studies
Monograph Series, no. 3).

This collection of twenty-three essays on Mongolian history is significant because it is
the work of a Mongolian historian who uses source materials not available in the west.
He handles a wide range of subjects and periods including Chinggis Khan and the
Mongol Empire, folklore, shamanism and the Inner Mongolian nationalist movement.
Jagchid presents his subjects from a Mongolian perspective and, in the case of the 20th
century nationalist movement, with the benefit of personal experience.

73 **Imperial nomads: a history of Central Asia, 500-1500.**
Luc Kwanten. Leicester, England: Leicester University Press, 1979.
352p. maps. bibliog.

This monograph is a history of the nomadic empires of Central Asia for students and non-specialists. It was written with the intention of updating R. Grousset's *The empire of the steppes: a history of Central Asia* (see item no. 71) but its coverage of empires from the 6th to the 12th century, especially those in western Asia, is brief. The larger part of the book is, in fact, devoted to the Mongol Empire which the author regards as the culmination of the steppe tradition.

74 **The Mongol chronicle Altan Tobči: text, translation, and critical notes.**
Charles Roskelly Bawden. Wiesbaden, Germany: Harrassowitz, 1955.
205p. bibliog. (Göttinger Asiatische Forschungen Band 5).

This work is based on the author's doctoral thesis at Cambridge University, 1954/55, and comprises a romanized text of the Mongolian chronicle *Altan Tobchi* 'Golden Summary' with an English translation. It was written in about 1655 and records the lives and achievements of Mongol khans from Chinggis Khan (ca. 1167-1227) to Lighdan, the last Great Khan, who died in 1636. As a native source of Mongolian history it is generally reliable and agrees with other native sources such as the *Secret History of the Mongols* (see item no. 84). It was, however, compiled after the Mongols became Buddhists and Chinggis Khan, who was actually a shamanist, was provided with a Buddhist genealogy dating back to the ancient kings of India.

75 **The modern history of Mongolia.**
Charles Roskelly Bawden, with afterword by Alan Sanders. London: KPI; New York: Routledge, Chapman & Hall, 1989. 2nd rev. ed. 476p. maps. bibliog.

This is a very comprehensive history of Khalkh Mongolia, from 1691, when the Khalkh Mongols came under Manchu rule, to the present. It is the most detailed and authoritative account in a western language of Mongolia in the Manchu period and owes much to the author's wide reading of Mongolian sources. Mongolian autonomy after 1911, the revolution of 1921 and the early years of single party rule are also well covered but the events from the mid-1930s onward are examined in less detail because of the scarcity of reliable information at the time of writing. For the Manchu period and the early 20th century, however, this remains the standard textbook providing a critical analysis of the political and social institutions and trends. The book is essential background for comprehending the dynamics and development of Mongolia in the 20th century.

Area handbook for Mongolia.
See item no. 1.

Information Mongolia.
See item no. 3.

Die Mongolen. (The Mongols.)
See item no. 7.

Mongolia: a country study.
See item no. 9.

Studies on Mongolia: proceedings of the first North American conference on Mongolian studies.
See item no. 23.

A lost civilization: the Mongols rediscovered.
See item no. 461.

The Mongol chronicles of the seventeenth century.
See item no. 462.

Works of Mongolian historians (1960-1974): trudy mongol'skikh istorikov (1960-1974).
See item no. 489.

Mongolia and the Mongols before Chinggis Khan

76   **The Cambridge history of early Inner Asia.**
     Edited by Denis Sinor.   Cambridge, England; New York: Cambridge
     University Press, 1990. 518p. maps. bibliog.

The most recent work of scholarship on the states and empires of Central Asia from earliest times to the twelfth century by various scholars. Many of the empires described, for example that of the Xiongnu (200 BC - 48 AD), the fourth century Ruanruan, the fifth century Turkic empire and the eighth century Uigur state, had their centres in or included Mongolia. Each chapter has its own bibliography and an index is provided.

77   **Khitan settlements in northern Mongolia: new light on the social and cultural history of the pre-Chingisid era.**
     Keith Scott.   *Canada-Mongolia Review*, vol. 1, no. 1 (1975) p. 5-28.

The Khitan controlled a large empire in northeast Asia in the tenth century and their rule, which extended to North China, is called the Liao dynasty by the Chinese. Some scholars believe that the Khitan were a Mongol people and spoke a Mongolian dialect. In this study of Khitan towns in Mongolia this author suggests that the history of the Mongols did not begin with Chinggis Khan and his immediate predecessors and that the Khitan settlements of Mongolia are a legitimate part of the Mongols' early history.

78 **L'histoire des Mongols avant Gengis-Khan d'après les sources chinoises et mongoles, et la documentation conservée par Rašidu-d-'Din.** (The history of the Mongols before Chingis Khan according to Chinese and Mongol sources and the documents preserved by Rashīd Al-Dīn.)
Louis Hambis. *Central Asiatic Journal*, vol. 14, nos. 1-3 (1970), p. 125-33.

The name 'Mongol' was first mentioned in Chinese documents of the Tang dynasty (6th-10th century). In this article written in French the author examines early reports of the Mongols in Chinese sources from the Tang dynasty to the 10th century Liao (Khitan) dynasty of China and compares these with Mongolian traditions as preserved by the Persian historian Rashīd Al-Dīn Tabib (see item no. 97). He identifies the earliest locations of the Mongols and their migrations to the southwest into Mongolia. For a more concise discussion of this topic in English see item no. 79.

79 **Mongolia before Genghis Khan: the native tradition.**
John Andrew Boyle. *Journal of the Anglo-Mongolian Society*, vol. 2, no. 1 (June 1974), p. 60-69.

A retelling of the legend of the origin of the Mongolian nation as preserved by the Persian historian Rashīd Al-Dīn (see item no. 97) and in the *Secret history of the Mongols* (see item no. 84). Rashīd says that the Mongol people were imprisoned in a narrow mountain valley from which they broke out by melting the iron-ore in the mountain. Boyle argues that the story is not incompatible with that in the *Secret history of the Mongols* which says that the Mongols were the progeny of the union of a Grey Wolf and a Fallow Deer.

Die Mongolen. (The Mongols.)
See item no. 7.

The empire of the steppes: a history of Central Asia.
See item no. 71.

Imperial nomads: a history of Central Asia, 500-1500.
See item no. 73.

The history and the life of Chinggis Khan. (The Secret History of the Mongols.)
See item no. 84.

The history of the Mongol conquests.
See item no. 85.

The Mongols.
See item no. 91.

Chinggis Khan, ca. 1167-1227 and the Mongol Empire, 1206-1368

80 **Conquerors and Confucians: aspects of political change in late Yüan China.**
John W. Dardess.   New York, London: Columbia University Press, 1973. 245p. map. bibliog.

This is the only monograph in English to deal specifically with the closing years of Mongol rule in China (the Yuan dynasty) and the collapse of the Mongol Empire, 1328-68. The author discusses the decline of steppe politics in the Empire and traces the events that led to the eviction of the Mongol court from Beijing by Chinese forces of the Ming. A violent debate about Confucianism in the state among Mongol and other non-Chinese officials was a prominent feature of these years which the author treats in some detail.

81 **The devil's horsemen: the Mongol invasion of Europe.**
James Chambers.   London: Cassell, 1988. Rev. ed. 214p. maps. bibliog.

An account of the Mongol reconnaissance and the campaign against Europe, which began in 1221, and of Mongol relations with the papacy. The book is ideal for the older schoolchild, students or the general reader.

82 **Genghis Khan.**
Michel Hoang, translated from the French by Ingrid Cranfield.
London: Saqi Books, 1990; New York: New Amsterdam Books, 1991. 323p. maps. bibliog.

One of several recent biographies of Chinggis Khan, (ca. 1167-1227), founder of the Mongol Empire. This one, written by a journalist and first published in French (Librairie Arthème Fayard, 1988), makes absorbing reading for the student or popular audience. The author examines the character of his subject and analyses his achievements against the background of Inner Asian geography, politics and society.

83 **Genghis Khan: his life and legacy.**
Paul Ratchnevsky, translated and edited by Thomas Nivison Haining.
Oxford: Blackwell, 1991; Cambridge, Massachusetts: Blackwell, 1992. 313p. map. bibliog.

This biography of Chinggis Khan was first published in German (Wiesbaden, Germany: Franz Steiner, 1983). It is an objective study of the youth, rise to power, rule and personality of its subject and of the structure of the Mongol Empire under his rule. The author supports all statements and conclusions with extensive references and endnotes, although some of the notes which appeared in the German edition have been omitted from the English version. An essential text for the serious student of Chinggis Khan and the Mongols' rise to power, this well-written English translation has much to interest a wider audience also.

84   **The history and the life of Chinggis Khan.** (The secret history of the
     Mongols).
     Translated and annotated by Urgunge Onon.   Leiden, Netherlands,
     New York: Brill, 1990. 183p. map. bibliog.

The *Secret history of the Mongols*, which chronicles the ancestry and life of Chinggis
Khan, is the only extant, contemporary native source on the mediaeval Mongols. Some
scholars, including Onon, believe it to have been written in 1228 while others prefer
1240. The author is a native Mongolian speaker who writes in a plain style and
language which is acceptable both to scholars and laymen. Another excellent version
by F. W. Cleaves (Cambridge, Massachussetts: Harvard University Press, 1982) has
been translated in the style of the Authorized Version of the Bible which is less
appealing, especially to the general reader.

85   **The history of the Mongol conquests.**
     John Joseph Saunders.   London: Routledge & Kegan Paul; New York:
     Barnes & Noble, 1971. 275p. maps. bibliog.

Recent scholarship has outdated this monograph to some extent, but it still remains a
useful and generally sound introduction to the Mongol conquests for students and
laymen. The author examines the history and geography of Inner Asia from 750 to
1200 before describing the conquests, the administration of conquered territories and
the disintegration of the Empire in the early 14th century. There are extensive
footnotes, genealogies, glossary, notes on transliteration and appendices on the *Secret
history of the Mongols* (see item no. 84) and the Mongols' use of firearms.

86   **The history of the world conqueror.**
     'Ala-ad-Din' Ata-Malik Juvaini, translated from the text of Mirza
     Muhammed Qazvini by John Andrew Boyle.   Manchester, England:
     Manchester University Press, 1958. 2 vols. maps. bibliog. (Unesco
     Collection of Representative Works, Persian series).

Juvaini (b. 1226) was a Muslim in the service of the Il-Khans, the Mongol rulers of
Persia, and he became the governor of Baghdad. He travelled widely in the Mongol
Empire and compiled this record of the life and achievements of Chinggis Khan, the
Mongol conquests up to the reign of Möngke Khan (1251-59) and the subject peoples
of the Empire from what he observed personally or learned from other eye-witnesses.
The book is written in a rhetorical style of Persian with many quotations from poetry
and the Koran. Although not always accurate in detail it is an important contemporary
source on the Mongol conquests by someone who lived close to the events described.

87   **Khubilai Khan: his life and times.**
     Morris Rossabi.   Berkeley, Los Angeles, California; London:
     University of California Press, 1988. 322p. maps. bibliog.

Khubilai, (1215-1294) a grandson of Chinggis Khan became Great Khan of the Mongol
Empire in 1260. During his reign the political centre of the Empire shifted to China
and the western territories began to break away as independent states. This major
biography attempts to treat Khubilai not so much as a Chinese emperor, as many
previous historians have done, but as a Mongol leader who sought to continue the
traditions and policies of his predecessors while acknowledging that much of his
population was sedentary rather than nomadic. The book is also a partial history of

China under Mongol rule. It acknowledges Khubilai's achievements in government and public works and as a patron of arts and religion but also indicates weaknesses of policy which caused the Empire to decline after Khubilai's death. The book will appeal to a wide audience and its bibliography includes many works of recent scholarship on the period.

88 **Mission to Asia.**
Compiled by Christopher Dawson. Toronto, London: Toronto University Press, 1986. Rev. ed. 246p. (Medieval Academy Reprints for Teaching).

This book was first published in 1955 and has been reissued under various imprints since then. It comprises a collection of reports by mediaeval European travellers whom the Pope sent on fact-finding missions to the Mongol court with the ultimate goal of converting the Mongols to Christianity. Included in the collection are excellent translations of John of Plano Carpini's history of the Mongols and William of Rubruck's account of his journey to the court of Möngke Khan at Kharkhorin (Karakorum) in 1253-55. The travellers provide lively, first-hand information on the territories, lives and customs of many of the populations of the Empire, as well as accounts of conversations with personalities such as Batu Khan of the Golden Horde (Russia) and the Great Khan Möngke.

89 **The Mongol empire: Genghis Khan: his triumph and his legacy.**
Peter Brent. London: Weidenfeld & Nicholson, 1976. 264p. maps. bibliog.

This entertaining and reliable account of the Mongol conquests and rule has been written by a journalist and can be recommended for a popular audience or older schoolchildren. The book is attractively illustrated in colour and black-and-white, and a chronology of contemporanous events in Western Europe and Eastern Asia is also included.

90 **Mongolian imperialism: the policies of the Grand Qan Mönke in China, Russia, and the Islamic lands, 1251-1259.**
Thomas T. Allsen. Berkeley, Los Angeles, California; London: University of California Press, 1987. 278p. map. bibliog.

This is an exceptional monograph on the Mongol Empire because the author examines Mongol rule throughout the empire as a whole, whereas most major studies have restricted their attention to specific regions. Allsen studies the reign of Möngke Khan (1251-59) and demonstrates how human and material sources were tapped through institutions such as the census, taxation, mobilization and a range of administrative systems, to create and control the world's largest land-based empire. The book is based on the author's doctoral thesis at the University of Minnesota in 1979 and a selective bibliography of Chinese, Persian and Russian sources, as well as western language materials, is included.

91 **The Mongols.**
David Morgan.   Oxford: Basil Blackwell, 1990. Reprinted ed.
Cambridge, Massachusetts: Basil Blackwell, 1987. 238p. map. (The
Peoples of Europe).

Students and other readers with no previous knowledge will find in this book an
excellent introduction to the mediaeval Mongols and their empire. The author provides
a brief but cogent survey of the origins, conquests and rule of the Mongols and he
analyses past and present judgements on these in the light of contemporary sources
and recent historical scholarship. The bibliography and footnotes are excellent guides
to further reading.

92 **The Mongols and Russia.**
George Vernadsky.   New Haven, Connecticut: Yale University Press,
1953. 462p. maps. bibliog. (A history of Russia, vol. 3).

A standard textbook study of the Mongol conquests of Russia and the history of the
Golden Horde as Mongol rule in Russia was called. Genealogical tables of the khans of
the Golden Horde are also provided. For a new evaluation of the impact of Mongol
rule in Russia, see item no. 95.

93 **The Muslim world: a historical survey. Part 2: the Mongol period.**
Berthold Spuler, translated from the German by F. R. C. Bagley.
Leiden, Netherlands: Brill, 1969. Reprinted ed. 125p. map. bibliog.

This book was first published in German in 1953 by Brill. The author has added further
passages and notes in the English version however. The work is a survey of the Mongol
conquests and rule of Islamic countries of central and western Asia, which include
Iran, Egypt and the Chagatai Khanate between the River Oxus and Mongolia, Russia
and India are also referred to. Several genealogies and dynastic charts are provided
and there is a guide to further reading in several languages.

94 **The rise of Chingis Khan and his conquest of North China.**
Henry Desmond Martin, introduction by Owen Lattimore, edited by
Eleanor Lattimore.   New York: Octagon, 1971. Reprinted ed. 360p.
maps. bibliog.

This is the most comprehensive account of the Mongol army and Chinggis Khan's East
Asian conquests. The author discusses the size of the army, its organization and the
military techniques and strategy of the Mongols and he provides detailed descriptions
of important battles. Martin's conclusions are based chiefly on Chinese sources. He
believes that China was the main object of the Mongols' military campaigns and that
for political reasons, rather than because of a deterioration in the Mongolian climate as
some writers have suggested.

95 **Russia and the Golden Horde: the Mongol impact on medieval Russian
history.**
C. J. Halperin.   Bloomington, Indiana: 1985; London: Tauris, 1987.
Reprinted ed. 180p. maps. bibliog.

This author re-examines traditional evaluations of the Mongol conquest and rule of
Russia and concludes that they are misleading. This is because Russian Christian

writers have deliberately remained silent about facts that were inconvenient from a religious point of view. Halperin demonstrates that relations between the two peoples were varied and not uniformly hostile, and that the Mongols made a considerable contribution to politics, society and commerce in Russia. He suggest that recent Soviet scholarship, in spite of its own ideological prejudices, also supports this thesis and he provides an extensive bibliography of relevant publications in Russian as well as in western European languages.

96 **Some remarks on the ideological foundations of Chingis Khan's empire.**
    Igor de Rachewiltz. *Papers on Far Eastern History*, vol. 7 (Mar. 1973),
    p. 21-36. bibliog.
This is a lucid study of Chinggis Khan's belief that Eternal Heaven had bestowed on him the right to rule the whole world. His successors used the same idea to justify the continuation of campaigns of conquest and their aggressive style of foreign policy. Rachewiltz suggests that this ideology was essentially derived from the Chinese belief in the Mandate of Heaven and transmitted to the Mongols by Chinese and other East Asians in the service of Chinggis Khan.

97 **The successors of Chingis Khan.**
    Rashīd Al-Dīn Tabib, translated by John A. Boyle.   New York,
    London: Columbia University Press, 1971. 372p. bibliog.
Rashīd (born ca. 1247) was chief minister to the Il-khan Ghazan of Persia. His account, written in Persian, of the rule of Great Khans and khans, from the death of Chinggis Khan in 1227 to the end of the 13th century, is one of the most important contemporary sources on the history of the Empire. It is based extensively on a lost Mongol work *Altan Debter* 'Golden Notebook'. It provides valuable information on the Mongol campaigns in Russia, Eastern Europe and South China, genealogical data on the imperial family and much of what is known about the administrative and financial systems of the empire.

98 **The travels of Marco Polo.**
    Marco Polo, translated by Ronald Latham.   Harmondsworth,
    England: Penguin, 1965. Reprinted ed. 379p. (Penguin Classics).
The best known mediaeval travel account by a European to the Mongol Empire. Polo (1254-1324) was a Venetian who served Khubilai Khan (r. 1260-1294) as an imperial emissary for seventeen years. His lively and colourful accounts of the customs and institutions he observed, including a contemporary view of the court of Khubilai at Khanbalic (Beijing), has remained a popular European classic ever since and inspired later generations of travellers to 'go east'. (For example, see item no. 31.) Several translations of Polo's book are available in English. This one is widely available and is indexed.

The empire of the steppes: a history of Central Asia.
See item no. 71.

Essays in Mongolian studies.
See item no. 72.

Imperial nomads: a history of Central Asia.
See item no. 73.

The Altan Tobči: text, translation and critical notes.
See item no. 74.

La condition de la femme mongole au 12e/13e siècle. (The position of the Mongol woman in the 12th and 13th centuries.)
See item no. 151.

Turkish and Mongol shamanism in the Middle Ages.
See item no. 217.

The political role of Mongol Buddhism.
See item no. 227.

Fundamental principles of Mongol law.
See item no. 271.

L'architecture mongole ancienne. (Old Mongolian architecture.)
See item no. 415.

Post-imperial Mongolia: the Age of Fragmentation, 1368-1691

99 **Dictionary of Ming biography, 1368-1644.**
Edited by L. Carrington Goodrich. New York, London: Columbia University Press, 1976. 2 vols.

Most of the individuals cited in this dictionary are Chinese but several good biographies of Mongols with whom the Chinese Ming government (1368-1644) had dealings are also included. Among these are Arughtai and the Oirat Mongol Esen Khan contributed by M. Rossabi, Batu Möngke, who was also known as Dayan Khan, by R. A. Miller and Altan Khan by H. Serruys.

100 **The fragmentation of the Mongols during the Ming dynasty and their step-by-step conquest by the Manchus and Russians. Part 1. The Mongols and Ming China. Part 2. The Mongols and the Manchus.**
Joseph S. Sebes. *Canada-Mongolia Review*, vol. 2, no. 2 (winter 1976), p. 127-49; vol. 3, no. 1 (May 1977), p. 22-32. bibliog.

A concise survey of Mongol politics after the fall of the Empire in 1368. The first part covers the fragmentation of Mongol unity and the alliance of various groups of Mongols with one another and with the Chinese Ming dynasty (1368-1644). In the second part the author examines political tensions in northeast Asia in the 17th century which were caused by the appearance of Russians in eastern Siberia and by the pressure of the rising Manchus.

101 **An historical sketch of Köke-khota city capital of Inner Mongolia.**
Paul V. Hyer. *Central Asiatic Journal*, vol. 26, no. 1-2 (1982),
p. 56-77.
Hohehot, the modern administrative centre of the Inner Mongolian Autonomous
Region of China, was founded by the Mongolian khan Altan in the 16th century and it
became an important Buddhist centre. This article gives a short account of the history
of the town from its beginnings until 1949.

102 **History of the Eastern Mongols during the Ming dynasty from 1368 to
1634.**
Dmitrii Dmitrievich Pokotilov. Philadelphia, Pennsylvania:
Porcupine Press, 1976. 243p. Reprinted ed.
The history of the eastern Mongols from the fall of the Empire in 1368 to the rise of
the Manchus in the 17th century is imperfectly known. This work, first published in
Russian in 1893 and in English translation in 1947 (Studia Serica Monographs, series
A, nos. 1 & 5, 1947 & 1949), is the only historical monograph on the period in English.
The author relies extensively on the Chinese Ming dynastic history, the *Ming shi*,
which he supplements with information drawn from other Chinese records and
Mongolian chronicles. Mongol-Ming relations and relations between different groups
of Mongols in this period are emphasized rather than the internal affairs and social
history of the Mongols. Part I is a translation of the Russian text by Rudolf
Loewenthal and part II contains addenda and corrigenda by Wolfgang Franke.

103 **The Mongols and Ming China: customs and history.**
Henry Serruys, edited by Françoise Aubin. London: Variorum
Reprints, 1987. 245p. bibliog. (Collected Studies Series no. CS262).
A collection of reprinted articles by an outstanding western scholar of Mongol relations
with the Ming dynasty of China. It includes a translation in French of a contemporary
Chinese account of Mongols, *Bei lou fengsu* 'Customs of the northern captives', by Xia
Tasheng besides articles on the survival of Mongol customs in the early Ming period,
Mongol oaths, Mongols in China 1400-50, and the biographies of two Mongolian
princesses, who were known as the Third Lady Erketü Khatun and Dayiching Beyiji.

104 **Notes on Esen's pride and Ming China's prejudice.**
Morris Rossabi. *Mongolia Society Bulletin*, vol. 9, no. 2 (fall, 1970),
p. 31-39. bibliog.
Conflict between the eastern Mongols and the Oirat Mongols was a recurring factor in
Mongol politics from the 14th to the 17th century. Esen Khan was a prominent leader
of the Oirats in the early 15th century. It was his ambition to reunite all Mongols under
his rule after the fashion of Chinggis Khan. To this end he formed an alliance with the
Ming government of China but when he was refused a Chinese princess for a bride he
attacked China in 1449. The article examines this incident and the motivations of the
sides involved which were characteristic of Mongol-Chinese relations in this period.

105 **Oirat-Chinese tribute relations, 1408-1446.**
David Miller Farquhar. In: *Studia Altaica, Festschrift für Nikolaus Poppe zum 60. Geburtsdag am 8. August 1957.* (Studia Altaica: festschrift for Nicholas Poppe on the occasion of his 60th birthday on 8 August 1957.) Wiesbaden, Germany: Harrassowitz, 1957, p. 60-68. (Ural-Altaische Bibliotek, Band 5).

In this paper Farquhar examines Oirat Mongol expansion from the Altai mountains to the borders of Korea in the early 15th century, with particular emphasis on Oirat relations with Ming China. The Oirat sent forty-three tribute missions to China in thirty-nine years, not because the Chinese Ming government forced them to do so but because they wanted to obtain Chinese goods in exchange.

106 **The political ideas of Lindan Khan.**
Junpei Hagiwara. In: *Proceedings of the Third East Asian Altaistic Conference August 17-24, 1969, Taipei, China*, edited by Chen Jiexian Sechin Jagchid. Taibei: National Taiwan University, 1969. p. 97-106.

Lighdan or Lindan Khan of the Chakhar, who died in 1636, was the last Great Khan of the Mongols. He has been condemned as weak, greedy, cunning and cowardly in Mongol, Chinese and western historiography. This author presents a more sympathetic and considered view, based on the evidence of contemporary documents, that Lighdan tried to deal with the Ming dynasty and the rising Manchus as an equal. Hagiwara argues that Lighdan's ultimate desire was to establish a genuine nomadic state with security of external trade and tribute and gives reasons why.

107 **Sino-Mongol relations during the Ming. Vol 1: the Mongols in China during the Hung-wu period (1368-1398).**
Henry Serruys. Brussels: Institut Belge des Hautes Études Chinoises, 1959. 329p. map. bibliog. (Mélanges Chinoises et Bouddiques, vol. 11).

This work is based on the author's PhD thesis at Columbia University in 1955. In spite of its scholarly content this and the companion volumes cited as items no. 108-09 are extremely well written and might appeal to a wider audience than that of the scholar and student. The first volume is a study of Mongol relations with China during the reign of the first Ming emperor, Hung-wu. Contrary to popular belief 3/4 of the Mongolian army remained behind when the last Great Khan of the Mongols, Togon Temür, fled China in 1368. Serruys describes the services of Mongols in the Ming army and bureaucracy, the distribution of the Mongols in China and the extent to which some of them were Sinicized.

108 **Sino-Mongolian relations during the Ming. Vol 2: the tribute system and diplomatic missions (1400-1600).**
Henry Serruys. Brussels: Institut Belge des Hautes Études Chinoises, 1967. p. 650. bibliog. (Mélanges Chinoises et Bouddhiques, vol. 14).

A companion volume to items no. 107 and 109. Various groups of Mongols were allowed to present tribute to the Ming emperors of China and in return received luxury articles and everyday consumer goods which the Mongolian economy did not produce. The book provides a wealth of information about these missions and the impact this type of exchange had on Mongolia.

109   **Sino-Mongolian relations during the Ming. Vol 3: trade relations: the horse fairs. (1400-1600).**
Henry Serruys.   Brussels: Institut Belge des Hautes Études Chinoises, 1975. 288p. bibliog. (Mélanges Bouddhiques et Chinoises, vol. 17).
The third volume in Serruys' monumental study of Mongol-Ming relations (see also items no. 107-08) in which he describes the political background to the fairs the Mongols demanded in order to exchange horses for Chinese luxury goods. The Ming authorities of China organized such fairs from time to time if the Mongols agreed not to raid northern China. The author discusses the importance of these fairs to the economies of Mongolia and China and provides details of the trade at Liaotung, Tatung and Hsüanfu, including the prices of horses. Although all three volumes are detailed and scholarly works they are beautifully written and might be appreciated by general readers also.

The empire of the steppes: a history of Central Asia.
See item no. 71.

Essays in Mongolian studies.
See item no. 72.

Imperial nomads: a history of Central Asia, 500-1500.
See item no. 73.

The Mongol chronicle Altan Tobči: text, translation, and critical notes.
See item no. 74.

A Mongolian source to the lamaist suppression of shamanism in the 17th century.
See item no. 213.

Early lamaism in Mongolia.
See item no. 220.

The political role of Mongol Buddhism.
See item no. 227.

Fundamental principles of Mongol law.
See item no. 271.

China and Inner Asia from 1368 to the present day.
See item no. 289.

Mongolia under the Manchu (Qing) dynasty, 1691-1911

110 **The Čahar population during the Ch'ing.**
Henry Serruys. *Journal of Asian History*, vol. 12, no. 1 (1978),
p. 58-79.

This is a study of one particular group of Mongols, the Chakhar of Inner Mongolia,
under Manchu (Qing) control. The modern Chakhar live in the district of Kalgan to
the north of Beijing and the Great Wall. Their ancestors were once subjects of
Lighdan Khan, the last Great Khan of all the Mongols whom the Manchus defeated in
1634 (see item no. 106). Thereafter, the Chakhar were not allowed autonomy under
their own princes because, unlike the Khalkh and some other Mongol groups, they did
not submit to the Manchus voluntarily. This article is a study of the relationship of the
Chakhar with the Manchu government and describes the administrative system with its
eight units or banners by which the Manchu controlled the Chakhar.

111 **The Ch'ing administration of Mongolia up to the nineteenth century.**
David Miller Farquhar. PhD thesis, Harvard University,
Cambridge, Massachusetts, 1960. 380p. bibliog. (Available from
Harvard University Library, Microfilm no. 2260.)

Farquhar's thesis is a clear and detailed exposition of the political and military
administrative system by which the Manchu (Qing) government of China organized
and controlled its Mongol populations. He describes the various levels of local
government with its officials, its privileges and obligations, and the central bureaucratic
apparatus, from 1691 to 1800. A chapter is also devoted to the prestigious religious
sector of Mongolian society which included both lamas and lay families who worked
for the monasteries. The religious sector was administratively quite separate from the
banner populations and their ruling princes. The bibliography provided with this work
is extensive and multi-lingual.

112 **Ch'ing policies in Outer Mongolia 1900-1911.**
Thomas Esson Ewing. *Modern Asian Studies*, vol. 14, no. 1 (1980),
p. 145-57.

Before 1900 the Mongol populations under the Manchu (Qing) government of China
enjoyed considerable autonomy under their own princes and the Chinese were not
allowed to intermarry or settle in Mongol lands. In the first decade of the 20th century
a series of extensive administrative and economic reforms, already in force among the
Chinese population, were introduced in Inner Mongolia and then ordered to be
implemented in Khalkh. The author of this article examines the impact this decision
had on the Khalkh Mongols arguing that they greatly feared cultural assimilation with
the Chinese and the extinction of the Mongol nation. These fears were important
factors in the decision of the Khalkh Mongols to declare independence in 1911.

113   **The city of Urga in the Manchu period.**
      Robert Arthur Rupen.   In: *Studia Altaica: Festschrift für Nikolaus Poppe zum 60. Geburtsdag am 8. August 1957. (Studia Altaica: festschrift for Nicholas Poppe on the occasion of his 60th birthday on 8 August 1957.)* Wiesbaden, Germany: Harrassowitz, 1957, p. 157-69. bibliog. (Ural-Altaische Bibliothek Band 5).

Before the capital of Mongolia was renamed Ulaanbaatar in 1924, Europeans called it Urga. The Mongols themselves called it 'Ikh Khüree' or 'Da Khüree' (Great Monastery). It was founded in 1649 as a tent monastery with no fixed location and it was a residence for the first Javzandamba Khutagt, a prominent 'Living Buddha' (see item no. 222). By the beginning of the 19th century Ikh Khüree was a small town located on its present site in the Tuul valley and had a population of 7,000, a fifth of which were lamas. This article examines the city's development as a centre for religion, education, commerce and administration until 1911. Further information on the history of the town is provided in item no. 10.

114   **The Dungan uprising and Mongolia.**
      Michael Raymond Underdown.   *Archív Orientální (Prague)*, vol. 58 (1990), p. 238-42.

Between 1864 and 1869 the Manchu (Qing) government of China called up Mongol troops to suppress a number of revolts by Dungans who were Chinese Muslims. The mobilization caused considerable economic hardship among the Mongols of Khalkh and Inner Mongolia at a time when their economy was in decline generally. Furthermore, Uliastai and Khovd in the west of Khalkh were attacked by Dungans in 1879 and Ikh Khüree (now Ulaanbaatar) was threatened. Although this article discusses these events without drawing specific conclusions, the impact of the Dungan uprising on the Mongols is clearly a contributory factor to the revolutionary situation that led to the Mongolian revolution of 1911.

115   **Manchu Chinese colonial rule in Northern Mongolia.**
      M. Sanjdorj translated from the Mongolian and annotated by Urgunge Onon. Preface by Owen Lattimore.   London: Hurst; New York: St. Martins, 1980. 118p. map. bibliog.

Mongols have exchanged goods with the Chinese for many centuries but it was only from the 17th century, after the Mongols had been absorbed into the Manchu empire, that this trade was conducted in Mongolia rather than China. A Mongolian historian traces the expansion of Chinese private trade, which included barter, credit and the loan of silver at high rates of interest, from 17th-20th centuries. Sanjdorj argues that the Mongols derived no benefit from this form of commerce but only crippling debts and that it was a contributory factor in the nationalist independence movement of the 19th and early 20th centuries. This book is of particular interest because it examines Mongol-Chinese relations from a Mongolian viewpoint albeit with a Marxist-Leninist bias.

116 **The Mongol rebellion of 1756-1757.**
Charles Roskelly Bawden. *Journal of Asian History*, vol. 2, no. 1 (1968), p. 1-31.

In 1756 there was an armed rebellion in Khalkh against Manchu (Qing) rule. This was crushed by a large Manchu force in 1757 and the Manchu government tightened its control over the Mongols as a consequence. This detailed article is based on Mongolian studies of the rebellion but its author disagrees with the Mongolian historians' assessment of the rebellion as nationalist and anti-feudal. Bawden argues that the rebel leader Prince Chingunjav was a minor figure who only had a vague notion of independence and was supported by a group of malcontents. However the affair was a turning point in Mongolian history. The previous close alliance that had existed between the senior Mongolian cleric, the Javzandamba Khutagt, and the Manchu emperor was broken and the Manchu government declared that all future incarnations must be discovered in Tibet. From this time there was no significant opposition to Manchu rule until 1911.

117 **Petitions of grievances submitted by the people (18th- beginning of 20th century).**
Translated from the Mongol by Sh. Rashidondog in collaboration with Veronika Veit. Wiesbaden, Germany: Harrassowitz, 1975. 209p. bibliog.

This is a collection of forty-two documents, translated and abridged from Mongolian into English, pertaining to cases brought before the Mongolian courts, mainly during the Manchu (Qing) period. Many concern debt and the non-payment of taxes and some of the cases were brought by commoners against their ruling princes. These documents draw attention to the harsh living conditions of many ordinary Mongols and illustrate the Mongolian legal process in the Manchu period. Most of the documents are preserved in the Mongolian State Central Archives.

118 **Some new information on peasant revolts and people's uprisings in eastern (Inner) Mongolia in the 19th century (1861-1901).**
Walther Heissig. In: *Analecta Mongolica: dedicated to the seventieth birthday of Professor Owen Lattimore*. Edited by John Gombojav Hangin, Urgunge Onon. Bloomington, Indiana: Mongolia Society, 1972, p. 77-99. (Occasional Papers, no. 8).

A series of anti-Chinese revolts in Inner Mongolia in the late 19th century are the subject of this article. Using archival documents and eye witness accounts Heissig exposes the reaction of contemporary Mongols to Chinese immigration, the sale of Mongol pastureland, railway building and to rising taxes. These factors contributed to the growth of nationalism in Inner and Khalkh Mongolia in the early 20th century.

Mongolia and the Mongols.
See item no. 10.

Essays in Mongolian studies.
See item no. 72.

The modern history of Mongolia.
See item no. 75.

The Mongols of the West.
See item no. 168.

The Diluv Khutagt: memoirs and autobiography of a Mongol Buddhist reincarnation in religion and revolution.
See item no. 219.

The Jebtsundamba Khutuktus of Urga: text, translation and notes.
See item no. 222.

Monasteries and cultural change in Inner Mongolia.
See item no. 224.

Mongolian lamaist quasi-feudalism during the period of Manchu domination.
See item no. 225.

The political role of Mongol Buddhism.
See item no. 227.

Mongol community and kinship structure.
See item no. 233.

Fundamental principles of Mongol law.
See item no. 271.

Aspects of Mongolian history, 1901-1915.
See item no. 276.

China and Inner Asia from 1368 to the present day.
See item no. 289.

The struggle for independence: 1911-21

119 **Asia's first modern revolution: Mongolia proclaims its independence.**
Urgunge Onon, Derrick Pritchatt.   Leiden, Netherlands; New York: Brill, 1989. 203p. map. bibliog.

In 1911 the Mongols of Khalkh (Outer) Mongolia broke free from the control of the Manchu (Qing) dynasty of China to establish an independent state of Khalkh Mongols and Inner Mongols. This monograph is a study of events from 1911-14 and efforts to confirm and consolidate the new state. The outstanding feature of the book is the inclusion of numerous and extensive quotations in English translation from official documents and the correspondence between Mongols and Russians who played a central role in the struggle for independence. These translations provide unique insights into the aims and aspirations of the Mongols and tensions amongst individuals at this time. They also challenge a traditional western view that the 1911 revolution was planned and executed by the Tsarist government. Some of the letters were also

History. The struggle for independence: 1911-21

published in the *Journal of the Anglo-Mongolian Society*, (vol. 7, no. 1 [Dec. 1981],
p. 3-72).

120 **Between the hammer and the anvil? Chinese and Russian policies in
     Outer Mongolia 1911-1921.**
     Thomas Esson Ewing. Bloomington, Indiana: Research Institute for
     Inner Asian Studies, 1980. 300p. bibliog. (Uralic and Altaic Series
     vol. 138).
This is the only monograph in English on Mongolia from 1911-21. It is an abridged
version of the author's much longer PhD thesis at Indiana University in 1977 (*Russian
and Chinese policies in Outer Mongolia, 1911-1921* available from University
Microfilms no. 78-5596). Ewing examines the efforts of Mongols to establish an
independent Mongolian state in Khalkh (Outer) Mongolia and shows how Mongolian
affairs and aspirations at that time were manipulated by the Russian and Chinese
governments to protect their own policy interests. Ewing emphasizes the Mongols' own
efforts to control their future, in spite of the obstacles, and provides much evidence to
suggest that the revolutions of 1911 and 1921 were genuine manifestations of Mongol
aspirations and not masterminded and directed by Russia or the Soviet Union.

121 **A contemporary Mongolian account of the period of autonomy.**
     Charles Roskelly Bawden. *Mongolia Society Bulletin*, vol. 9, no. 1
     (spring 1970), p. 8-29.
This Mongolian account of the autonomy (1911-1919) was first published in the 1920s
in the Mongolian script and reprinted in the Cyrillic script in 1962. This English
translation is valuable because it provides English readers with a rare contemporary
Mongolian view of the decision to declare independence in 1911, and a description of
the administrative system that was established as a result.

122 **G. J. Ramstedt and the Mongolian independence movement.**
     Pentti Aalto. *Suomalais-Ugrilainen Seuran Aikakauskirja* (*Journal
     de la Société Finno-Ougrienne*), vol. 72 (1973), p. 21-32. bibliog.
Ramstedt (1873-1950) was a Finnish Mongolist who was acquainted with some of the
leading figures in the Mongolian revolution of 1911. As a European with some
understanding of and sympathy for Mongol aspirations he was a rarity. This article is a
critical study of passages of Ramstedt's memoirs *Seven journeys eastward 1898-1912*
(Bloomington, Indiana: Mongolia Society, 1978), an important source on the
Mongolian revolution of 1911. These describe meetings that took place in 1899-1901
between Ramstedt and an Inner Mongolian official called Khaisan and a Khalkh prince
Khanddorj. They also give an account of Ramstedt's services as an interpreter to the
Mongol delegation which was sent to the St. Petersburg government to seek support
for Mongolian independence in 1911.

123 **Mongolia's renegade monk: the career of Dambiijantsan.**
     John Gaunt. *Journal of the Anglo-Mongolian Society*, vol. 10, no. 1
     (July 1987), p. 27-41.
Dambiijantsan, also known as the Ja Lama, was a Kalmyk who claimed to be the
reincarnation of Amursana, leader of an anti-Manchu rebellion of 1756-57 (see item
no. 116). At the turn of the 20th century Dambiijantsan established a power base in

44

western Mongolia among the Oirat Mongols who believed he had magic powers. He was involved in the Mongolian nationalist movement, sometimes supporting the government in Niislel Khüree (now Ulaanbaatar) and at other times challenging it. He was assassinated by the Mongolian Secret Police in 1923. This article traces Dambiijantsan's life and career which constitute an important dimension in early 20th century Mongolian history.

124   **The Mongolian revolution of 1921.**
Fujiko Isono.   *Modern Asian Studies,* vol. 10, no. 3 (1976), p. 375-94. bibliog.

In 1919 Mongolian princes agreed to end the country's autonomous status under Chinese suzerainty and join the Chinese state. A Chinese force entered the country to implement the change and the following year White Russian forces also occupied Mongolia in their struggle against the Bolsheviks. The occupations were important contributory factors to the formation of the Mongolian People's Party and the revolution of 1921 which established the Party in power. Using rare Mongolian documents of the period this author traces the origins and progress of the revolution and presents compelling reasons why this was a Mongolian rather than a Soviet initiative. See also items no. 127-28 by the same author.

125   **Nationalism and revolution in Mongolia, with a translation from the Mongol of Sh. Nachukdorji's life of Sukhebator.**
Owen Lattimore, Urgunge Onon.   New York: Oxford University Press, 1955. 186p. bibliog.

This is the only biographical monograph in English on D. Sükhbaatar (1894-1923), commander-in-chief of the Mongolian forces during the revolution of 1921. It has been superseded by a more recent study by L. Bat-Ochir and D. Dashjamts which was published in Mongolian and Russian in 1967, but is only available in English in an abridged form (see item no. 14). The new work does discredit some of Natsagdorj's statements in this biography, for instance his claim that lamas caused Sükhbaatar's death by poisoning him in 1923. Lattimore's lengthy introduction is an important feature of this monograph. He analyses Mongolian satellite politics and, although, like the biography, some of his conclusions are now dated, he provides some valid insights into events and conditions in Mongolia at the beginning of the 20th century that brought about two revolutions.

126   **Sendegijn Zagd, reminiscences of a Mongol soldier.**
Veronika Veit.   *Zentralasiatische Studien,* vol. 5 (1971), p. 199-224. maps.

The English translation of a memoir of a Mongolian partisan from a collection published in Ulaanbaatar in 1961. This document illustrates the way soldiers were recruited into Sükhbaatar's army of liberation in 1921 and gives an eye-witness account of some of the military action. The memoir also includes biographical information on Sükhbaatar, alongside whom Zagd fought.

127   **Soviet Russia and the Mongolian revolution of 1921.**
Fujiko Isono.   *Past and Present,* no. 83 (May 1979), p. 114-40.

In this article the author examines the background to the 1921 revolution and the reasons why the Soviet army intervened in Mongolia at that time. She does not agree with those who maintain that this was part of a Russian policy of expansion in East Asia. Rather it was a defensive act to prevent Mongolia being used as a base by counter-revolutionary White Russians who were occupying the country at the time. Soviet fears that the Japanese might also become embroiled in the region was also a factor. The article complements items no. 124 and no. 128 by the same author.

128 **Ungern, le 'baron fou' de la révolution mongole.** (Ungern, the 'mad baron' of the Mongolian revolution.)
Fujiko Isono.   *L'histoire*, no. 49 (Oct. 1982), p. 62-70.

Baron Ungern Sternberg, known as the 'Mad Baron' because of his great brutality, invaded Mongolia in 1920 with an army of anti-communist White Russians. He planned to set up a base there from which to attack eastern Siberia and the TransSiberian railway. The Soviet government regarded his action as a threat to the survival of the Soviet state and and for that reason instructed the Fifth Red Army to enter Mongolia in 1921. A number of sensational accounts of doubtful reliability (for instance F. Ossendowski: *Beasts, men and gods in Mongolia*, New York: Dutton, 1922) have been written about Ungern. This article, which is written in French, is a historian's view of the man and his Mongolian adventure.

129 **With the Russians in Mongolia.**
H. G. C. Perry-Ayscough, R. C. Otter-Barry, with a preface by Claude Macdonald.   London: John Lane & The Bodley Head; New York: John Lane, 1914. 344p. map.

Perry-Ayscough and Otter-Barry were British Army officers who visited Mongolia just before and just after the revolution of 1911. As Europeans with little previous knowledge of Mongolia and the Mongols their analysis of contemporary Mongolian affairs is not always valid but their descriptions of the Mongolian capital, Niislel Khüree (now Ulaanbaatar), other settlements and contemporary economic life are of interest. Other useful features of the book are the discussion of Mongolia's international status from a contemporary European viewpoint and English translations of the texts of the Mongol-Tibetan Treaty of 1912 and the Mongol-Russian Agreement and Protocol of 1912. The book is illustrated with contemporary photographs including some of Mongolian and Russian dignitaries of the period.

130 **Von Cinggis Khan zur Sowjetrepublik: eine kurze Geschichte der Mongolei unter besonderer Berücksichtigung der neuesten Zeit.** (From Chinggis Khan to Soviet republic: a short history of Mongolia with special attention to the contemporary period.)
Ivan Jakovlevich Korostovetz, Erich Hauer.   Berlin, Leipzig: Walter der Gruyter, 1926. 351p. map.

Although this German monograph provides an introduction to Mongolian history, life and society from the Middle Ages to the 20th century, it is chiefly of interest today as an eye-witness account of the period of autonomy, 1911-19, and, in particular, the Sino-Russian negotiations on Mongolia's political status. As Russian Minister in Peking with responsibility for matters pertaining to Mongolia, Korostovetz was closely involved in these negotiations. His book reveals the attitude of Tsarist Russia towards the Khalkh Mongols and their desire for full for independence at this time.

Mongolian heroes of the twentieth century.
See item no. 14.

The pre-revolutionary culture of Mongolia.
See item no. 21.

Sovremennaya Mongolia: otchet Mongol'skoi Ekspeditsii snaryazhennoi Irkutskoi kontori Vserossiiskogo Tsentral'novo Soyuza Potrebitel'nykh obshchestvo 'Tsentrosoyuz'. (Contemporary Mongolia: report of the Mongolian Expedition equipped by the Irkutsk office of the All-Russian Central Union of Consumer Cooperatives 'Tsentrosoyuz'.)
See item no. 22.

Weideplätze der Mongolen im Reich der Chalcha. (Mongolian pastures in Khalkh.)
See item no. 40.

The modern history of Mongolia.
See item no. 75.

Ch'ing policies in Outer Mongolia 1900-1911.
See item no. 112.

History of the Mongolian People's Republic.
See item no. 134.

Mongols of the twentieth century. Part 1.
See item no. 139.

The Diluv Khutagt: memoirs and autobiography of a Mongol reincarnation in religion and revolution.
See item no. 219.

The political role of Mongol Buddhism.
See item no. 227.

How Mongolia is really ruled: a political history of the Mongolian People's Republic, 1900-1978.
See item no. 245.

Japanese involvement in Mongol independence movements 1912-1919.
See item no. 264.

Aspects of Mongolian history, 1901-1915.
See item no. 276.

From 1921 to the present

131 Chinese agent in Mongolia.

Ho-t'ien Ma. Translated by John de Francis. Baltimore, Maryland:
Johns Hopkins Press, 1949. 215p. map.

Ma Ho-t'ien visited Mongolia in 1926-27 as a political agent of the Chinese
Guomindang party. Since he was a rightwing Chinese his view of the country under a
pro-Marxist government is an unusual one. His account of the visit brings to life the
political and social conditions and the prominent individuals of the day. Ma also
provides much information on the new administrative, educational and financial
institutions and the fledgling trade unions. He gives detailed descriptions of schools he
visited and the regulations for primary schools are printed in an appendix. A second
appendix lists local government divisions (banners) in Mongolia, Inner Mongolia and
Uriankhai (now Tannu Tuva).

132 Choibalsan and the Mongolian revolution.

Fujiko Isono. *Journal of the Anglo-Mongolian Society*, vol. 7, no. 2
(Dec. 1981), p. 50-77.

Khorloogiin Choibalsan (1895-1952), a hero of the revolution of 1921 and head of state
from the 1930s until his death, has been dubbed the 'Stalin of Mongolia'. There is no
full-length, objective biography of him in any language and the limited factual
information available about him is not easy to assess. This author examines
Choibalsan's life and career after the revolution of 1921 in the light of his own writings,
most of which are available only in Mongolian. She suggests that the harsher
characteristics of Choibalsan's personality were thrust upon him by external
circumstances and that he remained close to the common people to the end. Not
everyone would agree, but the article is a rare attempt to analyse one of the most
prominent individuals in 20th century Mongolian history.

133 From serf to sage: the life and work of Jamsrangiin Sambuu.

Owen Lattimore. *Journal of the Anglo-Mongolian Society*, vol. 3,
no. 1 (Dec. 1976), p. 1-23.

This short biography of J. Sambuu, (1895-1972), who rose from a poor background in
prerevolutionary society to become the Prime Minister of Mongolia, is drawn largely
from his own writings which are only available in Mongolian. In this article Lattimore
has turned the subject of a rather dry socialist biography into a human being and he
examines the life and achievements of Sambuu against the background of the changing
times in which he lived.

134 History of the Mongolian People's Republic.

Translated and edited by William A. Brown, Urgunge Onon.
Cambridge, Massachusetts; London: East Asian Research Centre,
Harvard University, 1976. 910p. maps. bibliog. (Harvard East Asian
Monographs, no. 65).

An English translation of the third volume of the official history of the MPR for the
years 1917-65 which was first published by the Mongolian Academy of Sciences in
1968. It has a very comprehensive coverage of the political, economic, social and
cultural history of the country with the underlying theme of progress from a feudal

system to a socialist one without going through a capitalist stage (Lenin's theory of 'by-passing capitalism'). In spite of the political bias of the book, it does explain clearly the internal workings of a young and struggling state in the first half of the twentieth century and includes much valuable data not available elsewhere. In addition, the English version contains extensive annotations provided by the translators, an index and an additional bibliography of works mainly in English, which make this book a first and authoritative source of reference for the period it covers.

135 **Inside Outer Mongolia.**
Robert Arthur Rupen. *Foreign Affairs*, vol. 37, no. 2 (Jan. 1959), p. 328-33. map.

A concise but perceptive view of Mongolia in the 1950s by a sympathetic American scholar and one of the first westerners to visit the country in the post war period (1959). He describes the conditions of the time, the political structure, party control, economy, education, urban development and survival of religion and illuminates a hitherto obscure period of contemporary Mongolian history. Rupen was impressed by the strength of the Mongols' sense of independence and national identity and recommended Mongolia's admission to the United Nations.

136 **Mongolia yesterday and today.**
Tianjin, Mongolia: Tianjin , 1924. 69p.

This document is a contemporary translation of the protocols of the Third Congress of the Mongolian People's Revolutionary Party which met in 1924. The record provides unique information on the conditions of the time and the aspirations of ordinary Mongols for their country and its future. During the congress a political coup took place and Danzan the Chairman was shot as a counter-revolutionary. An account of this coup is missing from this version but there is ample evidence of the contemporary pressures on the Mongols to conform to Comintern (Communist International) and Soviet ideology and politics that were the real reason for Danzan's removal. The Mongolian record of the congress (Ulaanbaatar: 1966) does cover Danzan's ouster. For an account of that in English see items no. 75 and 137.

137 **The Mongolian People's Republic, 1924-1928, and the Right Deviation.**
Judith Nordby.   PhD thesis, University of Leeds, England, 1988.
(Available from the British Library Documents Centre, Wetherby, England, order no. BLDSC D86315).

Although this thesis is a comprehensive history of Mongolia from 1924-28, it is also the most detailed study in English of the period 1921-24. In the 1920s, Mongolian society was emerging from a traditional herding society of princes, commoners and lamas and the Mongolian government and people were searching for an acceptable political form. At the same time the regime was under increasing pressure to conform to models and policies laid down by the USSR and the Comintern (Communist International). This is made clear by the train of events that led to the exposure of so-called Rightwing opportunists in the Mongolian Party and Government in 1928 which, as the author demonstrates, was engineered largely by agents of the Comintern working in the Mongolian government.

138 **The Mongolian People's Republic today.**
Thomas Esson Ewing. *Asian Affairs*, vol. 67, no. 3 (Oct. 1980),
p. 309-21.

A historian analyses Mongolian society and the extent of Mongolian development by
the late 1970s. He pays particular attention to the contribution of foreign aid to this
development and questions some of the claims made by communist writers. The author
draws on personal observations made during a four-month visit to Ulaanbaatar in 1979.

139 **Mongols of the twentieth century. Part 1.**
Robert Arthur Rupen. Bloomington, Indiana: Indiana University
Press, 1964. 570p. bibliog. (Uralic and Altaic Series vol. 37).

An extensive collection of information and data pertinent to the history of
contemporary Mongolia from 1917 to the early 1960s, much of which has been drawn
from Russian sources. The author pays particular attention to key individuals and
discusses their life and work in the context of Russian and Chinese policies and activity
in the region. He provides many illustrations, seventeen appendices, including lists of
party and government officials and a text of the 1960 constitution, detailed endnotes
and an index, all of which render this book a valuable reference work on modern
Mongolian history. The second volume of the work is a bibliography which is cited as
item no. 487.

140 **Soviet-Japanese confrontation in Outer Mongolia: the battle of
Nomonhan-Khalkhin Gol.**
Larry William Moses. *Journal of Asian History*, vol. 1, (1967)
p. 64-85. maps. bibliog.

In 1939 Russian and Mongolian forces defeated a Japanese army on the Mongolian
border with Manchuria at the battle of Khalkhyn gol (or Nomonkhan, as it is known in
Japan). Although there are more recent studies of this battle in western scholarship
this is the only one to examine the conflict from a Mongolian perspective. The author
discusses military strategies and considers the implications of the battle for the political
aspirations of Mongols both in independent Mongolia and in Inner Mongolia. He
argues that the defeat of Japan dashed the hopes of some Mongols that Japan would
support the formation of a Greater Mongolian state and that this was an important
reason why Mongolia was to remain in the Soviet camp.

141 **Soviet Mongolia: a study of the oldest political satellite.**
George Gregory Stanislaus Murphy. Berkeley, Los Angeles,
California: University of California Press; London: Cambridge
University Press, 1966. 224p. bibliog.

This is a history of Mongolia and its relationship with the USSR from 1921 to 1960 and
it is an expanded version of the author's doctoral dissertation at the University of
Washington in 1957. The author's chief interest is the political and economic
relationship of the country with the Soviet Union. Although outdated in many respects
the work is still useful as a general history of modern Mongolia and supplements other
20th century histories because the author has consulted some important secondary
sources in Russian which other scholars did not have access to. His analysis of the first
three economic plans (1948-52, 1953-57 and 1958-60) and the collectivization of
livestock herding economies under the interim plan of 1958-60 are useful.

142 **Soviet-Mongolian cooperation during the Second World War.**
Ch. Pürevdorj. *Far Eastern Affairs*, no. 4 (1985), p. 35-43.
An informative article on Mongolia's Second World War effort which provided the
Soviet Union with food, clothing, 530,000 horses, money and troops. It also includes a
brief account of the military action of Mongolian forces and Soviet forces in Inner
Mongolia in August 1945 which routed the occupying Japanese.

Area handbook of Mongolia.
See item no. 1.

Mongolia: a country study.
See item no. 9.

Mongolia: politics, economics and society.
See item no. 11.

Mongolia today.
See item no. 12.

Mongolian heroes of the twentieth century.
See item no. 14.

The new Mongolia.
See item no. 36.

The modern history of Mongolia.
See item no. 75.

**Nationalism and revolution in Mongolia, with a translation from the Mongol
of Sh. Nachukdorji's life of Sukhebator.**
See item no. 125.

**The Diluv Khutagt: memoirs and autobiography of a Mongol reincarnation in
religion and revolution.**
See item no. 219.

The political role of Mongol Buddhism.
See item no. 227.

**How Mongolia is really ruled: a political history of the Mongolian People's
Republic, 1900-1978.**
See item no. 245.

Mongolia's measured steps.
See item no. 248.

Short history of the Mongolian People's Revolutionary Party 1940-1961.
See item no. 254.

Mongolia: fast forward.
See item no. 302.

Mongolian educational venture in western Europe (1926-1929).
See item no. 354.

History. From 1921 to the present

US Joint Publications Research Service: East Asia: Mongolia.
See item no. 466.

Outer Mongolia, 1911-1940: a bibliographical review.
See item no. 488.

Population

General, including minorities

143 **An analysis of the situation of children and women in Mongolia – 1990.**
Ulaanbaatar: Ministry of Health and Social Services; New Delhi:
Unicef, ROSCA, 1990. 26p. map.
Forty-six per cent of the Mongolian population is below the age of sixteen. The birth
rate is high, contraception limited, and health services and the food supply are not
adequate to alleviate the situation. As a result, there is some malnutrition and the child
mortality rate is high. This publication examines these factors in the light of official
data and statistics. Information and tables on the nutritional status of school children
are also provided.

144 **Les chamanistes du Bouddha vivant.** (The shamanists of the Living
Buddha.)
Sandagsürengiin Badamkhatan, translated and adapted by Marie-
Dominique Even. *Études Mongoles et Sibériennes*, vol. 17 (1986),
207p. map. bibliog.
A definitive study in French of the history, social organization, culture, lifestyle and
shamanism of the Darkhad minority who live around Lake Khövsgöl in northwest
Mongolia. A bibliography of publications mainly in Russian and Mongolian is
provided.

145 **Ethnic boundaries in western Mongolia: a case study of a somon in the Mongol Altai region.**
   Slawoj Szynkiewicz. *Journal of the Anglo-Mongolian Society*, vol. 10, no. 1 (July 1987), p. 11-16.

This is a population study of a local government district (sum) in south western Mongolia where 7,000 Mongols and Kazakhs live. The Mongols include the Torguud, Khoshuud, Zakhchin and Uriankhai sub-groups and the Kazakhs are also subdivided. The article examines the way the various groups are differentiated, how they interact and how they relate to the political community.

146 **Les langues mongoles.** (The Mongolian languages.)
   Marie-Lise Beffa, Roberte Hamayon. *Études Mongoles et Sibériennes*, vol. 14 (1983), p. 121-69, bibliog.

This article provides an inventory of Mongolian populations in Mongolia, the USSR and in China by language and dialect. The authors classify the Mongolian languages in four groups, Central (which includes Khalkh Mongolian and its sub-groups in Inner Mongolia), Eastern (other Inner Mongolian dialects), Northern (Buryat) and Western (Oirat). Additional data on other isolated groups of Mongolian speakers is also included. The article has an appendix in which the administrative divisions of Mongols in their respective states are listed, and a bibliography is provided.

147 **La mode de vie des Caatan, éleveurs de rennes du Xövsgöl.** (The lifestyle of the Tsaatan, reindeer herders of Khövsgöl.)
   Sandagsürengiin Badamkhatan, translated and adapted by Roberte Hamayon, Marie-Lise Beffa. *Études Mongoles et Sibériennes*, vol. 18 (1987), p. 99-127.

This article by a Mongolian ethnologist first appeared in Mongolian in *Studia Ethnologica* (Tom. 2 fasc. 1 [1962]). Its subject is the life of the Tsaatan reindeer herders, who are a Mongolized Turkic people living in the region of Lake Khövsgöl in northwest Mongolia. The author studied the Tsaatan during a visit in 1959-60, just before they were organized into collectives. He describes their hunting and herding practices, their mode of transport, tents, clothing and shamanism. (A recent photographic record of the Tsaatan appeared in the Daily Telegraph [London] colour supplement of 27 April 1992.)

148 **Mongol ard ulsyn ugsaatny sudlal, khelnii shinjleliin atlas; etno-lingvisticheskii atlas MNR; atlas ethnologique et linguistique de la République Populaire de Mongolie.** (Ethnological and linguistic atlas of the Mongolian People's Republic.)
   Ulaanbaatar: Academy of Sciences, 1976. 2 vols.

A loose leaf atlas of seventy-seven maps comprising two volumes in a single board folder. An introduction and a list of the maps are provided in Mongolian, Russian and French. Although the quality of production is rather poor, these maps contain a wealth of information on administration, archaeology, ethnography, monasteries, languages and the distribution of the peoples of Mongolia.

149 **La R.P.M.: rappel de quelques données.** (The MPR: a reminder of
some data.)
J. P. Attali, A. Slanovski. *Études Mongoles*, vol. 1 (1970), p. 1-8. map.
bibliog.

In 1970, 76.2 per cent of the population of Mongolia or 775,400 individuals were
Khalkh Mongols. The remainder comprised other eastern Mongols, Oirats, Buryats
and non-Mongols, who are chiefly Kazakhs. This article presents concise data and
information on the various ethnic groups of Mongolia with a map indicating where
each group lives.

Area handbook of Mongolia.
See item no. 1.

Information Mongolia.
See item no. 3.

Mongolia: a country study.
See item no. 9.

**Paralipomena Mongolica: wissenschaftliche Notizen über Land, Leute und
Lebenweise in der Mongolischen Volksrepublik.** (Paralipomena Mongolica:
scientific notes on the country, people and way of life in the Mongolian
People's Republic.)
See item no. 19.

The pre-revolutionary culture of Mongolia.
See item no. 21.

**Sovremennaya Mongolia: otchet Mongol'skoi Ekspeditisii snaryazhennoi
Irkutskoi kontori Vserossiiskogo Tsentral'nogo Soyuza Potrebitel'nykh
ovshchestvo 'Tsentrosoyuz'.** (Contemporary Mongolia: report of the Mon-
golian Expedition equipped by the Irkutsk office of the All-Russian Central
Union of Consumer Cooperatives 'Tsentrosoyuz.')
See item no. 22.

Economic-geographical sketch of the Mongolian People's Republic.
See item no. 46.

Die mongolische Volksrepublik: physisch-geographische Beschreibung. (The
Mongolian People's Republic: description of physical geography).
See item no. 47.

Problems of Mongolian shamanism. (Report of an expedition made in 1960 in
Mongolia.)
See item no. 215.

The geography of education and health in the Mongolian People's Republic.
See item no. 240.

National economy of the MPR for 65 years: anniversary statistical collection.
See item no. 339.

National economy of the MPR for 70 years (1921-1991).
See item no. 340.

A contribution to the anthropology of Khalkh-Mongols. (The anthropologists'
and physicians' report on the Czechoslovak-Mongolian archeological expedition in the year 1958.)
See item no. 360.

Women

150 **The active builders of socialism.**
S. Udval.   *US Joint Publications Research Service*: *Translations on
Mongolia*, no. 57 (17 Sept. 1964), p. 29-35. (JPRS 26,443).
The Chairman of the Mongolian Women's Commitee describes Mongolian women's
participation in the workplace, on committees and in other organizations. She names
women of outstanding achievement and remarks on facilities such as childcare which
are available to women. The article was first published in the Mongolian political
journal *Namyn Am'dral* (no. 7 1964, p. 32-37).

151 **La condition de la femme mongole au 12e/13e siècle.** (The position of the
Mongol woman in the 12th and 13th centuries.)
Paul Ratchnevsky.   In: *Tractata Altaica Denis Sinor sexagenario
optime de rebus altaicis merito dedicata*.   Wiesbaden, Germany:
Harrassowitz, 1976, p. 509-30.
The subject of this carefully researched study in French is the position and status of
Mongol women in the 12th and 13th centuries. Using contemporary sources
Ratchnevsky explains the important social and economic roles of women in the
nomadic society which gave Mongol men the liberty to devote themselves to military
activities. The article also covers the gender distribution of responsibilities in the
Mongol family, polygamy, bride price, the status of widows and the political role of
strong and influential women of the imperial clan such as Hö'elün, the mother of
Chinggis Khan and Sorkhaghtani, the mother of Khubilai Khan.

152 **Consideration of reports submitted by states parties under Article 18
of the convention: initial report of states parties: Mongolian People's
Republic.**
Committee on the Elimination of Discrimination Against Women
(CEDAW).   New York: United Nations, 1983. (V.83 64119).
This report was prepared for the fourth session of the United Nations Committee on
the Elimination of Discrimination against Women (CEDAW) in 1983. It summarizes
Mongolia's progress in eliminating discrimination against women in society, public life
and the workplace as required by various international conventions. Clauses from the

Mongolian Constitution of 1960 and some other laws which refer to women are printed in an appendix.

153 Emancipation of Mongolian women praised.

E. Chimidtseren. *US Joint Publications Research Service: Translations on Mongolia*, no. 221 (19 May 1970), p. 31-36. (JPRS 505,442).

A Mongolian specialist on women's history describes the development of women's status since 1921 and their achievements in public service, politics, the economy, science and education.

154 The life of a Mongol woman in a Khorchin Mongol village.

Kuo-yi Pao. *Mongolian Studies*, vol. 13 (1990) p. 133-41.

This article is based on the author's observations in his native village of Bayin Man, a farming community 160 km east of Mukden in Manchuria. He emphasizes the harshness of women's lives in such communities where they were set to work at the age of seven or eight. He discusses arranged marriages, the strict treatment of women by their inlaws, relations of wives with their husbands and the effect on a woman of her becoming a mother-in-law. See item no. 230 on childbirth and child training in the same village.

155 Mongol girls.

James Gilmour. *Journal of the Anglo-Mongolian Society*, vol. 3, no. 2 (Dec. 1976), p. 1-13.

Gilmour was an English missionary in Mongolia in the 1880s and he wrote this account for the *Girl's Own Paper* in 1884. He describes the domestic life of a Mongolian camp and the tasks traditionally performed by girls and women, such as milking, spinning thread and gathering dried dung for fuel. He also provides a detailed account of a traditional Mongolian wedding. Further information on girls and women may be found in Gilmour's book *Among the Mongols* (see item no. 25).

156 Status of women: Mongolia.

B. Dolgormaa, S. Zambaga, L. Oyuungerel. Bangkok: Unesco, 1990. 43p. bibliog. (RUSHSAP Series on Monograph and Occasional Papers, no. 27).

This short report for Unesco by officials of the Mongolian Women's Committee presents a favourable view of the development of the status of Mongolian women in the family, employment, health and welfare, public service and culture since the revolution of 1921. The report makes reference to government provision for women and includes some statistical data.

157 Women's rights in MPR detailed.

L. Choijil. *US Joint Publications Research Service: Mongolia Report*, MON-85-005 (2 May 1985), p. 146-49.

This article was written for a popular audience and it praises the right of women in Mongolia to work. Benefits for pregnant women and working mothers and the 'Motherhood Glory' title which is awarded to women with large families are mentioned.

158 **Women, taboo and the suppression of attention.**
Caroline Humphrey. In: *Defining females*. Edited by Shirley Ardener.
London: Croom Helm, 1978, p. 89-108. bibliog.

A study of the rules of behaviour and the relationships of women in traditional
Mongolian families by a social anthropologist. Linguistic taboos, especially those
imposed on a daughter-in-law in the presence of her father-in-law, and the
psychological effects of prescribed behaviour are also discussed.

The Mongols and Ming China: customs and history.
See item no. 103.

The Mongolian People's Republic, 1924-1928, and the Right Deviation.
See item no. 137.

An analysis of the situation of children and women in Mongolia – 1990.
See item no. 143.

Inside a Mongolian tent.
See item no. 232.

Mongols Living
Outside Mongolia

159 The Buryat intelligentsia.
Robert Arthur Rupen. *Far Eastern Quarterly*, vol. 15, no. 3 (May 1956), p. 383-98.

A study of the achievements of a group of Buryat scholars of the late 19th and early 20th centuries. They include Agvan Dorzhiev, Dorji Banzarov, Tseveen Zhamtsrano and Elbegdorj Rinchino. Each contributed to or was affected by the rise of national consciousness among the Buryats and other Mongols during their lifetime and the last two worked for the Mongolian government in the 1920s.

160 China's Inner Mongolia.
Inner Mongolian Association of Foreign Cultural Exchange, translated by Chang Chenhua, Yan Yishen, Chang Naijun. Hohehot, China: Inner Mongolian People's Publishing House, 1987. 118p. map.

This is the only extensive publication in English on the contemporary Inner Mongolian Autonomous Region (IMAR), its history, geography, culture, and economic development. It is a useful introduction for tourists and specialists and contains descriptions of places and features of interest to tourists, including three maps of Hohehot, the administrative centre of the IMAR.

161 The Daurs of China: an outline.
Henry Guenter Schwarz. *Zentralasiatische Studien*, vol. 17 (1984), p. 154-71. bibliog.

Today, approximately 78,000 Daur Mongols live in China's Heilongjiang Province and in the Inner Mongolian Autonomous Region. This article is an excellent introduction to this distinct group of Mongols. It includes a brief account of their history from the 10th century and describes their language, society, economy and religion. An excellent bibliography of the Daurs comprising fifty-nine items in Chinese, Japanese, Russian, Mongolian and western languages is also provided.

162 **Inner Mongolia: the haos and the huais of Chinese policy towards the Mongols.**
William R. Heaton. *Mongolian Studies*, vol. 3, (1976), p. 97-115. bibliog.

A study of Chinese policy in Inner Mongolia from the point of view of two Mongols, one a member of the Chinese People's National Assembly who takes a positive view of life under Chinese communist leadership, and the other a dissident and lifelong supporter of the Mongolian autonomous movement in Inner Mongolia. The article focuses on issues of integration, power, and social and cultural transformation affecting the Mongols.

163 **A journey in Southern Siberia: the Mongols, their religion and their myths.**
Jeremiah Curtin. Boston, Massachusetts; London: Sampson Low & Marston, 1909. 319p. map.

The author of this monograph travelled to Siberia in 1900, learned the language of the Buryats and collected data on their history, myths, folklore and religion. Photographs and a collection of folk tales are included in the book.

164 **Les Kalmak de l'Issyk-kul'.** (The Kalmyks of Issyk-kul.)
N. L. Zhukovskaya. Translated and adapted by Françoise Aubin. *Études Mongoles et Sibériennes*, vol. 16 (1985), p. 91-106.

In 1864, some Ölöd, a group of western Mongols, migrated to Issyk-kul in Kirgizstan. In 1970 their descendents numbered 3,500. This article describes their present agricultural lifestyle, which they adopted, together with Islam, from their Kirgiz neighbours. A short introduction to the article is provided by the translator, p. 81-86.

165 **The Mongolian nation within the People's Republic of China.**
Paul V. Hyer. In: *Case studies on human rights and fundamental freedoms: a world survey.* Edited by Willem A. Veenhoven. The Hague: Nijhoff, 1975. vol. 1, p. 472-507. (Foundation for the Study of Plural Societies.)

This is a clearly written and well-informed article which examines the status of the Mongols of China, the historical aspects of Mongol nationhood and the contemporary problems of discrimination and integration of this minority with the majority Han Chinese.

166 **Mongolia's population: from sharp decline to steady increase.**
Kao Yun, Xiang Rong. *Peking Review*, no. 47 (18 Nov. 1977), 14-18.

The Chinese authors of this article discuss population growth and improved life expectancy among Mongols living in China during the 1970s. These benefits are attributed to Chinese government policies of land reclamation, collectivized herding and improved health care.

167 **The Mongols of Manchuria.**
Owen Lattimore. New York: John Day, 1934. 2nd ed.; London:
Allen & Unwin, 1935. 311p. maps. bibliog.

The author of this book was fluent in Mongolian and writes from his own experience and from conversations with Mongols during his travels in the 1920s and 1930s. The work is a classic study of the Mongols of China and their problems in the early 20th century. In spite of its age the book is well worth reading today because it provides an excellent background for understanding different Mongolian groups, their histories and their nationalist aspirations.

168 **The Mongols of the west.**
Stephen A. Halkovic, Jr. Bloomington, Indiana: Indiana University,
1985. 226p. bibliog. (Uralic and Altaic Studies vol. 148).

An introduction to the history of the Oirat Mongols of western Mongolia and Xinjiang, China. The author surveys the origins and fragmentation of the Oirats, and describes the 17th century wars of the Oirats with the eastern Mongols and Oirat interaction with Tibet. A facsimile edition of the manuscript of the *History of the Kalmyk Khans* with an English translation is included.

169 **My childhood in Mongolia.**
Urgunge Onon. Oxford: Oxford University Press, 1972. 112p.

Urgunge Onon (1919-), the subject of this autobiography, is a Daur Mongol. He was born and brought up in a small village on the Nonni River in China's Heilongjiang Province, and now lives in England. He writes of his daily life and escapades during his childhood and of the individuals who were his relatives and his neighbours. This book will appeal to young and old alike.

170 **Some notes on the Mongols of Yunnan.**
Henry Guenter Schwarz. *Central Asiatic Journal*, vol 28, nos. 1-2
(1984), p. 100-18.

The Tonghai Mongols number about 4,700. They live in China's Yunnan Province and are descendants of Mongol soldiers who were stationed in the region in the 13th century. This is the only study of the group in English and is based on the report of a research team from the Inner Mongolian Teachers' College in 1976. It includes a brief account of the history, language, culture and society of this group and the only bibliography on the Tonghai Mongols in western scholarship. The works cited are in Chinese or Mongolian.

171 **A travel survey of China's Mongolian regions. Part 1.**
Christopher Atwood. *Mongolia Society Newsletter* (new series), no. 6
(Jan. 1989), p. 11-21.

An American attending the Inner Mongolian Normal University in Hohehot compiled this information for the benefit of travellers to the Inner Mongolian Autonomous Region of China. He advises on travel regulations, geography, demography, administration and society, providing information which is not available elsewhere in English.

Mongols Living Outside Mongolia

Mongolia's culture and society.
See item no. 13.

Buryat religion and society.
See item no. 212.

Monasteries and culture change in Inner Mongolia.
See item no. 224.

A Mongolian living Buddha: biography of the Kanjurwa Khutughtu.
See item no. 226.

Social organization of the Mongol-Turkic pastoral nomads.
See item no. 237.

La Mongolie intérieure et les Mongols de Chine: élements de bibliographie.
(Inner Mongolia and the Mongols of China: selected bibliography).
See item no. 486.

Language

General

172 Comparative study of postpositions in Mongolian dialects and the written language.
Frederick Holden Buck.   Cambridge, Massachusetts: Harvard University Press, 1955. 158p. map. bibliog. (Harvard-Yenching Institute Studies, no. 12).
This monograph is a survey of the use of postpositions in historical and contemporary Mongolian dialects with a general discussion of the Mongolian language. Examples are given in romanization. The work has been written for the general scholar, including Mongolists and linguists and is based on the author's doctoral dissertation at Harvard University.

173 Compendium of Mongolian suffixes.
Serge Kassatkin.   New York: American Council of Learned Societies, 1960. 112p. bibliog. (Research and Studies in Uralic and Altaic Languages Project, no. 29).
Mongolian is an agglutinative language and suffixes play a central role in word formation and syntax. The formative and inflectional suffixes of Mongolian are the subject of this study and many examples are given in romanization and in the Cyrillic script. The work is a by-product of Lessing's Mongolian-English dictionary project (see item no. 185). Kassatkin was one of the compilers of that dictionary and he has based this study of Mongolian suffixes on materials collected by the project.

174 Khalkha structure.
John Street.   Bloomington, Indiana: Indiana University Press; The Hague: Mouton, 1963. 255p. bibliog. (Uralic and Altaic Series vol. 24).
This is a linguistic study of Khalkh Mongolian which is the standard language of contemporary Mongolia. In his introduction the author states that he has deliberately

adopted a mixed approach and written each section with a different audience in mind. His examination of morphographemics is mainly for the structural linguist. It is very technical and would probably confuse the student or general reader. However his chapter on syntax is excellent, especially for anyone who already knows a little Mongolian. It is illustrated with many examples in the Cyrillic script with English translations. The book also has a good index which aids easy reference.

175 The modern Mongolian language.
Garma D. Sanzheyev. Moscow: Nauka, 1973. 129p.

This is a concise description of modern Khalkh Mongolian phonology, morphology and syntax with examples in the Cyrillic script. The book was first published in Russian in 1961 and the author, a Buryat Mongol, is a prominent Soviet Mongolist.

176 Modern Mongolian: a transformational syntax.
Robert I. Binnick. Toronto, London: University of Toronto Press, 1979. 133p. bibliog.

An analysis of Mongolian syntax, both for the linguist and the non-linguist, based on the generative semantic version of transformational syntax with limited use of technical terms and diagrams. The book covers basic sentence structure, coordinate structure, complex sentences, pronominalization and sentence-level rules. The information is well organized and there is an index of Mongolian forms.

177 Introduction to Altaic linguistics.
Nicholas N. Poppe. Wiesbaden, Germany: Harrassowitz, 1965. 212p. bibliog. (Ural-Altaische Bibliothek, vol. 14).

Most scholars accept that the Mongolian languages belong to the Altaic group of languages, together with the Turkic and Tungus languages and perhaps Korean. This monograph is a manual for students. It provides a brief history and description of the Altaic languages and their investigation, and the relationships of the various members of the group are analysed. The book is included in this bibliography because it provides a linguistic context for Mongolian languages and dialects.

178 Introduction to Mongolian comparative studies.
Nicholas N. Poppe. Helsinki: Suomalais-Ugrilainan Seura, 1987. 2nd impression. 300p. bibliog. (Suomalais-Ugrilainan Seuran Toimituksia, Mémoires de la Société Finno-Ougrienne, no. 110).

A detailed study of Mongolian phonology and morphology for linguists and others, which compares the dialects of Khalkh, Inner Mongolia, the Buryats and the Kalmuks. It was first published in 1955 and although the author admits in his new introduction that some interpretations of the data are outdated much of the content is still valid.

179 Mongolian language handbook.
Nicholas N. Poppe. Washington, DC: Center for Applied Linguistics, 1970. 175p. map. bibliog. (Language Handbook Series, no. 4).

Students and non-specialists are the target audience of this monograph. It contains a brief description of the history and characteristic features of Mongolian followed by a more detailed account of the phonology, morphology and syntax of the language. A short chapter on prerevolutionary and modern literature is also included.

Les langues mongoles. (The Mongolian languages.)
See item no. 146.

Computer requirements of Mongolian handwriting: from bamboo to laser.
See item no. 358.

Written Mongolian from its transliteration to its automatic writing: analysis and coding of the traditional Mongolian script for computer-processing.
See item no. 370.

Dictionaries

180   **Glossary of Mongolian technical terms.**
Frederick H. Buck.   New York: American Council of Learned Societies, 1958. 79p. bibliog. (American Council of Learned Societies' Program in Oriental Languages Publications Series B, no. 13.)

The glossary comprises 4,500 entries of selected political, administrative, economic, scientific, transport, agricultural, medical and military terms drawn from dictionaries and other glossaries. The citations are listed in Cyrillic Mongolian with English translation. Although dated it is the only work of its kind providing glosses in English. See also items no. 182, 188-89.

181   **A modern English-Mongolian dictionary.**
John Gombojab Hangin.   Bloomington, Indiana: Indiana University Press, 1987. Reprinted ed. 288p. (Uralic and Altaic Series vol. 89).

This is the only English-Mongolian dictionary currently available but it should be used with caution. It contains about 10,000 words but a significant proportion of these are not in regular use in the contemporary language of Mongolia. Mongolian words are printed in the Cyrillic script in this volume but the work was also published in the Mongolian script in 1986 by the Inner Mongolian Educational Press.

182   **A modern Mongolian-English dictionary.**
John Gombojab Hangin, John R. Krueger, Paul D. Buell, William V. Rozycki, Robert G. Service.   Bloomington, Indiana: Indiana University Press, 1986. 900p. bibliog. (Uralic and Altaic Series vol. 150).

This is the most comprehensive and up-to-date Mongolian-English dictionary available. It contains approximately 35,000 words used in the traditional and modern language of Mongolia and these are cited in the standard Mongolian Cyrillic script. The compilers have drawn extensively on the earlier Mongolian-English dictionary of Lessing (see item no. 185) and the standard Mongolian dictionary of Tsevel (Ulaanbaatar: 1966). In recent decades many new scientific and technical words and expressions have been introduced into Mongolia. A number have been included in this dictionary, although its coverage is not so extensive as that of the Mongolian-German dictionary cited as item no. 188. A useful feature of Hangin's dictionary is the list of about 250 commonly used abbreviations.

183 **A modern Mongolian-English-Japanese dictionary.**
D. Tömörtogoo, Shigeo Ozawa, Haruo Hazumi. Tokyo: Kaimei Shoin, 1979. 892p.

This dictionary draws heavily on Lessings' Mongolian-English dictionary (see item no. 185). However it has been produced in a much smaller format so it is easier to handle. Also unlike Lessing's work, this dictionary cites Mongolian words in the Cyrillic script with English and Japanese equivalents.

184 **Mongol-English practical dictionary: with English word reference list.**
Chicago: Evangelical Alliance Mission, 1953. 679p.

Although almost forty years old, this is still the only dictionary providing access to Mongolian, as written in the Mongolian script, both from English and Mongolian. It was produced to help Christian missionaries working in Inner Mongolia. See also item no. 181.

185 **Mongolian English dictionary.**
Edited by Ferdinand D. Lessing, compiled by Mattai Haltod, John Gombojab Hangin, Serge Kassatkin, Ferdinand D. Lessing.
Berkeley, Los Angeles, California: University of California Press, 1960. Reprinted ed. 1217p. bibliog.

An excellent and comprehensive dictionary for English speakers which is especially useful to those who wish to read texts in the Mongolian script. Headwords are listed alphabetically in a romanized spelling together with is equivalent in the Mongolian script and in the modern Cyrillic spelling. An index of words in Cyrillic is provided, which is helpful though cumbersome for the reader who only wishes to read Cyrillic texts. The dictionary is an essential tool for reading older Mongolian works, however, particularly Buddhist texts. It includes a considerable number of Buddhist terms, some of which are listed in a separate sequence.

186 **Mongolian-English-Russian dictionary of legal terms and concepts.**
Compiled and edited by William Elliott Butler, Alynn Joelle Nathanson. The Hague; Boston, Massachusetts: Nijhoff, 1982. 718p. (Studies on Socialist Legal Systems).

This dictionary is a companion volume to W. E. Butler's study of the Mongolian legal system (see item no. 273). Words and phrases are listed in Mongolian (Cyrillic script) with English and Russian equivalents. Indices of English and Russian legal words and phrases are provided.

187 **Mongol-Oros-Angli tol'; mongol'sko-russko-angliiskii slovar';**
Mongolian-Russian-English dictionary.
Ts. Tsedendamba, edited by B. Damdin. Ulaanbaatar: Ministry of Education Textbook and Periodical Office, 1986. 332p.

A selection of approximately 5,000 headwords with Mongolian and Russian glosses. In spite of its limited coverage of the contemporary Mongolian vocabulary this dictionary does supplement other dictionaries currently available because it includes a number of modern political, economic, scientific and technical terms as well as modern phrases and idioms.

188   **Wörterbuch mongolisch-deutsch.** (Mongolian-German dictionary.)
      Hans-Peter Vietze in collaboration with Klaus Koppe, Gabriele Nagy,
      Tümenbayaryn Dashtseden.   Leipzig, Germany: VEB Verlag
      Enzyklopädie, 1988. 417p. bibliog.
This dictionary, in the Mongolian Cyrillic script, contains 50,000 headwords including many modern technical words and expressions, with brief notes on Mongolian grammar and pronunciation. It is the most comprehensive dictionary of contemporary standard Mongolian in a western European language. See also the companion volume cited as item no. 189.

189   **Wörterbuch deutsch mongolisch.** (German-Mongolian dictionary.)
      Hans-Peter Vietze in collaboration with Tsendiin Damdinsüren,
      Gendengiin Luvsan, Gabriele Nagy.   Leipzig, Germany: VEB
      Enzyklopädie, 1987.
A dictionary from German into Mongolian which is the companion volume to item no. 188. It contains 35,000 headwords with introductory notes on Mongolian grammar and pronunciation.

Paralipomena Mongolica: wissenschaftliche Notizen über Land, Leute und Lebenweise in der Mongolischen Volksrepublik. (Paralipomena Mongolica: scientific notes on the country, people and way of life in the Mongolian People's Republic).
See item no. 19.

Grammars, textbooks and readers

190   **Basic course in Mongolian.**
      John Gombojab Hangin.   Bloomington, Indiana: Indiana University
      Press, 1987. 2nd revised ed. 208p. (Uralic and Altaic Series vol. 73).
A study course in the standard spoken and written language of independent Mongolia in the Cyrillic script. It comprises twenty chapters of sentences, arranged according to a series of subject categories of use to visitors to Mongolia. Each section also includes notes on grammar, drills and exercises. Additional features include reading texts, glossaries and an index of suffixes and particles. A set of audio-tapes to accompany the course is also available from the publishers. This is the only such course available for English speakers and can be used with or without a teacher.

191 **Buriat grammar.**
Nicholas N. Poppe. Bloomington, Indiana: Indiana University; The
Hague: Mouton, 1960. 129p. bibliog. (Uralic and Altaic Series, vol. 2).

A grammar of standard Buryat Mongolian, the literary language of the Autonomous
Buryat Socialist Republic in eastern Siberia. The book has sections on phonology,
inflections (i.e. suffixes), formal and functional classes of words, word formation, and
phrase and clause structure. Examples are given in romanization.

192 **Buriat reader.**
James E. Bosson. Bloomington, Indiana: Indiana University; The
Hague: Mouton, 1962. 249p. bibliog. (Uralic and Altaic Series vol. 8).

An introductory textbook for students of the language of the Buryat Mongols of
Eastern Siberia. The course is based on graded texts in the Cyrillic script with
additional notes on grammar. Romanized versions of the texts of the first ten chapters
are also provided.

193 **Dagur Mongolian: grammar, texts and lexicon.**
Samuel Elmo Martin. Bloomington, Indiana: Indiana University,
1961. 336p. (Uralic and Altaic Series vol. 4).

The Daur Mongolian dialect is spoken in China's Heilonjiang Province by 80-100,000
people. The author of this work based his analysis of the structure of the language on
the speech of Urgunge Onon, a native speaker (see item no. 169). Martin describes the
phonology and morphology of Daur and provides four romanized texts each with two
English translations. One follows the Mongolian word order and indicates case
endings. The other is in standard English. An English-Daur, Daur-English lexicon is
also provided.

194 **Élements de grammaire mongole.** (Elements of Mongolian grammar.)
Marie-Lise Beffa, Roberte Hamayon. Paris: Dunod, 1975. 286p.
map. bibliog. (Documents de Linguistique Quantitive, no. 26).

A standard grammar of Khalkh Mongolian in French. The phonology, morphology,
suffixes, parts of speech of the language and syntax are explained with many examples
and charts. Morphological examples and suffixes are given in the Cyrillic script and in
romanized Mongolian script. Sample sentences are in the Cyrillic script only. The book
is well indexed and there are many charts of linguistic features such as noun cases,
verbal suffixes, pronouns and postpositions, which make this a very useful reference
and study tool both for the linguist and the student of the language.

195 **Gesprächsbuch mongolisch-deutsch; Mongol German yariany devter.**
(Mongol-German phrasebook.)
Dugarsürengiin Gongor. Leipzig, Germany: VEB Verlag
Enzyklopädie, 1988. 128p.

A pocket Mongolian-German phrasebook originally intended for the use of Mongols
visiting the former German Democratic Republic. Mongolian words and phrases are
produced on the left with the German equivalent in Latin script and Cyrillic transcript
on the right. The phrases are grouped in subject categories such as social situations,

shopping, visits to the doctor, factories, and collectives. No comparable English-Mongolian phrasebook is available but this one would be useful to anyone who understands some German.

196   **A grammar of written Mongolian.**
       Nicholas N. Poppe.   Wiesbaden, Germany: Harrassowitz, 1974.
       Reprinted ed. 195p. (Porta Linguarum Orientalium).
This book has long been a standard textbook of the written Mongolian language. The author introduces the written language and describes the traditional Mongolian script which was the standard script in Mongolia until 1950. It is still the standard script in Inner Mongolia and is now being phased in to replace the Cyrillic script in Mongolia. The main section of the book explains the parts of speech and syntax which are markedly different from those of the modern spoken language of Mongolia. An index of grammatical forms and suffixes is useful for easy reference.

197   **Intermediate Mongolian.** (A textbook for modern Mongolian.)
       John Gombojab Hangin.   Bloomington, Indiana: Indiana University
       Press, 1975. 379p. (Uralic and Altaic Series vol. 125).
A course of thirty readings in the Cyrillic script with vocabularies, cultural and grammatical notes and exercises. It is intended for students who have completed the author's *Basic course in Mongolian* (see item no. 190). The passages have been selected to provide readers with an introduction to Mongolian life, culture and contemporary society.

198   **An introduction to classical (literary) Mongolian.**
       Kaare Grønbech, John R. Krueger.   Wiesbaden, Germany:
       Harrassowitz, 1976. 2nd ed.
A textbook to introduce students to the classical Mongolian written language with graded texts, grammar notes and glossary. The texts are printed in romanization and the Mongolian script versions of some of them are also included. Instructions on reading the script are provided. The grammar notes are extremely clear, and although classical grammar differs from modern Khalkh Mongolian grammar in certain respects, students of the modern language might find this book helpful also.

199   **Lesebuch der mongolischen Sprache.** (Textbook of the Mongolian
       language.)
       Hans-Peter Vietze.   Leipzig, Germany: VEB Verlag Enzyklopädie,
       1988. 263p.
An excellent Mongolian textbook based on thirty-six graded readings with grammatical notes in German and with glossaries. The texts include conversations, simplified literary readings and passages from newspapers in the standard language of Mongolia (Khalkh dialect).

200   **Modern Mongolian: a primer and reader.**
       James E. Bosson.   Bloomington, Indiana: Indiana University Press;
       The Hague: Mouton, 1964. 256p. (Uralic and Altaic Series vol. 38).
This primer has long been out of print but may be found in some libraries. The reading texts are dated but the description of the language is clear and students still enjoy

learning from from this book. It comprises thirty lessons with readings in the Cyrillic script and grammar notes, a Mongolian-English glossary and an index of suffixes and particles. The readings include some passages selected from modern Mongolian literature.

201 **Mongolian newspaper reader: selections from Ünen.**
David C. Montgomery. Bloomington, Indiana: Indiana University Press; The Hague: Mouton, 1969. 203p. (Uralic and Altaic Series vol. 102).

This reader is intended to familiarize language students with the style and vocabulary of the newspapers of Mongolia. It includes twenty passages on subjects ranging from politics and the economy to culture. These have been selected from articles which appeared in Ünen, ('Truth'), the newspaper of the Mongolian People's Revolutionary Party, between 1962 and 1966, and are based on a vocabulary of 2,000 words. Literal translations accompany the first ten passages and there are notes on difficult expressions and sentences. Some Mongolian newspapers have now adopted a more colloquial style but the style taught in this reader continues to be used in some of the government papers.

202 **Mongolisches Lesebuch: Lesestücke in Uigur-Mongolischer Schrift mit grammatikalischen Bemerkungen.** (Mongolian reader: reading passages in the Uigur-Mongolian script with grammatical notes.)
András Róna-Tas. Vienna: Arbeitskreis für tibetische und buddhistische Studien, University of Vienna, 1988. 65p. bibliog. (Wiener Studien zur Tibetologie und Buddhismuskunde, Heft 19).

A beginner's graded reader comprising ten texts in the traditional Mongolian script. The first two readings each have a romanized transcript and all texts are accompanied by notes on how to read the script and on grammar, all of which are in German. No similar textbook is available in English but this work does provide a very good introduction to a complicated script. It is suitable for classroom use or individual study by anyone who can read a little German.

Religion

General

203 Certain questions of atheistic propaganda.
    Ch. Jügder. *US Joint Publications Research Service: Translations on Mongolia*, no. 105 (5 April 1966), p. 15-19. (JPRS 34,880).

Under the 1960 Constitution Mongolian citizens were granted freedom of religion and the right to anti-religious propaganda. This brief article which first appeared in *Ünen* (22 July 1966), the newspaper of the Mongolian People's Revolutionary Party, encourages party members to be vigilant against manifestations of religion and to be active in the promotion of atheism. This indicates that, although the Buddhist church had been destroyed in the 1930s, religious belief and the practice of religion was by no means dead.

204 Dreams and paranormal experiences among contemporary Mongolians.
    David C. Lewis. *Journal of the Anglo-Mongolian Society*, vol. 13, nos. 1-2 (1991), p. 48-55.

Between 1986 and 1990 the author questioned twelve educated Mongolians about supernatural experiences and religious or superstitious beliefs. Here he describes their dreams, premonitions and telepathic experiences and concludes that religious feelings have survived beneath a veneer of atheism in contemporary Mongolia.

205 The encyclopedia of religion.
    Edited by Mircea Eliade. New York: Macmillan; London: Collier Macmillan, 1987. 16 vols.

This encyclopaedia contains an excellent article on Mongol religions covering shamanism and related folk religions, and Buddhism (vol. 10, p. 54-57). Other articles describe the cults of Chinggis Khan and Geser Khan, and various religious concepts of the Mongols such as *Tenger* 'Heaven', *ongon* (the dwellings of shamanist spirits) and the shaman. The articles were all written by Walther Heissig or Klaus Sagaster, who are experts on Mongolian religion, and collectively they provide a good survey of Mongolian religion for the non-specialist. Suggestions for further readings are also given. The encyclopaedia is arranged alphabetically by topic and there is an index to the whole work in volume 16.

206 **James Gilmour of Mongolia.**
Richard Lovett. London: Religious Tract Society, 1892. 190p.

An account of the life and work of James Gilmour (1843-1891), the only British missionary to serve in Outer Mongolia until recently. This is one of a number of biographies on the man and it was written for a Christian audience. Other works about Gilmour may be found in the bibliography of item no. 210. For Gilmour's own writings on Mongolia see items no. 25, 34 and 155.

207 **Manual of Mongolian astrology and divination.**
Edited by Francis Woodman Cleaves with a critical introduction by Antoine Mostaert. Cambridge, Massachusetts: Harvard University Press, 1969. 127p.

A textual analysis with a collection of English translations of materials on the twelve cycles of the Mongolian calender and a discussion of Mongolian astrology. This is a scholarly work but a general reader might also find it of interest because it provides information not readily available elsewhere in English.

208 **A need to intensify atheistic propaganda.**
Kh. Tsevegmid. *US Joint Publications Research Service: Translations on Mongolia*, no. 54 (19 Aug. 1964), p. 9-11. (JPRS 25,994.)

This article, first published in the Mongolian political journal *Namyn Am'dral* (no. 4, 1964), protests against religious practices such as fortune-telling, spiritism and mountain worship in Uvs *aimag* and describes Party measures undertaken to eradicate them. This indicates clearly the persistance of religious beliefs among Mongols after the destruction of the Buddhist church in the 1930s. (See also item no. 203.)

209 **The religions of Mongolia.**
Walther Heissig, translated from the German edition by Geoffrey Samuel. Berkeley, Los Angeles: University of California Press, 1980. 146p. map. bibliog.

In this monograph the chapters on Mongolian religion, which were first published in German in *Die Religion der Tibet und der Mongolei* 'The religion of Tibet and Mongolia' by Guiseppe Tucci and Walther Heissig in 1970, appear in English translation. They cover aspects of folk religion including shamanism, animism, fire worship, scapulimancy and the cult of Chinggis Khan as well as Mongolian Buddhism. Islam and Christianity, notably Nestorianism and Manicheeism, which have also been embraced by Mongols at various times are not included.

210 **Shamans, lamas and evangelicals: the English missionaries in Siberia.**
Charles Roskelly Bawden. London; Boston, Massachusetts: Routledge & Kegan Paul, 1985. 382p. maps. bibliog.

Christian missionary work among the Mongols of Russia, particularly the Buryats, is the subject of this extensive historical study. From 1818-40 the London Missionary

Society ran a mission to the Buryats of eastern Siberia. Among its workers were William Swan, Edward Stallybrass and Robert Yuille. They were active as teachers and evangelists but their main achievement was the translation of the Bible into Mongolian. James Gilmour revived the Society's work among the Khalkh Mongols and in Inner Mongolia in the 1870s (see item no. 206).

Mongolia's culture and society.
See item no. 13.

The modern history of Mongolia.
See item no. 75.

History of the Mongolian People's Republic.
See item no. 134.

The Mongolian People's Republic, 1924-1928, and the Right Deviation.
See item no. 137.

Mongols of the twentieth century. Part 1.
See item no. 139.

A journey in Southern Siberia: the Mongols, their religion and their myths.
See item no. 163.

Les Kalmak de l'Issyk-kul'. (The Kalmyks of Issyk-kul.)
See item no. 164.

Shamanism

211 **The black faith, or shamanism among the Mongols.**
Dorji Banzarov, translated from the Russian by Jan Nattier, John R. Krueger. *Mongolian Studies* vol. 7, (1981-1982), p. 53-91.
This is a classic study of Mongol shamanism, based on Mongolian texts, and was first published by the author, a Buryat scholar, in 1846. He argues that the origin of shamanism is to be found in the powers of nature. He discusses the Mongolian concept of *Tenger*, 'Heaven', and compares this with the God of other peoples. Reverence for fire, ancestor worship, secondary spirits, the shaman and the decline of shamanism are also explained.

212 **Buryat religion and society.**
Lawrence Krader. *Southwestern Journal of Anthropology.* vol. 10, no. 3 (autumn 1954), p. 322-51. bibliog.
An anthropologist examines the principle features of shamanism in the context of the social organization of the Buryat Mongols of Siberia. The study is based on the pioneering work of Buryat scholars of the late 19th and early 20th centuries, for instance item no. 211. The sacrificial ceremonies performed in kinship communities and the significance of the number three to society, the soul and the spiritual world of the Buryat Mongols, are given particular attention.

213 **A Mongolian source to the lamaist suppression of Shamanism in the 17th century.**
Walther Heissig. *Anthropos¸* vol. 48 (1953), p. 1-29, 493-536. map. bibliog.

There is little suggestion in Mongolian literature that shamanists offered any significant resistance to Buddhism when that religion was adopted by the Mongols in the 16th century. The 17th century texts discussed in this article are therefore of considerable importance to the history of shamanism and Buddhism in Mongolia. They celebrate the efforts of a proselytizing Mongolian lama, Neyichi toyin, (1557-1653), who was a zealous persecutor of shamanism in eastern Mongolia. The texts are in romanization with an English translation and they tell how Neyichi toyin defeated the shamans with powerful magic and general harrassment.

214 **Notes on shamanism in Ar-Xangai aimag.**
Caroline Humphrey. *Journal of the Anglo-Mongolian Society*, vol. 6, no. 2 (1980), p. 95-99.

The survival of shamanism in the socialist period is confirmed by this record of an interview with an old Mongol shaman in 1974. He talks about his drum, hat, music and mirror and tells how he is possessed by a powerful spirit whom he calls Dayan Deerxe Tenger. The author also gives some terms for rituals and ritual equipment.

215 **Problems of Mongolian shamanism. (Report of an expedition made in 1960 in Mongolia).**
Vilmos Diószegi. *Acta Ethnographica* (Budapest) vol. 10, no. 1-2 (1961), p. 195-206. map. bibliog.

A Hungarian expert on shamanism draws on information collected in Mongolia in 1960, when he located about thirty male and female shamans among different ethnic groups in Mongolia, to discuss interethnic relationships and the relationship of shamanism with lamaism. Like item no. 214 this article provides valuable evidence of the survival of shamanism in 20th century Mongolia.

216 **The shamanism of the Mongols.**
Marie-Dominique Even. In: *Mongolia today*. Edited by Shirin Akiner. London, New York: Kegan Paul International, p. 183-205. bibliog.

This article is ideal for the non-specialist interested in Mongol shamanism. It explains, clearly and concisely, the shamanist concepts of the universe, the soul and the spirits that inhabit natural phenomena. The author also discusses the shaman, his calling, his role as a mediator between men and spirits and the survival of shamanism in contemporary Mongolia.

217 **Turkish and Mongol shamanism in the Middle Ages.**
John Andrew Boyle. *Folklore*, vol. 83, (Autumn 1972), p. 177-93. bibliog.

Shamanism in the Mongol Empire (1206-1368) is the subject of this article. It examines the activity and powers of a shaman, his role in Mongol and Turkish society and his role in warfare. Mediaeval shamans were noted for their ability to control the weather as a military strategy. The author has drawn his information from the writings of mediaeval European travellers and Muslim historians and geographers and his article is suitable for students or the general reader.

Mongol journeys.
See item no. 30.

Essays in Mongolian studies.
See item no. 72.

Les chamanistes du Bouddha vivant. (The shamanists of the Living Buddha.)
See item no. 144.

La mode de vie des Caatan, éleveurs de rennes du Xövsgöl. (The way of life of the Tsaatan, reindeer herders of Khövsgöl).
See item no. 147.

The encyclopedia of religion.
See item no. 205.

The religions of Mongolia.
See item no. 209.

Buddhism

218 **The Dalai lamas and the Mongols.**
Paul V. Hyer. *Tibet Journal*, vol. 6, no. 4 (winter 1981), p. 3-12.
This article was written for a general audience and is an introductory survey of Mongol-Tibetan relations from 1576 when the Mongol Altan Khan met the Third Dalai Lama to 1979 when the Fourteenth Dalai Lama visited Ulaanbaatar. The relationship had both spiritual and political dimensions. When Altan Khan adopted Buddhism in 1576 he granted the title 'Dalai Lama' to this line of incarnations and subsequent Mongol rulers gave political and military support to the Tibetan theocracy as this article shows.

219 **The Diluv Khutagt: memoirs and autobiography of a Mongol reincarnation in religion and revolution.**
Owen Lattimore, Fujiko Isono. Wiesbaden, Germany: Harrassowitz, 1982. 279p. maps. bibliog. (Asiatische Forschungen Band 74).
A highranking Buddhist reincarnation, born in 1884, describes his daily life in the Narvanchin monastery in northern Mongolia and recalls political events in Mongolia up to 1931. These documents are quite unique for the period. Most extant Mongolian memoirs of the early 20th century concern people of whom the Mongolian Party and goverment approved. In contrast the Diluv Khutagt was seriously harrassed by the revolutionary regime. His personal property was confiscated in 1929-30 and he was the object of a show trial in 1930-31 when the Mongolian government launched an all-out

attack on religion. Unlike many other high lamas of the period, the Diluv Khutagt survived and he fled to China in 1931. He died in America in 1965.

220 **Early lamaism in Mongolia.**
Henry Serruys. *Oriens Extremus (Wiesbaden)*, vol. 10, no. 2 (Oct. 1963), p. 181-216. bibliog.

A detailed and well-written article on the history of Buddhism among the Mongols after 1368. It provides ample evidence that Buddhism continued to flourish among various groups of Mongols in the 14th and 15th centuries even though some earlier scholars believed that Buddhism died out with the collapse of the Mongol Empire. The author published an addendum to the article in the same journal (vol. 13 [1966], p. 165-75).

221 **An interview with the Hambo Lama.**
Holmes Welch. *Journal of the Royal Central Asiatic Society*, vol. 49, no. 2 (April 1962), p. 172-82.

The verbatim account of an interview given in 1961 by Samagiin Gombojav, the abbot of Gandan monastery. Until very recently Gandan was Mongolia's only working monastery. Gombojav talks about the contemporary practice of Buddhism in Mongolia and the activities of the monastery. Additional information and scholarly comment is added by Charles Bawden.

222 **The Jebtsundamba Khutuktus of Urga: text, translation and notes.**
Charles Roskelly Bawden. Wiesbaden, Germany: Harrassowitz, 1961. 91p. bibliog. (Asiatische Forschungen Band 9).

This scholarly monograph contains the Mongolian text in romanization and in English translation of the biographies of seven of the eight incarnations or 'Living Buddhas' of the Javzandamba Khutagt (Jebtsundamba Khutuktus) of Urga, (now Ulaanbaatar). The Javzandamba Khutagts were important political and religious figures in Mongolia from the birth of the first in 1635 to the death of the eighth in 1924. In the Tibetan Buddhist hierarchy they ranked third in holiness and prestige after the Dalai Lamas and Panchen Lamas of Tibet. Another translated version of this work is included in item no. 10.

223 **Life in a Khalka steppe lamasery.**
G. C. Binsteed. *Journal of the Royal Asiatic Society*, (1914) p. 847-900.

Binsteed was a British Army officer who visited monasteries in Jehol, in Inner Mongolia, and on the Kherlen river in northern Mongolia in 1913. He was a careful and interested observer and has left a clear account of monastic life with some general comment on the social conditions of the time. He describes the buildings, services and music of the monasteries and he gives Mongolian terms for various articles of lama clothing, temple equipment and musical instruments. Plans of two monasteries in Jehol are also provided.

224 **Monasteries and culture change in Inner Mongolia.**
Robert James Miller. Wiesbaden, Germany: Harrassowitz, 1959.
152p. bibliog. (Asiatische Forschungen Band 2).
The subject of this monograph is the administrative and economic organization of
Buddhist monasteries of Mongolia in the 18th and 19th centuries. Monasteries were
important autonomous units, a society within the secular Mongolian society, during the
period when Mongolia was controlled by the Manchu (Qing) government. The author
has based his study on the records of foundations in Inner Mongolia but the system
with its institutions, officials and activities was the same in Khalkh Mongolia. The book
is based on the author's PhD thesis at Washington University, 1956.

225 **Mongolian lamaist quasi-feudalism during the period of Manchu
domination.**
Sechin Jagchid. *Mongolian Studies*, vol. 1 (1974), p. 27-54. bibliog.
When monastic Buddhism became established among the Mongols in the 16th century
its high churchmen and incarnations constituted a religious aristocracy which was
recognized and encouraged by the Manchu emperors. This article discusses the Qing
(Manchu) regulations which defined and limited the titles, property, privileges and
duties of the Mongolian Buddhist hierarchy. The highest rank was that of khan and the
Living Buddha known as the Javzandamba Khutagt (see item 222) was the only
churchman to hold this title. This author suggests that it was precisely the rank of khan
that gave the Eighth Javzandamba Khutagt (1871-1924) the authority to become the
theocratic ruler of the Khalkh Mongols in 1911.

226 **A Mongolian living Buddha: biography of the Kanjurwa Khutughtu.**
Paul V. Hyer, Sechin Jagchid. Albany, New York: State University of
New York Press, 1983. 203p. map.
The Kanjurwa Khutughtu (Khutagt) (1914-78) was a senior incarnation in Inner
Mongolia and the leader of Inner Mongolian Buddhism from 1920 to 1945. This
account of his life is based on taped interviews which he gave in Taiwan where he lived
from 1949 until his death. His biography provides a model for understanding monastic
life and the role of a 'Living Buddhas' in Mongolian politics and society. The book is
also a valuable source of information on political events in Inner Mongolia during the
first half of the 20th century. For a life of another incarnation see item no. 219.

227 **The political role of Mongol Buddhism.**
Larry William Moses. Bloomington, Indiana: Indiana University
Press, 1977. 299p. bibliog. (Uralic and Altaic Series vol. 133).
The subject of this study is the involvement of Mongolian monasteries and Buddhist
incarnations in Mongolian internal and external politics from the Middle Ages to 1939
when the monasteries were destroyed by Mongolia's Marxist government. The larger
part of the text is devoted to the interaction of the monasteries with the Mongolian
People's Revolutionary Party and the post-revolutionary government. The book also
contains a quantity of data useful for understanding the economic and social role of
Mongolian Buddhism, particularly in the 20th century. This book is a published version
of the author's PhD thesis submitted to Indiana University in 1972.

228 **Religion and ritual in society: Lamaist Buddhism in late 19th- century Mongolia.**
Aleksei M. Pozdneyev, edited by John R. Krueger, translated from the Russian by Alo Raun and Linda Raun. Bloomington, Indiana: Mongolia Society, 1978. 694p. (Occasional Papers, no. 10).

A detailed study of the monasteries of Outer Mongolia by a Russian scholar who carried out extensive fieldwork in the country in the last century. The book was first published in Russian in 1887. Its author describes the architecture of temples, their furnishings and decoration, and statues and other religious objects. Other chapters cover the life, training and duties of the various ranks of the clergy, Buddhist incarnations and monastic services. Modern scholars have suggested that some of Pozdneyev's assumptions about ritual are misleading because he did not fully understand it. However, if read with caution, this book provides a wealth of information on Mongolian monastic Buddhism.

229 **Travels in Mongolia.**
Bandō Shōjun. *Eastern Buddhist* (Tokyo) vol. 3, no. 2, (Oct. 1970), p. 123-27. bibliog.

There are few accounts of Mongolian Buddhism in the fifty years since the destruction of the monasteries in the 1930s. This short article written in 1970 is of interest because in that year the Asian Buddhist Peace Conference (ABPC) was founded in Ulaanbaatar and a Buddhist college for the training of young monks was opened. The ABPC gave religion the limited but official role in Mongolia of promoting a peaceful foreign policy and establishing contacts with Buddhist countries, not all of which had friendly relations with Mongolia. The author of this article was a Japanese Buddhist who attended the inaugural meeting of the ABPC and he describes Gandan Monastery, the only functioning monastery in Mongolia at this time, its lamas and their training.

Mongolia and the Mongols. Volume One – 1892.
See item no. 10.

Mongolia's culture and society.
See item no. 13.

Mongolian journey.
See item no. 15.

Mongolie: textes et photographies. (Mongolia: text and photographs.)
See item no. 17.

Essays in Mongolian studies.
See item no. 72.

The Mongol chronicle Altan Tobči: text, translation, and critical notes.
See item no. 74.

The modern history of Mongolia.
See item no. 75.

The Ch'ing administration of Mongolia up to the nineteenth century.
See item no. 111.

History of the Mongolian People's Republic.
See item no. 134.

The Mongolian People's Republic, 1924-1928, and the Right Deviation.
See item no. 137.

Mongols of the twentieth century. Part 1.
See item no. 139.

The encyclopedia of religion.
See item no. 205.

The religions of Mongolia.
See item no. 209.

A Mongolian source to the lamaist suppression of shamanism in the 17th century.
See item no. 213.

Problems of Mongolian shamanism. (Report of an expedition made in 1960 in Mongolia.)
See item no. 215.

Some portraits of the First Jebtsundamba Qutugtu.
See item no. 413.

Vydayushchiisya mongol'skii skul'ptor G. Dzanabadzar; the eminent Mongolian sculptor – G. Zanabazar; G. Zanabazar eminent sculpteur mongol; G. Zanabazar, destacado escultor de Mongolia.
See item no. 414.

L'architecture mongole ancienne. (Old Mongolian architecture).
See item no. 415.

Erdeni-zuu, un monastère de XVI siècle en Mongolie. (Erdene Zuu: a 16th century monastery in Mongolia.)
See item no. 419.

Lamaistische Tanzmasken: der Erlik-Tsam in der Mongolei. (Lamaist dance masks: the Erlik Tsam in Mongolia.)
See item no. 421.

The music of the Mongols: an introduction.
See item no. 422.

Social Conditions

230 **Child birth and child training.**
Kuo-yi Pao. *Monumenta Serica*, vol. 25 (1966), p. 409-39.

A Khorchin Mongol describes birthing methods, care of the very young and of sick children, vaccination against smallpox, the upbringing of children, discipline and play in his native village of Bayin Man near Mukden in Inner Mongolia. Similar practices in the handling of the newborn and children have been observed among other groups of Mongols.

231 **Family and kinship structure of Khorchin Mongols.**
Kuo-yi Pao. *Central Asiatic Journal*, vol. 9, no. 4 (Dec. 1964),
p. 277-311. map. bibliog.

A study of the author's native village of Bayin Man near Mukden in Inner Mongolia, a settled community of Khorchin Mongols. This is a community based on a patrilocal extended family. The author describes interpersonal relationships within that community and gives terms for the generational relationships. For other studies of the same community see items no. 154, 230 and 433.

232 **Inside a Mongolian tent.**
Caroline Humphrey. *New Society*, vol. 30 (1974), p. 273-75.

An anthropologist explains the traditional arrangement of objects inside a Mongolian tent (ger) where areas are designated male and female. Continuity and change in these practices in socialist Mongolia are noted and plans of traditional and present day tent arrangements provided.

233 **Mongol community and kinship structure.**
Herbert Harold Vreeland III. Westport, Connecticut: Greenwood ,
1973. Reprinted ed. 327p. maps. bibliog.

A detailed analysis of three contrasting Mongolian communities, each based on the recollections of a single informant. The communities are the monastic centre of the

Diluv Khutagt (1884-1965) in northern Mongolia and the secular families that served it about 1920 (see also item no. 219); the Chakhar village in Inner Mongolia of J. G. Hangin (1921-89) ca. 1930; and the Daur village of U. Onon (1919-) in modern Heilongjiang Province, China, ca. 1930 (see also item no. 169). On the basis of the structures described, Vreeland concludes that a common prototype of the kinship model 'Normal Omaha' existed among Mongols for at least five centuries.

234 **Mongolia: coming to terms with family legislation.**
William Elliott Butler. *Journal of Family Law*, vol. 27, no. 1 (1988-89), p. 211-19.
A legal scholar discusses aspects of the Mongolian family, children and marriage in the context of the 1973 Family Code as amended in 1982. He also describes a marriage ceremony which he attended at the Palace of Marriages in Ulaanbaatar.

235 **Obok: a study of social structure in Eurasia.**
Elizabeth E. Bacon. New York, London: Johnson, 1966. Reprinted ed. 235p. maps. bibliog. (Viking Fund Publication in Anthropology no. 25).
This study by an anthropologist was first published in 1958. It is an analysis of kinship, social structure and social organization among the Hazara Mongols of Afghanistan, the mediaeval Mongols and various modern groups such as the Khalkh. The author identifies a simple tribal structure which she calls 'obok' (Mongolian *ovog*) and which she believes came into existence when an extended family acquired joint property. The thesis is also applied to other peoples of Eurasia such as the Romans, Germanic peoples and the Celts who are not ethnically or linguistically related to the Mongols. Bacon's views on traditional Mongol social structure may be compared with those of Krader (see item no. 237) and contrasted with Vladimirtsov's (see item no. 238).

236 **Social class structure of Mongolia.**
Ts. Balkhaajav. *US Joint Publications Research Service, Translations on Mongolia*, no. 306 (16 Feb. 1979), p. 1-12. (JPRS no. 72,833).
The Marxist-Leninist analysis of Mongolian society after the Second World War divides the population into two classes, the working class which comprises industrial workers and the working *ards* who herd livestock. Balkhaajav compares and contrasts their roles in the economy and society and he extends his discussion to the trade unions, the League of Revolutionary Youth and the intelligentsia. The article was first published in Russian in *Nauchnyi Kommunizm* (no. 4, 1976, p. 67-76).

237 **Social organization of the Mongol-Turkic pastoral nomads.**
Lawrence Krader. The Hague: Mouton, 1963. 412p. maps. bibliog. (Indiana University Publications Uralic and Altaic Series vol. 20).
This monograph is a study of kinship systems and related social structures from the 18th to 20th century. The subjects of the study share a common environment and economy as pastoral nomadic societies in Central Asia and they are linguistically related. They include the Ordos Mongols of Inner Mongolia, the Buryat Mongols of Siberia, the Volga Kalmyks, the Monguors of the Kansu-Tibetan border and the Turkic speaking Kazakhs. This author's views on the structure of traditional Mongolian society differ markedly from those of the author of item no. 238.

238 **Le régime sociale des mongols: le féodalisme nomade.** (The social
structure of the Mongols: nomadic feudalism.)
Boris Yakovlevich Vladimirtsov, introduction by René Grousset,
translated by Michel Carsow. Paris: Adrien Maisonneuve, 1948.
291p. map. bibliog.

There is no basic consensus among scholars on the character of traditional Mongolian
society. This book is a classic study and was first published in Russian in 1934. It argues
that from the Middle Ages, Mongolian society was feudalist rather than kinship based.
This view has caused great controversy among both communist and western scholars.
For the alternative analysis of Mongol social structure see items no. 235 and no. 237.
Although all three books are dated, taken together they can provide a starting point
and some useful data for a new examination of traditional Mongolian society.

Area handbook on Mongolia.
See item no. 1.

Information Mongolia.
See item no. 3.

Mongolia: a country study.
See item no. 9.

Mongolia: politics, economics and society.
See item no. 11.

Mongolia's culture and society.
See item no. 13.

**Paralipomena Mongolica: wissenschaftliche Notizen über Land, Leute unde
Lebenweisse der Mongolischen Republik.** (Paralipomena Mongolica: scientific
notes on the country, people and way of life of the Mongolian People's
Republic.)
See item no. 19.

An analysis of the situation of children and women in Mongolia – 1990.
See item no. 143.

The life of a Mongol woman in a Khorchin Mongol village.
See item no. 154.

Women, taboo and the suppression of attention.
See item no. 158.

Development and consolidation of the ranks, and composition of the MPRP.
See item no. 244.

The Mongolian legal system: contemporary legislation and documentation.
See item no. 273.

Social Services, Health and Welfare

239 **Activities of MPR Children's Fund.**
A. I. Tsedenbal-Filatova. *US Joint Publications Research Service*:
Mongolia Report, no. 366 (8 Aug. 1983), p. 21-27. (JPRS 84,068).
The Children's Fund was set up by the Mongolian government to channel the
voluntary efforts and donations of organizations and individuals to providing services
for children. These have included the provision and support of mother and child health
services, nurseries, sporting, cultural and leisure facilities, and exhibitions. The
Chairman of the Fund, wife of former Party and state leader Yu. Tsedenbal, describes
some of these projects for a popular audience. The article first appeared in the
Mongolian Russian-language newspaper *Novosti Mongolii* (26 Apr. 1983, p. 3).

240 **The geography of education and health in the Mongolian People's
Republic.**
Robert Ante. *Mongolia Society Bulletin*, vol 12, nos. 1-2 (1973),
p. 32-51.
This article analyses and evaluates the impact of Mongolia's sparse population and the
great distances between settled centres on the development and spatial distribution of
welfare facilities.

241 **Mongolia: a leap across the centuries.**
Lalit Thapalyal. *World Health*, (April 1976), p. 14-19.
This article is an overview of Mongolian health services, mother and child care,
mortality, incidence of specific diseases and diet for a popular audience.

242 **Payment of old-age pensions clarified.**
J. Badmajav. *US Joint Publications Research Service, Translations on
Mongolia*, no. 253 (1 Nov. 1971), p. 17-19. (JPRS 54,367).
An article on the provision of state pensions for the elderly according to a regulation of
1970. Benefits for people who work under hazardous conditions and women with more

Social Services, Health and Welfare

than four children are also mentioned, with information on the rates received. The article first appeared in the Mongolian government journal *Ardyn Tör*.

243 **Public health development reviewed.**
Dar'sürengiin Nyam-Osor. *US Joint Publications Research Service*: *Mongolia Report*, no. 340 (30 June 1982), p. 5-9. (JPRS 81,176).

This is an abridged translation of an article published in the periodical *Ekonomicheskoe Sotrudnichestvo Stran-chlenov SEV*, (no. 4, 1981, p. 78-81). It marks sixty years of public health services in Mongolia and notes progress in medical research, speciality services, drug production, mother and child services and outpatient services especially in the period 1960-80. The contribution of Comecon countries to public health in Mongolia is noted.

Area handbook of Mongolia.
See item no. 1.

Information Mongolia.
See item no. 3.

Mongolia: a country study.
See item no. 9.

Mongolia: politics, economics and society.
See item no. 11.

Paralipomena Mongolica: wissenschaftliche Notizen über Land, Leute und Lebenweise in der Mongolischen Volksrepublik. (Paralipomena Mongolica: scientific notes on the country, people and way of life in the Mongolian People's Republic.)
See item no. 19.

The wealth of mineral springs in our country.
See item no. 49.

An analysis of the situation of children and women in Mongolia – 1990.
See item no. 143.

National economy of the MPR for 65 years: anniversary statistical collection.
See item no. 339.

National economy of the MPR for 70 years (1921-1991): anniversary statistical yearbook.
See item no. 340.

US Joint Publications Research Service: East Asia: Mongolia.
See item no. 466.

Politics

244 **Development and consolidation of the ranks, and composition of the MPRP.**
R. Nansal. *US Joint Publications Research Service*: *Translations on Mongolia*, no. 249 (9 Sept. 1971), p. 40-49. (JPRS 54,021).
A concise review of statistical data on party membership from 1921-70 with information on overall membership, social composition, education, women and the distribution of party members and cells in the economy. The article was first published in Mongolian in 1971.

245 **How Mongolia is really ruled: a political history of the Mongolian People's Republic, 1900-1978.**
Robert Arthur Rupen. Stanford, California: Hoover Institution Press, 1979. 225p. bibliog. (Histories of Ruling Communist Parties).
A history of Soviet control of Mongolia through the agency of the Mongolian People's Revolutionary Party. The author focuses on ideological, economic and strategic issues and pays particular attention to the interaction of Mongolian nationalism and communism. As a history of 20th century Mongolia the book is of particular value because it extends the range of other histories to the 1960s and 1970s to include the Sino-Soviet dispute, urbanization and the development of heavy industry at the Erdenet Copper and Molybdenum combine. Other useful features are biographical notes on individuals who took part in the revolution of 1921 and lists of senior party officials elected in 1976. The extensive bibliography which includes many items in Russian updates the author's earlier bibliography of 20th century Mongolia which is cited as item no. 487 by the same author.

246 **Local government in the Mongolian People's Republic 1940-1960.**
George Ginsburgs. *Journal of Asian Studies*, vol. 20, no. 4
(Aug. 1961), p. 489-508.

This article traces the development of local government structures and functions in Mongolia. Ginsburgs describes the system as laid down in the second Constitution of 1940 and the reforms of 1949 when the number of tiers of local government were reduced and direct elections to local assemblies introduced. He concludes his study with the changes made under the 1960 constitution when local government boundaries and the territories under the control of the new herding collectives were harmonized. The 1960 system and divisions of local government are still in existence but reforms may be expected in the wake of the 4th Constitution which came into force in February 1992.

247 **Mongolia 1990: a new dawn?**
Alan John Kelday Sanders. *Asian Affairs*, vol. 22 (OS vol. 78), no. 2
(Jun. 1991), p. 158-66.

An overview of contemporary Mongolian affairs with a description of the democratic reforms of 1990 and economic and social conditions in Mongolia after the implementation of the reforms.

248 **Mongolia's measured steps.**
Paul V. Hyer. *Problems of Communism*, vol. 21, no. 6 (Nov.-Dec. 1972), p. 28-37. bibliog.

The author discusses Mongolia's internal and external affairs and development after the Second World War in the context of geopolitics. The extent to which the Mongolian government was able to formulate and pursue independent policies in the 1960s and 1970s is questioned.

249 **The Mongolian People's Republic in the 1980s: continuity and change.**
Judith Nordby. In: *Communism and reform in East Asia*. Edited by
David S. G. Goodman. London; Totowa, New Jersey: Cass, 1988,
p. 113-131. bibliog.

An analysis of communist rule in Mongolia in the 1980s. The author surveys trends in politics, economics and society and speculates on future developments in the wake of the economic and politic reforms that were introduced in the Soviet Union and Mongolia from 1986. The article was also published in *Journal of Communist Studies* (vol. 3, no. 4 [1988], p. 113-31).

250 **The Mongolian revolution of 1990: stability or conflict in Inner Asia?**
Marko Milivojević. London: Research Institute for the Study of
Conflict and Terrorism, 1990. 33p. map. bibliog. (Conflict Studies,
no. 242).

In 1990 Mongolia gave up communist party rule in favour of a democratic government and a market economy. The author of this pamphlet discusses the implications of the changes for Mongolian politics, economics and international relations. He pays special attention to the re-emergence of nationalism and traditional culture among Mongols and suggests that the possibility of a reunification of Mongols within a Greater Mongolian state is a serious question in a region of considerable strategic importance.

251 **Nomadism and revolution.**
Larry William Moses. *Mongolia Society Bulletin*, vol. 10, no. 2
(fall 1971), p. 35-41.

This author argues that Mongolia's traditional way of life, pastoral nomadism, is the
basis of, rather than a hindrance to, modernization and industrialization. He explains
how the Mongolian pastoral economy provides both raw materials and a class capable
of exploiting them for the ready market that exists in the Soviet Union. He suggests
that such a situation, as a central factor in promoting modern state development, is
quite unique.

252 **The program of the Mongolian People's Revolutionary Party.**
US Joint Publications Research Service: Translations on Mongolia,
no. 124 (22 Dec. 1966), 22p. (JPRS 39,236).

An English text of the 1966 Programme of the Mongolian People's Revolutionary
Party translated from the version published in the Party newspaper *Ünen* (14 June
1966, p. 1-4). The Programme was adopted by the 15th Congress of the Party in 1966
and remained the basis of all policy-making, domestic and foreign, and the
development of Mongolian society and the economy until 1990. Another text in
English was published in Ulaanbaatar in 1981.

253 **'Restructuring' and 'openness'.**
Alan John Kelday Sanders. In: *Mongolia today*. Edited by Shirin
Akiner. London, New York: Kegan Paul International, 1991,
p. 57-75. bibliog.

In this article Sanders examines the political and economic reforms of 1986-88. They
were modelled on the Soviet reforms of the period of *glasnost* ('openness'), and
perestroika ('reconstruction') initiated by Soviet President M. Gorbachev and
introduced into Mongolia by the then Party and state leader, J. Batmönkh. The
reforms were intended to revive a stagnant economy by giving enterprises greater
control of and responsibility for their own finances.

254 **Short history of the Mongolian People's Revolutionary Party 1940-1961.**
US Joint Publications Research Service: Translations on Mongolia,
no. 74 (14 June 1965), 82p. (JPRS 30,598).

This is a translation of chapters six to eight of the official history of the Mongolian
People's Revolutionary Party which was edited by B. Lkhamsüren and published in
serial form in the party's journal *Namyn Am'dral* in 1964. Chapters one to five (1917-
1940) were published in English in the same translation series, JPRS 25,224 (23 June
1964) and chapters ten to eleven (1961-66) in JPRS 43,790 (21 Dec. 1967). The entire
book also appeared in Mongolia as a monograph in 1966.

255 **Struggle of the MPRP to develop along non-capitalist lines.**
B. Baldoo. *Joint Publications Research Service, Translations on
Mongolia*, no. 60 (24 Nov. 1964), p. 1-21. (JPRS no. 27,522.)

An official statement of the political theory of by-passing capitalism which was
formulated by V. I. Lenin. (See item no. 134). This concept underpinned Mongolian
development from the 1960s to the 1980s and was used to justify Mongolia's heavy
political and economic reliance on the USSR. The article was written for the

instruction of MPRP members and first appeared in the Party journal *Namyn Am'dral* (no. 8, 1964, p. 31-49).

Area handbook of Mongolia.
See item no. 1

Mongolia: a country study.
See item no. 9.

Mongolia: politics, economics and society.
See item no. 11

Mongolia today.
See item no. 12.

Mongolian heroes of the twentieth century.
See item no. 14.

Paralipomena Mongolica: wissenschaftliche Notizen über Land, Leute und Lebenweise in der Mongolischen Volksrepublik. (Paralipomena Mongolica: scientific notes on the land, people and way of life in the Mongolian People's Republic.)
See item no. 19.

The People's Republic of Mongolia: general reference guide.
See item no. 20.

The modern history of Mongolia.
See item no. 75.

Between the hammer and the anvil? Russian and Chinese policies in Outer Mongolia 1911-1921.
See item no. 120.

A contemporary account of the period of autonomy.
See item no. 121.

The Mongolian revolution of 1921.
See item no. 124.

Nationalism and revolution in Mongolia, with a translation from the Mongol of Sh. Nachukdorji's life of Sukhebator.
See item no. 125.

Soviet Russia and the Mongolian revolution of 1921.
See item no. 127.

From serf to sage: the life and work of Jamsrangiin Sambuu.
See item no. 133.

History of the Mongolian People's Republic.
See item no. 134.

The Mongolian People's Republic, 1924-1928, and the Right Deviation.
See item no. 137.

Mongols of the twentieth century. Part 1.
See item no. 139.

Soviet Mongolia: a study of the oldest political satellite.
See item no. 141.

The political role of Mongol Buddhism.
See item no. 227.

The reevaluation of Chinggis Khan: its role in the Sino-Soviet dispute.
See item no. 294.

Mongolia: fast forward.
See item no. 302.

The Mongolian People's Republic: toward a market economy.
See item no. 304.

Leaders and leadership roles in a Mongolian collective: two cases.
See item no. 323.

Ideological struggle reflected in MPR literature.
See item no. 393.

Proceedings of the Fourth Congress of Mongolian Writers' Union, opened 27 June 1967, in Ulan Bator.
See item no. 395.

Asia yearbook.
See item no. 480.

The Far East and Australasia.
See item no. 481.

Yearbook on international Communist affairs.
See item no. 483.

Mongolian Nationalism and Panmongolism

256 **Buryats.**

Caroline Humphrey. In: *The nationalities question in the Soviet Union.*
Edited by Graham Smith. New York, London: Longman, 1990.
p. 290-303. bibliog.

This study examines recent manifestations of nationalism and the survival of Mongol
culture among the Buryat Mongols of Siberia. These are particularly apparent in
cultural organizations that were formed in the late 1980s. The growing consciousness of
Buryat Mongol history, Buddhism and the Buryat Mongol language parallels similar
trends in Mongolia in the same period.

257 **Chinese Communist administration and local nationalism in Inner
Mongolia.**

William R. Heaton. *Mongolia Society Bulletin*, vol. 10, no. 1 (spring
1971), p. 11-47. bibliog.

Inner Mongolian nationalism since 1921 and Chinese nationality policies from 1947 to
1966 are treated in this article. The author gives particular attention to the Chinese
government policy of autonomy for the Inner Mongolian Autonomous Region
(IMAR) and the impact of the Chinese Cultural Revolution on the IMAR from 1966.
He argues that these policies have fomented nationalism among the Mongols of China
rather than controlled it as the government intended.

258 **De Wang's independent Mongolian Republic.**

Michael Raymond Underdown. *Papers in Far Eastern History*
(Canberra), no. 40 (Sept. 1989), p. 123-32. map. bibliog.

This author describes the last stand of Inner Mongolian nationalism before the whole
of Inner Mongolia fell to the Chinese communists. The influential and popular Inner
Mongolian Prince De (Demchugdongrub) set up a constitutional state in the southern
and western parts of Inner Mongolia in 1949 but this had been swept away by 1950 and
Prince De was imprisoned.

259 **Documents on Inner Mongolia: selected US intelligence reports
(declassified) on leaders and factions in Inner Mongolia, 1946-1949.**
Washington, DC: Centre for Chinese Research Materials, Association
for Research Libraries, 1972. 74p. map.

This is a collection of thirty-three United States government documents of which
twenty-eight were formerly classified as political and the remainder as military
information. They include biographies, and information on the organizations,
governments and military leaders of the Mongols of China from 1946 to 1949. The
information was supplied by lamas, Japanese language instructors, Chinese civil
administrators and Communist underground workers. Collectively the documents give
valuable insights into Mongolian nationalism in Inner Mongolia and inter-Mongol
relations in the mid 20th century.

260 **Inner Mongolia: aftermath of the Cultural Revolution.**
Alan John Kelday Sanders. *Journal of the Anglo-Mongolian Society*,
vol. 6, no. 1 (1980), p. 42-49.

During the Chinese Cultural Revolution the Inner Mongolian Autonomous Region
was reduced to half its former size and many Mongols were persecuted. The author
discusses this and describes the subsequent restoration of the Region's borders and
normalization of relations between the government and Mongol minority.

261 **Inner Mongolia: 'Local nationalism' and the cultural revolution.**
William R. Heaton. *Mongolia Society Bulletin*, vol. 10, no. 2
(fall 1971), p. 2-34. bibliog.

The author of item no. 257 provides additional information to support his contention
that the autonomous status of the IMAR failed to integrate that region and its Mongol
population into Chinese society, as was intended, but increased demands for genuine
autonomy. In this article he examines the experiences of Inner Mongols during the
Chinese Cultural Revolution and the use of military force in the region to crush
whatever the Red Guards regarded as local nationalism.

262 **Inner Mongolia under Japanese occupation, 1935-1945.**
Sechin Jagchid. *Zentralasiatische Studien*, vol. 20 (1987), p. 140-72.

Jagchid's analysis of the background and events of the Japanese occupation of Inner
Mongolia are significant because he writes as an eye witness and as a Mongol. He
suggests that the experiences of the Mongols of Inner Mongolia in this period have had
an important influence on subsequent Mongolian history and the survival of the
Mongol nation in China.

263 **Inner Mongolia 1912: the failure of independence.**
Robert B. Valliant. *Mongolian Studies*, vol. 4 (1977), p. 56-119.
bibliog.

There was a strong nationalist movement among Mongols of Inner Mongolia in the
early part of the present century but they did not achieve their aim of becoming
citizens of an independent state. The author seeks reasons for this in the many
Japanese archival documents of the period.

264 **Japanese involvement in Mongol independence movements 1912-1919.**
Robert B. Valliant. *Mongolia Society Bulletin*, vol. 11, no. 2
(fall 1972), p. 1-32.

Inner and Outer Mongolian affairs were closely affected by foreign interests between 1912 and 1919. The author of this article examines the interaction of Mongols, Chinese, Japanese and Russians in this period as revealed in Japanese documents. He argues that the Inner Mongolian princes, by opting for alliance with the Chinese at this time, gave up the best opportunity they ever had to achieve independence.

265 **Mongolian nationalism.**
Robert Arthur Rupen. *Journal of the Royal Central Asiatic Society*,
vol. 45 (1958), p. 157-202, 245-68.

A rather rambling account of the nationalist and Panmongolist aspirations of Buryat, Khalkh and Inner Mongols in the early 20th century. However it does provide much factual information, identifying prominent individuals and events relevant to the topic. The article is in two parts and is based on the author's PhD thesis at the University of Washington, 1954.

266 **Ulanfu and Inner Mongolian autonomy under the Chinese People's Republic.**
Paul V. Hyer. *Mongolia Society Bulletin*, vol. 8, nos. 1-2 (1969),
p. 24-62. bibliog.

Ulanfu (1904-88) was a Tümet Mongol of Inner Mongolia. He was educated in the Soviet Union, joined the Chinese Communist Party and became a Vice President of China. This article traces his life and career, aspects of which throw light on the history of nationalist and revolutionary movements in Inner Mongolia before 1949 and the Inner Mongolian autonomous movement.

Studies on Mongolia: proceedings of the first North American conference on Mongolian studies.
See item no. 23.

Essays in Mongolian studies.
See item no. 72.

Some new information on peasant revolts and people's uprisings in eastern Inner Mongolia in the 19th century (1861-1901).
See item no. 118.

Asia's first modern revolution: Mongolia proclaims its independence.
See item no. 119.

Nationalism and revolution in Mongolia, with a translation from the Mongol of Sh. Nachukdorji's life of Sukhebator.
See item no. 125.

The Mongolian People's Republic, 1924-1928, and the Right Deviation.
See item no. 137.

Mongols of the twentieth century. Part 1.
See item no. 139.

The Mongols of Manchuria.
See item no. 167.

A Mongolian living Buddha: biography of the Kanjurwa Khutughtu.
See item no. 226.

How Mongolia is really ruled: a political history of the Mongolian People's Republic, 1900-1978.
See item no. 245.

The Mongolian revolution of 1990: stability or conflict in Inner Asia?
See item no. 250.

Constitution and Legal System

267 **The advocate in the Mongolian People's Republic.**
William Elliott Butler. *Journal of the Anglo-Mongolian Society*,
vol. 6 (1980), p. 73-88.

A western legal scholar describes the work of Mongolian lawyers which includes the provision of legal advice to individuals and institutions, criminal case work and the preparation of materials to educate the public in matters of law. An English translation of the 1978 statute on the College of Mongolian Advocates is also provided. This article is a revised version of one which appeared under the same title in *Review of Socialist Law*, (vol. 6, 1980, p. 193-97).

268 **Constitutions of the communist party-states.**
Edited by Jan Francis Triska. Stanford, California: Hoover
Institution, 1969. 2nd printing. 541p.

The texts of the Mongolian constitutions of 1924, 1940 and 1960 are reproduced in this book. The version of the 1940 constitution contains amendments to 1959 and the version of the 1960 constitution is in an English translation supplied by the Permanent Mission of the Mongolian People's Republic to the United Nations. See also item no. 269.

269 **The constitutions of the communist world.**
Edited by William B. Simons. Boston: Lancaster; The Hague;
Nijhoff, 1984. 2nd printing. 644p.

This book contains the text of the Mongolian Constitution adopted on 6 July 1960 as amended by the 1 October 1979. It has been translated into English from the Russian version by W. E. Butler who has also provided a brief introduction with notes on the two earlier constitutions of 1924 and 1940. Another version of the 1960 constitution translated from the Mongolian text with amendments to 1973, was published in the JPRS translation series JPRS 74,814 (26 Dec. 1979). (See item no. 466). Readers should be aware that there are significant differences in the various translated versions, particularly of the 1960 constitution. See also item no. 268.

94

270 **Courts of the Mongolian People's Republic (historical notes).**
D. Sangidanzan, introduction by William Elliott Butler, translated from
the Mongolian by Alynn Joelle Nathanson. London: University
College Faculty of Laws, 1980. (Studies on Socialist Legal Systems
Monograph Series, no. 1).
The Mongolian text of this work was published in 1967 and describes the development
of courts and the judicial system in Mongolia from 1921-66. In his introduction, Butler
extends the study to the end of the 1970s. He also examines the nature of the
Mongolian system, pointing out the differences between it and the judicial systems of
the Soviet Union and China and comments on legal officials and the way the
Mongolian system functions.

271 **Fundamental principles of Mongol law.**
Valentin Aleksandrovich Ryazanovskii. Bloomington, Indiana:
Indiana University Press; The Hague: Mouton, 1965. 343p. bibliog.
(Uralic & Altaic Series vol. 43).
This publication is an English translation of a Russian monograph published in Tianjin,
China, in 1937 and includes texts of the legal codes discussed, as available. The author
examines the mediaeval law code, the *Yasa* (see item no. 272) and the *bilegs* or 'wise
sayings' of Chinggis Khan, the Mongol-Oirat Regulations of 1640, the 18th century
code of Khalkh, the *Khalkha Jirum*, Buryat law and some of the laws of the
autonomous state (1911-19). He discusses the sources and content of the various codes
and argues that they are based on the customary law of the Mongol tribes and predate
the Mongol Empire. They show the influence of the Mongols' nomadic, herding
lifestyle and, to some extent, of Chinese law. This study is somewhat dated but it is the
only monograph on pre-revolutionary Mongol law in English.

272 **The 'Great Yasa of Chingiz Khan' and Mongol law in the Ilkhanate.**
David O. Morgan. *Bulletin of the School of Oriental and African
Studies (London)*, vol. 49, no. 1 (1986), p. 163-76.
The author challenges the views of earlier scholars, including V. A. Ryazanovskii (see
item no. 271), who believe that Chinggis Khan promulgated a law code, known as the
Great *Yasa*, in 1206. Morgan argues that there is insufficient evidence for this but he
suggests reasons why a belief in the existence of such a law code developed. He also
discusses the practice of justice during the Mongol empire period (1206-1368). A more
concise statement of Morgan's views, which are generally accepted by contemporary
scholars, is to be found in his book *The Mongols* cited as item no. 91.

273 **The Mongolian legal system: contemporary legislation and
documentation.**
Edited by William Elliott Butler, translated by Alynn Joelle
Nathanson, William Elliott Butler. Boston, Massachusetts: Nijhoff,
1982. 995p. (Studies on Socialist Legal Systems).
A comprehensive study of the legal framework that underpinned the political, social
and economic life of Mongolia under the socialist system. The book includes texts of
the civil, criminal, labour and other codes, analyses the legal system, its institutions
and the administration of justice, and describes the training of the legal profession.
Although many aspects of the Mongolian system were modelled on those of the Soviet

Constitution and Legal System

Union, as Butler points out, there are also significant differences. A dictionary of legal terms and concepts has also been published as a companion to this book and is cited as item no. 186.

274 **Mongolia's new constitution: blueprint for democracy.**
Alan John Kelday Sanders. *Asian Survey*, vol. 32, no. 6 (June 1992), p. 506-20.

No English version of Mongolia's fourth constitution, which came into force on 12 February 1992, has yet been published. This article traces the drafting of this constitution, the heated debates that accompanied its progress through the Great *Khural* (National Assembly) and summarizes the provisions of its final form. The author bases his analysis on the Mongolian version published in the Mongolian government newspaper, *Ardyn Erkh* (14 Jan. 1992).

275 **Mongolia's 'socialist constitution'.**
George Ginsburgs. *Pacific Affairs*, vol. 34, no. 2 (summer 1961), p. 141-56.

In this article the author presents a very favourable view of the Mongolian constitution of 1960 and suggests that it is more innovative than the contemporary constitutions of other countries in the Soviet bloc. He argues that it is a model constitution because it formulates all essential propositions of domestic and foreign policy within the bloc, acknowledges Mongolia's debt to the USSR for the existence of proletarian internationalism, and identifies the dominant role of the communist party in the state and society. National and local government structures as laid down in the 1960 constitution are also discussed in this article.

Mongolia today.
See item no. 12.

Petitions of grievances submitted by the people (18th-beginning of 20th century).
See item no. 117.

Mongols of the twentieth century. Part 1.
See item no. 139.

Mongolian-English-Russian dictionary of legal terms and concepts.
See item no. 186.

Mongolia: coming to terms with family legislation.
See item no. 234.

Local government in the Mongolian People's Republic 1940-1960.
See item no. 246.

International position of the Mongolian People's Republic.
See item no. 280.

Outer Mongolia and its international position.
See item no. 286.

Peoples' education law of the MPR.
See item no. 356.

Foreign Relations

General

276 **Aspects of Mongolian history, 1901-1915.**
Michael Raymond Underdown. *Zentralasiatische Studien*, vol. 15
(1981), p. 151-240.

This article examines Mongolian internal and external affairs at the beginning of the
20th century as revealed in the dispatches of German diplomats in Beijing, St.
Petersburg and elsewhere. The documents show that Mongolia was by no means
isolated from the rest of the world at this time. On the contrary, great power politics
deeply affected the country and contributed to the growth of Mongolian nationalism.

277 **Brezhnev at signing of the Soviet-Mongolian Treaty.**
Current Digest of the Soviet Press, vol. 210 (Sept. 1966), p. 3-9, 44.

In 1966 a Treaty of Friendship, Cooperation and Mutual Aid was signed in
Ulaanbaatar by the respective heads of state of Mongolia and the USSR, Yu.
Tsedenbal and L. Brezhnev. This collection of articles translated from the Soviet Press
includes a text of the treaty and extracts from the speeches of Tsedenbal and Brezhnev
at the signing. The treaty secured Mongolia's support for Soviet foreign policy for the
next twenty years, and facilitated the mobilization of many thousands of Soviet troops
into Mongolia during that period.

278 **Cooperation beween MPR and other CEMA countries detailed.**
Dumaagiin Sodnom. *US Joint Publications Research Service: Mongolia
Report*, no. 370 (8 Nov. 1983), p. 1-5. (JPRS 84,699).

From 1970 members states of Comecon planned their economies in cooperation and
many joint projects were undertaken in Mongolia. The Chairman of the Mongolian
State Planning Commission refers to several such ventures in this article, including the
International Geological Expedition, irrigation for the Kharkhorin State Farm and the
study of alternative forms of power generation. He also comments on cooperation for

long-range planning of labour distribution and the food supply, and on various projects set up in Mongolia with Soviet assistance. Several articles on Comecon cooperation in Mongolia have been published in English in the JPRS translation series (see item no. 466).

279 **Ensuring peace in Asia and the Pacific: the Mongolian initiative.**
Jargalsaikhany Enkhsaikhan. *Asian Survey*, vol. 25, no. 10 (Oct. 1985), p. 1031-38.
The author of this article was the Mongolian ambassador to the United Nations and he writes about a Mongolian initiative of 1981 for an international convention on mutual non-aggression and the non-use of force in Asia and the Pacific. This initiative was promoted at the United Nations and on other international platforms. The article provides a clear statement of the Mongolian government's views on peace, security and the arms race in the 1980s, which were important aspects of foreign policy in that period.

280 **International position of the Mongolian People's Republic.**
Jiří Síma. *Pacific Community*, vol. 4, no. 4, (July 1973), p. 562-87.
Mongolia's attempts to secure the worldwide recognition of its independent status are traced in this article. The author is a specialist in Mongolian affairs and was recently the Czech ambassador to Mongolia. He identifies three periods: 1921-45 when only the USSR recognized Mongolia; 1946-61 when diplomatic relations were opened with China and other socialist countries; and from 1961 when Mongolia joined the United Nations and was recognized by a much wider range of states. A list of sixty-one countries with whom Mongolia had relations up to 1971 is included. For a more recent list see item no. 282.

281 **Mongol-Tibetan treaty of January 11, 1913.**
Parshotam Mehra. *Journal of Asian History*, vol. 3, no. 1 (1969), p. 1-22. bibliog.
A treaty between Mongolia and Tibet was signed in the Mongolian capital, Niislel Khüree (now Ulaanbaatar), in 1913 but it was of no importance in promoting Mongolia's international status and has been largely ignored in western studies of Mongolia's political history. In this article, an Indian scholar examines the background, context and terms of the treaty arguing that it had a powerful impact on Central Asia in the following decade. A text of the treaty may be found in item no. 129.

282 **Mongolia has diplomatic relations with 93 countries.**
US Joint Publications Research Service: *Mongolia Report*, MON-85-002 (4 March 1985), p. 41-44.
A list of ninety-three countries with whom Mongolia has diplomatic relations and the date of commencement. The first friendly country listed is the Soviet Union as of 1921 and the most recent was Ecuador which entered into relations in 1982. Since this list was published the number of friendly countries has risen to 125, including the USA and South Korea, in 1987 and 1989 respectively. The most recent was Brunei in 1992.

283 **The Mongolian army.**
Robert Arthur Rupen. In: *Communist armies in politics*. Edited by
Jonathan R. Adelman. Boulder, Colorado: Westview Press; Epping,
England: Bowker, 1982, p. 167-83. bibliog.

In this article the author surveys the formation, development and activity of the
Mongolian army from 1921 in the context of Mongolian politics and international
strategic issues. The influence and control of the USSR over the Mongolian armed
forces is emphasized.

284 **The Mongolian People's Army.**
Marko Milivojević. *Armed Forces*, vol. 6, no. 12 (Dec. 1987),
p. 562-65. map.

The Mongolian armed forces are discussed in the context of Sino-Soviet relations in
this article. A chart illustrating the organization of the armed forces is provided.

285 **Nomonkhan: Japan against Russia, 1939.**
Alvin D. Coox. Stanford, California: Stanford University Press, 1985.
2 vols.

The battle of Nomonkhan is known to Mongols and Russians as the battle of Khalkhyn
gol (Khalkh river). In 1939, on Mongolia's border with Manchuria, the Japanese
Kwantung army was soundly defeated by a joint Soviet and Mongolian force. Coox's
study is a military history which examines border skirmishes from 1936 and the
creation of the Kwantung army and then gives a detailed description of the strategy
and progress of the battle. The author has made extensive use of Japanese sources and
he views the war from a Japanese perspective giving little consideration to the
significance of this conflict for either Mongolia or the Soviet Union. Mongolia's
involvement at Khalkhyn gol is discussed in item no. 140.

286 **Outer Mongolia and its international position.**
Gerard Martin Friters, edited by Eleanor Lattimore, with an
introduction by Owen Lattimore. New York: Octagon, 1974.
Reprinted ed. 358p. bibliog.

This book has appeared under several imprints since it was first published in 1949. The
author examines Mongolia's relations with Russia, China and Japan from the point of
view of international law. Although the book is dated, its explanation of the reasons
why the international community was unwilling to accept Mongolia as an independent
and sovereign state before the Second World War are clearly explained and still valid.
A text of the Mongolian constitution of 1940, translated from the Russian version, is
provided in an appendix.

287 **Russian and Soviet policy in Manchuria and Outer Mongolia 1911-1931.**
Peter Shenghao Tang, introduced by Philip E. Mosely. Duke, North
Carolina: Duke University Press, 1959. 494p. maps. bibliog.

This author presents a critical analysis of Tsarist Russian and Soviet diplomatic
strategies for territorial expansion in northeast Asia, which he argues has led, in
Mongolia's case, to Soviet economic dominance and a political protectorate. Tang
identifies a basic continuity in Russian and Soviet intentions vis-à-vis Mongolia and
suggests that these policies were to have important implications in the 1960s. He also

argues that Mongolian affairs have been and are determined by the Soviet Union and gives little consideration to the view that the Mongols have played some part in their own destiny in the early 20th century. For an alternative view of Russian policies in Mongolia see item no. 120.

288 **The Russo-Japanese treaties of 1907-1916 concerning Manchuria and Mongolia.**
Ernest Batson Price.   Baltimore, Maryland: Johns Hopkins Press 1933. 164p. map. bibliog.

Events in Mongolia have, from time to time, been determined by the conflicting strategic interests of Russia and Japan. This was the case at the beginning of the 20th century when the two governments concluded secret treaties assigning Mongolia to the Russian sphere of influence and Manchuria and Inner Mongolia to the Japanese sphere. These agreements were to determine the kind of support the Tsarist government was prepared to give the Khalkh Mongols when they declared independence in 1911. The secret treaties are the subject of this monograph and English translations of the documents are included in appendices.

Area handbook of Mongolia.
See item no. 1.

Mongolia: a country study.
See item no. 9.

Mongolia: politics, economics and society.
See item no. 11.

Mongolia today.
See item no. 12.

Between the hammer and the anvil: Chinese and Russian policies in Outer Mongolia 1911-1921.
See item no. 120.

With the Russians in Mongolia.
See item no. 129.

History of the Mongolian People's Republic.
See item no. 134.

The Mongolian People's Republic, 1924-1928, and the Right Deviation.
See item no. 137.

The Mongolian People's Republic today.
See item no. 138.

Soviet-Japanese confrontation in Outer Mongolia: the battle of Nomon-Khan-Khalkin gol.
See item no. 140.

Soviet-Mongolia cooperation during the Second World War.
See item no. 142.

Foreign Relations. Mongolia and the Sino-Soviet dispute

The Dalai lamas and the Mongols.
See item no. 218.

Mongolia's measured steps.
See item no. 248.

The Mongolian revolution of 1990: stability or conflict in Inner Asia?
See item no. 250.

National economy of the MPR for 70 years (1921-1991): anniversary statistical yearbook.
See item no. 340.

Mongolia and the Sino-Soviet dispute

289 **China and Inner Asia from 1368 to the present day.**
Morris Rossabi. London: Thames & Hudson, 1975. 320p. maps.
bibliog.

China's relations with its neighbours from the end of the Mongol empire to the 20th century are the subject of this textbook for students. It explains the traditional relationship of China and the Mongols, the development of Chinese and Russian relations from the 17th century and provides valuable background material for comprehending the interaction of Mongolia, the Soviet Union and China in the 20th century.

290 **China and Mongolia: recurring trends and prospects for change.**
Elizabeth E. Green. *Asian Survey*, vol. 26, no. 12 (Dec. 1986),
p. 1337-63.

A clear and perceptive analysis of Mongol-Chinese relations since 1921. The author argues that these are determined by historical factors as well as Mongolia's fear of Chinese expansion, China's vacillating policy towards minorities, particularly the Inner Mongols, and the Sino-Soviet dispute. She demonstrates this by tracing events from the end of the Second World War, when Chiang Kai-shek recognized Mongolian independence, to 1986 when Soviet President Mikhail Gorbachev offered to withdraw Soviet troops from Mongolia.

291 **Inner Asia in international relations: the role of Mongolia in Russo-Chinese relations.**
Larry William Moses. *Mongolia Society Bulletin*, vol. 11, no. 2
(fall 1972), p. 55-75.

This author argues that Mongolia took the side of the USSR in the Sino-Soviet dispute, as a matter of choice, on the basis of traditional Inner Asian relations and because it felt threatened by China. In this article he examines Mongolia's perception of the world and the way the Mongolian government makes positive decisions for survival which are based on historical precedents dating back to 1691. He suggests that the

102

benefits Mongolia has received since 1911 as a result of its alliance with Tsarist Russia and the Soviet Union have outweighed the disadvantages of domination by the latter.

292 **Mongolia between China and Russia.**
Ram Rahul. *Asian Survey*, vol. 18, no. 7 (July 1978), p. 659-65.

A brief analysis of Mongolian relations with the USSR and China since the signing of the Sino-Soviet Treaty of 1950. The author concludes that the Mongols opted for alliance with the USSR in the 1960s because they were suspicious of China's intentions towards their country.

293 **The Mongolian People's Republic and Sino-Soviet competition.**
Robert Arthur Rupen.   In: *Communist strategies in Asia*. Edited by
A. Doak Barnett.   London: Pall Mall; New York, London: Praeger,
1963, p. 262-92.

In the 1950s China and the Soviet Union vied with one another to win the favour of Mongolia by providing developmental aid. In this article Sino-Soviet competition is discussed in the context of Mongolian domestic politics, destalinization in Mongolia, and Panmongolism. Rupen published a similar analysis in *China Quarterly* (no. 16 1963 p. 75-85) and further information may be found in his monograph 'How Mongolia is really ruled' (see item no. 245).

294 **The reevaluation of Chinggis Khan: its role in the Sino-Soviet dispute.**
Paul V. Hyer.   *Asian Survey*, vol. 6 (Dec. 1966), p. 696-705.

After the death of the hard-line Mongolian leader, Kh. Choibalsan, in 1952 and of Stalin in 1953, there was greater freedom of policy-making and national expression in Mongolia for a short time. In 1962, the Mongolian government planned a series of celebrations to mark the 800th anniversary of the birth of Chinggis Khan but these were called off soon after commencement under pressure from the USSR and several senior government officials were sacked. This article, based on rare Mongolian sources, traces the events surrounding the celebrations and demonstrates that the outcome was intimately connected with deteriorating relations between the Soviet Union and China. The article also provides a good example of the way Mongolian perceptions of Chinggis Khan in a given period can indicate the extent of the country's dependency on the USSR.

295 **The Soviet armed forces and Mongolia.**
Marko Milivojević.   *Jane's Intelligence Review*, vol. 3 no. 7
(July 1991), p. 306-10. maps. bibliog.

In 1989 the Soviet Union began to withdraw its estimated 50,000 troops from Mongolia. This article comments on the presence of this force in Mongolia in the context of the Sino-Soviet dispute and the events in the 1980s that led to troop withdrawal. The author makes the additional suggestion that changing political circumstances in Mongolia and Inner (Central) Asia render future military cooperation between Mongolia and Russia unlikely. See also item no. 284 on the Mongolian army by the same author.

296 **The two phases in Mongolian-Chinese relations (1949-1972).**
O. Chuluun. *Far Eastern Affairs*, no. 1 (1974), p. 24-32.

A Mongolian view of Sino-Mongol relations. The author describes the period of close and friendly exchanges between Mongolia and China from 1949 to 1960 which brought Mongolia many economic benefits. In the 1960s relations deteriorated and during the Chinese Cultural Revolution, which began in 1966, Chinese citizens demonstrated violently against Mongolia on several occasions. From statements made by Chinese and maps and textbooks published in China in the 1960s, the author identifies a covert desire by Mao Zedong to absorb Mongolia into China. This, and the belief that the Soviet Union was ideologically correct in the Sino-Soviet dispute, are given as important reasons for the sharp decline in Mongolian-Chinese relations by 1972.

History of the MPR.
See item no. 134.

Mongols of the twentieth century. Part 1.
See item no. 139.

How Mongolia is really ruled: a political history of the Mongolian People's Republic, 1900-1978.
See item no. 245.

The Mongolian revolution of 1990: stability or conflict in Inner Asia?
See item no. 250.

Brezhnev at the signing of the Soviet-Mongolian Treaty.
See item no. 277.

The Mongolian People's army.
See item no. 284.

The influence of railway construction in Mongolia: the shift from Chinese to Russian/Soviet protection.
See item no. 331.

Economy

297 **An attempt to delimit the main economic zones of the Mongolian People's Republic.**
P. M. Alampiyev, V. V. Kistanov, M. B. Mazanova, D. C. Chumichev. *Soviet Geography*, vol. 3 (1962), p. 16-29.
This article identifies the long-term aims of Mongolian economic planning from the early 1960s when Mongolia became a member of Comecon. In 1961 a joint Mongolian-Soviet team surveyed the country and its economic potential. The territory was divided into three economic zones, the western, central and eastern zones, to facilitate planning for agricultural and industrial development. The geography, resources and potential of each zone are described here.

298 **Certain points of land utilization laws clarified.**
T. Sengedorj. *US Joint Publications Research Service: Translations on Mongolia*, no. 240 (5 Mar 1971), p. 58-60. (JPRS 52,547).
From 1991, many of Mongolia's state and cooperative assets were privatized and this has led to a reconsideration of concepts of ownership and use of land. This article explains the legal and practical aspects of land utilization and land organization during the years of single party rule, with reference to the land laws of 1933 and 1943, the development of state farms, and the reorganization of local government boundaries in 1960.

299 **The economic and social development of the Mongolian People's Republic: a Siberian colony?**
Michael Perrins. In: *Sibirica II: British Universities Siberian Studies Seminar: report of the third meeting held at the Scott Polar Research Institute, University of Cambridge 28-30 September 1984*, Lancaster, England: British Universities Siberian Studies Seminar, 1986. p. 41-58.
In this paper the author analyses industrial and agricultural development and the growth of urban centres that took place in Mongolia in the 1970s, in accordance with

Economy

Comecon policies for economic integration. He argues that this was both a continuation and an intensification of the neo-colonialist development encouraged by the USSR in the 1950s and 1960s defined by G. G. S. Murphy in his book *Soviet Mongolia: a study of the oldest political satellite* (see item no. 141). The ultimate goal of Mongolian planned development was the integration of Mongolia in the Siberian economy.

300 **Finances of the Mongolian People's Republic.**
B. Dolgormaa, edited by A. M. Aleksandrov, K. N. Plotnikov. *US Joint Publications Research Service: Translations on Mongolia*, no. 267 (16 Oct. 1972), 47p. (JPRS 57,269).

This publication is an English translation of selected chapters of a monograph by a Mongolian author writing in Russian. The chapters cover the Mongolian national budget, capital investment, credit and foreign exchange relations, the monetary system, and the financing of Mongolian agriculture and industry. A number of statistics for the late 1960s are provided.

301 **Monetary, credit system of MPR.**
B. Dolgormaa. *US Joint Publications Research Service: Translations on Mongolia*, no. 306, (16 Feb. 1979), p. 13-22. (JPRS 72,833).

A concise account of banking in Mongolia from 1924 to the era of the planned economy. In 1924 the Mongolian Trade and Industrial Bank opened. It was owned jointly by the Mongolian and Soviet governments and in 1925 it began issuing the national currency, the *tögrög*. The article was first published in Russian in *Deng'i i Kredit* (no. 2 Feb. 1978, p. 72-79).

302 **Mongolia: fast forward.**
Leslie Holstrom. *Euromoney*, supplement (July 1991), 21p.

Mongolia's plans for wide-ranging reforms and transfer to a market economy, which were formulated in 1990, are the subject of the entire issue of this special edition of *Euromoney*. The articles cover privatization, price liberalization, banking, transport, tourism, trade and opportunities for foreign investment in the 1990s.

303 **Mongolia: moves towards perestroika.**
Michael Faber. *Development Policy Review*, vol. 8, (1990), p. 411-28.

This article was written at the end of the 1980s when Mongolia was cautiously introducing economic reforms. The author explains how the planned, centralized economy was managed in Mongolia and speculates on methods and problems for transfer to a system that would allow enterprises to have greater control of their own financial affairs and increase their productivity. While the article was being written, Mongolia abandoned economic planning altogether and opted for a market economy. This study provides an interesting glimpse of a transitional period and background to a number of issues and problems the Mongolian government is grappling with in the 1990s.

304 **The Mongolian People's Republic: toward a market economy.**
Elizabeth Milne, John Leimone, Franek Rozwadowski, Padej
Sukachevin.   Washington, DC: International Monetary Fund, 1991.
81p. map. (Occasional Paper, no. 79).

The information and data in this study were collected by officials of the International
Monetary Fund (IMF) in Mongolia in 1990, in preparation for the country's admission
to the IMF in February 1991. Mongolia's financial and economic conditions are
described, particularly from 1985 when some reforms were introduced, and the authors
make projections for the immediate future. A large part of the book comprises
appendices on government structure, budgetry structure, banking, tables of social and
economic indicators and a selection of economic statistics based on Mongolian
government sources, some of which have been adjusted by the IMF. Another detailed
and up-to-date account is available in *Mongolia: a centrally planned economy in
transition*. (New York: Oxford University Press, for the Asian Development Bank,
1992. 250p. map).

305 **Planning in the MPR.**
George Gregory Stanislaus Murphy.   *Journal of Asian Studies*, vol. 18,
no. 2 (Feb. 1959) p. 241-58.

Mongolia agreed to adopt the Soviet system of centralized planning in 1940 but the
commencement of the first five-year plan was delayed by the Second World War.
Using Russian sources the author of this article analyses the first two plans, (1948-52
and 1952-57), the problems the planners faced and the results. Item no. 141 by the
same author also provides information on the interim three-year plan of 1958-60.

Area handbook of Mongolia.
See item no. 1.

Information Mongolia.
See item no. 3.

Mongolia: a country study.
See item no. 9.

Mongolia: politics, economics and society.
See item no. 11.

Mongolia today.
See item no. 12.

**Paralipomena Mongolica: wissenschaftliche Notizen über Land, Leute und
Lebenweise in der Mongolischen Volksrepublik.** (Paralipomena Mongolica:
scientific notes on the land, people and way of life in the Mongolian People's
Republic.)
See item no. 19.

The People's Republic of Mongolia: general reference guide.
See item no. 20.

Sovremennaya Mongolia: otchet Mongol'skoi Ekspeditsii snaryazhennoi Irkutskoi kontori Vserossiiskogo Tsentral'novo Soyuza Potrebitel'nykh oshchestvo 'Tsentrosoyuz'. (Contemporary Mongolia: report of the Mongolian Expedition equipped by the Irkutsk office of the All-Russian Central Union of Consumer Cooperatives 'Tsentrosoyuz').
See item no. 22.

Land of the blue sky: a portrait of modern Mongolia.
See item no. 28.

Economic-geographical sketch of the Mongolian People's Republic.
See item no. 46.

Chinese agent in Mongolia.
See item no. 131.

History of the Mongolian People's Republic.
See item no. 134.

The Mongolian People's Republic, 1924-1928, and the Right Deviation.
See item no. 137.

Mongols of the twentieth century. Part 1.
See item no. 139.

Soviet Mongolia: a study of the oldest political satellite.
See item no. 141.

National economy of the MPR for 65 years: anniversary statistical collection.
See item no. 339.

National economy of the MPR for 70 years (1921-1991): anniversary statistical yearbook.
See item no. 340.

National economy of the MPR in 1967: a compilation of statistics.
See item no. 341.

Asia 1992 yearbook.
See item no. 480.

The Far East and Australasia 1992.
See item no. 481.

Trade

306 **MPR-Soviet foreign trade history.**
Yondongiin Ochir. *US Joint Publications Research Service*: *Mongolia Report*, no. 316 (6 Aug. 1979), p. 16-24. (JPRS 73,963).

An overview of Mongolia's trade with the USSR from 1921. The article identifies trade agreements, categories of goods exchanged, joint ventures and summary turnover figures. Other types of cooperation with the USSR and Soviet aid to Mongolia are also mentioned. The article first appeared in the Comecon journal *Ekonomicheskoe Sotrudnichestvo Stran-chlenov SEV*, (no. 4, 1978).

307 **MPR trade with CEMA countries examined.**
Yondongiin Ochir. *US Joint Publications Research Service*: *Mongolia Report* (30 July 1982), p. 47-51. (JPRS 81,407).

In the 1980s ninety-seven per cent of Mongolia's foreign trade was with the Comecon countries. The article is a concise survey of this trade and makes reference to the agreements and bodies that governed the exchange of goods with specific countries under the 1981-85 plan.

308 **Development of domestic trade outlined.**
B. Sharavsambuu. *US Joint Publications Research Service*: *Mongolia Report*, MON-85-005 (2 May 1985), p. 109-13.

A brief survey of the growth and organization of the state internal trading system by the Minister of Trade and Procurement. The article was written for a popular audience and first appeared in Russian in the Mongolian newspaper *Novostii Mongolii* (24 Aug. 1984, p. 2).

Area handbook for Mongolia.
See item no. 1.

Mongolia: a country study.
See item no. 9.

Mongolia: politics, economics and society.
See item no. 11.

Mongolia today.
See item no. 12.

The People's Republic of Mongolia: general reference guide.
See item no. 20.

Weideplätze der Mongolen im reich der Chalcha. (Mongol pastures in Khalkh.)
See item no. 40.

Narrative of a journey through Western Mongolia, July 1872 to January 1873.
See item no. 48.

Manchu Chinese colonial rule in Northern Mongolia.
See item no. 115.

Chinese agent in Mongolia.
See item no. 131.

History of the Mongolian People's Republic.
See item no. 134.

The Mongolian People's Republic, 1924-1928, and the Right Deviation.
See item no. 137.

Mongols of the twentieth century. Part 1.
See item no. 139.

Soviet Mongolia: a study of the oldest political satellite.
See item no. 141.

National economy of the MPR for 70 years (1921-1991): anniversary statistical yearbook.
See item no. 340.

Industry

309 Development of Baga Nuur coal mine detailed.
Dorjiin Dondov. *US Joint Publications Research Service*: *Mongolia Report*, no. 370 (8 Nov. 1983), p. 38-41. (JPRS 84,699).

In 1974 large deposits of coal suitable for use in power stations were found at Baga Nuur in the Central Economic Zone. Construction of the mine began in 1978 and four years later a new town of 10,000 inhabitants had come into existence. The director of the mine describes the coal and its extraction which was expected to amount to six million tonnes per annum when fully operational and support a new industrial centre. The article first appeared in Russian in *Ekonomicheskoe Sotrudnichestvo Stran-Chlenov SEV* (no. 2 (Mar. 1983) p. 49-51). A number of other articles on Mongolian industrial development have appeared in the same journal, some of which have been translated into English in the JPRS translation series (see item no. 466).

310 Efficient utilization of wood and firewood resources required in the MPR.
US Joint Publication Research Services: *Translations on Mongolia*, no. 291 (1 June 1976), 8p. (JPRS 67,387).

A discussion of forest resources in Mongolia based on the findings of a Soviet study in the 1950s and on other research. The author comments on forestry management, the uses of wood in the national economy, in particular as firewood, and he concludes that supplies are sufficient for the country's needs. A number of other articles on the timber industry have been published in the JPRS translation series (see item no. 466).

311 Erdenet mining complex development outlined.
R. I. Semigin. *US Joint Publications Research Service*: *Mongolia Report*, no. 336 (21 Jan. 1982), p. 33-38. (JPRS 97,709).

The Erdenet Copper and Molybdenum combine in northern Mongolia is the largest mining and concentrate complex in Asia. Developed as a joint venture with the USSR in the 1970s it accounted for a considerable proportion of Mongolia's exports to the

USSR in the 1980s and the new town of Erdenet is now the third largest city in Mongolia. In this article the general director of the combine describes the mineral deposits, the technology and methods used to extract and semi-process them, the labour force and training. A table of main indicators for the years 1979-81 is provided. This article was first published in Russian in *Gorny Zhurnal* (Sept. 1981, p. 15-18).

312 **Fifty years of construction materials industry reviewed.**
S. Luvsangombo. *US Joint Publications Research Service, Translations on Mongolia*, no. 256 (12 Jan. 1972), p. 71-80. (JPRS 54,916).

This article describes and charts the production of bricks, adhesives and precast concrete in Mongolia. It first appeared in the Mongolian professional journal *Barilgachin* (no. 4 1970, p. 1-6).

313 **Significance of cooperation in the development of the MPR power network.**
Galsantsedengiin Nyam-Ochir. *US Joint Publications Research Service, Mongolia Report*, no. 360 (31 March 1983), p. 33-37. (JPRS 83,170).

This is a concise survey of the development of power plants and electricity networks in cooperation with other members of Comecon and of Mongolia's links with the Siberian United Power Network. The article first appeared in *Ekonomicheskoe Sotrudnichestvo Stran-Chlenov SEV* (no. 10 1982, p. 33-35).

314 **Status of MPR and CEMA countries jointly owned enterprises discussed.**
Davaasürengiin Dariimaa. *US Joint Publications Research Service: Mongolia Report*, no. 349 (3 Dec. 1982), p. 15-20. (JPRS 82,386).

Several industrial enterprises which are owned jointly by Mongolia and other members of Comecon are identified in this article. The author explains their legal status, organization and management and compares them with enterprises owned wholly by Mongolia. This article first appeared in the Soviet journal *Khozyaistvo i Pravo* (no. 2 June 1982, p. 72-75).

Area handbook of Mongolia.
See item no. 1.

Mongolia: a country study.
See item no. 9.

Mongolia: politics, economics and society.
See item no. 11.

The People's Republic of Mongolia: general reference guide.
See item no. 20.

Economic-geographical sketch of the Mongolian People's Republic.
See item no. 46.

History of the Mongolian People's Republic.
See item no. 134.

The Mongolian People's Republic, 1924-1928, and the Right Deviation.
See item no. 137.

Mongols of the twentieth century. Part 1.
See item no. 139.

How Mongolia is really ruled: a political history of the Mongolian People's Republic, 1900-1978.
See item no. 245.

US Joint Publications Research Service: East Asia: Mongolia.
See item no. 466.

Agriculture

315 **Les activités rurales en République Populaire de Mongolie.** (Rural activities in the Mongolian People's Republic.)
Jean-Pierre Accolas, Jean-Pierre Deffontaines, Françoise Aubin.
Études Mongoles, vol. 6 (1975), p. 7-98.

Accolas and Deffontaines examined the rural economy during a study visit to Mongolia in 1974. The first part of their report concerns cooperative livestock raising and fodder crop cultivation. In the second part they discuss the production and processing of milk, including the preparation of cheeses, kumiss and milk spirit and provide data on milk analysis. The article is in French. See also item no. 326 by the same authors.

316 **Communist agriculture: farming in the Far East and Cuba.**
Edited by Karl-Eugen Wädekin. London, New York: Routledge, 1990. 131p.

This collection of articles includes two which concern Mongolia: 'Agrarian policies in China, Vietnam, Mongolia and Cuba' by Karl-Eugen Wädekin and 'Socialist agriculture outside Europe: new ways in Mongolian agriculture?' by Günter Jähne. They were presented at a conference on socialist agricultural development and demonstrate how Marxist-Leninist theories of agriculture have been put into practice in Mongolia and with what results.

317 **Going with the grain: Mongolia's state farms.**
Caroline Humphrey. *Inside Asia*, no. 8 (April-May 1986), p. 29-31.

In 1984 this author visited the Darkhan State Farm in northern central Mongolia. She discusses the structural, economic and social aspects of wheat production on this farm in the context of economic change in the Mongolian countryside since 1921.

318   **Fraternal cooperation in plant protection, parasite prevention.**
       B. Badmajav, N. Tronj. *US Joint Publications Research Service*:
       Translations on Mongolia, no. 314, (8 June 1979), p. 1-4. (JPRS
       73,648).

This article describes Comecon cooperation and other measures to combat some of the problems of arable farming in Mongolia. It includes a discussion of Brandts fieldmouse *Microtus Brandti Radok*, which is a serious pest in the grasslands and a problem for the herding collectives. The article first appeared in the East German periodical *Internationale Zeitschrift der Landwirtschaft* (no. 3, 1977, p. 243-44). Many articles on Mongolian agriculture were published in that serial in the 1970s. They are a valuable source of information and a number have appeared in English translation in the JPRS translation series (see item no. 466).

319   **Historical development of state farms.**
       Kh. Banzragch. *US Joint Publications Research Service: Translations
       on Mongolia*, no. 250 (28 Sept. 1971). 8p. (JPRS 54,141).

A Mongolian agronomist provides information on the development, size, location, crops, livestock and technical methods of state farms in Mongolia after ten years of Virgin land policies and extensive state farm development. The information in this article may be updated by that of B. Rachkov in the same translation series *Mongolia Report* (no. 340, [12 Aug. 1982], p. 32-36 [JPRS 81,520]) which also includes a description of a visit to the Nomgon State Farm near Ulaanbaatar.

320   **Influence of irrigation, fertilizer on barley yields, quality.**
       D. Dashdendev. *US Joint Publications Research Service: Translations
       on Mongolia*, no. 293 (13 Aug. 1976), 9p. (JPRS 67,757.)

Barley has been grown in Mongolia since ancient times and is used as a food and fodder crop and for brewing. This article reports field tests carried out at the Jargalant State Farm using four strains of barley, Nutans 47, Viner, Noyët and Altay 1. The quality and quantity of yields produced when potassium and phosphorus fertilizers or irrigation are used are noted.

321   **International cooperation in development of Mongolian agriculture.**
       D. Dugar. *US Joint Publication Research Service: Translations on
       Mongolia*, no. 304 (14 Nov. 1978), p. 33-41. (JPRS 72,232).

This article describes the work of agricultural research institutions which includes selective breeding, veterinary research, crop trials, pest and weed control, and production systems. It was first published in Russian in *Mezhdunarodnyi Sel'skokhozyaistvennyi Zhurnal* (no. 1, 1978, p. 9-12). Articles in Russian periodicals are an important source of information on Mongolian agriculture, and a number of these have been published in English translation in the JPRS translation series (see item no. 466).

322   **Labour organization in livestock breeding.**
       S. Luvsandorj. *US Joint Publications Research Service: Translations
       on Mongolia*, no. 65 (18 Feb. 1965), p. 5-16. (JPRS 28,806).

Herd management in the newly established herding collectives is the subject of this article. It explains task specialization and the organization of the working day at different seasons of the year. The article first appeared in the Mongolian economic journal *Ediin Zasag, Erkhiin Asuudal* (Oct. 1964, p. 13-23). Several other articles on the organization of collectives have appeared in English translation in the JPRS translation series (see item no. 466).

323 **Leaders and leadership roles in a Mongolian collective: two cases.**
Daniel Rosenberg. *Mongolian Studies*, vol. 7, (1981-82), p. 17-51.

The two men who are the subjects of this article are the director of the Ikh Tamir herding collective in Arkhangai *aimag* (province) and the local First Party Secretary. Both grew up in poor rural families and rose to their present offices through service in the army and the Party. Through their biographies and the way each approaches his job, the organization and problems of collectives are explained. The article also demonstrates the nature of politics generally in a developing nation under a communist regime and the effect on politics of Mongol behaviour in particular.

324 **'Negdel' development: a socio-cultural perspective.**
Daniel Rosenberg. *Mongolian Studies*, vol. 1, (1974), p. 62-75.

This article reports on twelve Mongolian herding collectives (*negdels*) a decade after they were formed. The author describes the organization of the collectives, how labour is used and Party involvement. He finds much to praise in the system and the way it is linked with an industrial sector that uses its product. By the 1980s most observers agreed that the collectivized herding economy had not performed as well as this author predicted they would. Nevertheless the article is still worth reading for its factual information on the organization and management of the collectives and on rural development generally in the period concerned.

325 **Pastoral nomadism in Mongolia: the role of herdsmen's cooperatives in a national economy.**
Caroline Humphrey. *Development and Change*, vol. 9, no. 1 (Jan. 1978), p. 133-60. bibliog.

This article shows how the traditional Mongolian herding economy evolved and became a fully collectivized system. The author examines the organization and practices of collective livestock herding and considers how the Mongolian economy and society have been affected by two decades of collectivized herding.

326 **Quelques données sur l'élevage du yak en République Populaire de Mongolie.** (Some data on yak herding in the Mongolian People's Republic.)
Jean-Pierre Accolas, Jean-Pierre Deffontaines. In: *Le yak: son role dans la vie materielle et culturelle des éleveurs d'Asie Centrale.* (The yak: its role in the material and cultural life of the herdsmen of Central Asia.) Paris: Société d'Ethnozootechnie, 1976, p. 133-41.

In Mongolia yaks are herded mainly in the nine western *aimags* (provinces) which lie 1500m above sea level. In 1974 500,000 yaks, that is one fifth of the bovine population of Mongolia, were owned by herding collectives. The authors describe the physical characteristics of the yak and the production and utilization of yak's milk to satisfy the needs of a growing population and rapid urbanization in these *aimags*. The *khainag*, which is a yak crossed with a bull or cow, is also mentioned. The study is based on field work in Mongolia in 1974 and the report is in French. See also item no. 315 by the same authors.

327 **Socialist organization of Mongolian agriculture described.**
　　D. Myobuu. *US Joint Publications Research Service: Mongolia Report*, no. 317 (23 Aug. 1979), p. 13-21. (JPRS 74,069).
A concise survey of the formation and development of the Mongolian herding collectives by a Mongolian author for a German audience. He remarks on the role of the government in setting up the collectives, government investment in collectives and the growth of settled centres where social, cultural and economic services are provided for members of collectives. The article first appeared in *Internationale Zeitschrift für Landwirtschaft* (vol. 22, no. 6, 1978, 539-42), and marks twenty years of the collective movement.

328 **Some aspects of the history of land rights in Mongolia.**
　　Bazaryn Shirendev. *Journal of the Anglo-Mongolian Society*, vol. 3, no. 1, (1976) p. 44-55; no. 2 (1976), p. 41-57.
A Mongolian historian discusses the use of land, especially for agricultural purposes, during the autonomous period (1911-1919) and the development of the concept of state owned land in the 1920s. He draws attention to the fact that Mongols raised crops in Mongolia, in addition to herding animals, long before the 20th century.

Area handbook for Mongolia.
See item no. 1.

Mongolia: a country study.
See item no. 9.

Mongolia: politics, economics and society.
See item no. 11

The People's Republic of Mongolia: general reference guide.
See item no. 20.

Economic-geographical sketch of the Mongolian People's Republic.
See item no. 46.

History of the Mongolian People's Republic.
See item no. 134.

The Mongolian People's Republic, 1924-1928, and the Right Deviation.
See item no. 137.

Mongols of the twentieth century. Part 1.
See item no. 139.

Soviet Mongolia: a study of the oldest political satellite.
See item no. 141.

Agriculture

Certain points of land utilization laws clarified.
See item no. 298.

Soils of Outer Mongolia (Mongolian People's Republic).
See item no. 368.

Transport

329 **The development of transport.**
Alan John Kelday Sanders. *Focus*, vol. 20, no. 5 (Jan. 1970), p. 8-11.
In this brief article the pre-revolutionary methods of travel and freight transport by caravan and on horseback are contrasted with the road, river, rail and air services of the 20th century.

330 **Fifty years of Mongolia's transport.**
Mongolia, no. 3 (24) (1975), p. 10-23.
An illustrated, popular feature in a magazine published in Mongolia for English speakers. Its subject is motor and air transport in Mongolia with remarks on the training of personnel and system maintainence.

331 **The influence of railway construction in Mongolia: the shift from Chinese to Russian/Soviet protection.**
Alpo Juntunen. *Transport History*, vol. 12, 3rd Series, no. 2, (Sept. 1991), p. 169-86. map. bibliog.
The author of this article examines the railway construction debate from the late 19th century to 1955, when the Trans-Mongolian line (now called the Ulaanbaatar railway) was completed, in the context of Mongol-Sino-Soviet relations.

332 **Rail transport in the Mongolian People's Republic.**
V. Bömbög. *US Joint Publication Research Service: Translations on Mongolia*, no. 299 (3 May 1978), p. 19-26. (JPRS 71,058).
The construction of the Ulaanbaatar Railway (formerly the Trans-Mongolian railway), begun in 1947, and of the branch lines serving the Sharyn Gol and Erdenet industrial complexes is the subject of this article. Passenger and freight services, the economic benefits of the railway and the training of personnel are also covered. The same author has written a similar article on motor transport which was translated in the JPRS

translation series (JPRS no. 73,249). Both articles emphasize the assistance of the Soviet Union in the development of transport.

Area handbook for Mongolia.
See item no. 1.

Mongolia: a country study.
See item no. 9.

Economic-geographical sketch of the Mongolian People's Republic.
See item no. 46.

Asien/Asia/Asie.
See item no. 50.

History of the Mongolian People's Republic.
See item no. 134.

The Mongolian People's Republic, 1924-1928, and the Right Deviation.
See item no. 137.

Mongolia: fast forward.
See item no. 302.

Employment, Manpower and the Trade Unions

333 **The activities of the Mongolian trade unions for the good of the working people.**
Ulaanbaatar: [n.p.], 1970. 44p. (50 years of trade unions in P.R.M. [MPR]).
There is no comprehensive study of the Mongolian Trade Unions in western scholarship. This booklet marking the 50th anniversary of the Mongolian trade unions provides some details of wages, pensions and other benefits, the regulation of female labour and the cultural and leisure facilities promoted by the unions. See also items no. 335-36.

334 **Manpower policy and planning in the Mongolian People's Republic.**
M. Lkhamsüren. *International Labour Review*, vol. 121, no. 4, (July-Aug. 1982), p. 469-80.
According to the Constitution of 1960, Mongolian citizens had a right to work. Manpower policies aimed to provide full employment and to fill all jobs. In this article the former Chairman of the State Committee on Labour and Wages discusses these policies, the development of labour resource planning, vocational training and the allocation of skilled manpower. He also remarks on the special problems of labour distribution in a society with a high birth rate and a high proportion of young people.

335 **Mongolian Trade Unions.**
Ulaanbaatar: Trade Unions Council, [n.d.], 24p. (The magazine of the Mongolian Trade Unions, Special Publication).
A propaganda publication for English readers on the work of the Mongolian Trade Unions. It contains short, illustrated articles on worker safety, socialist competition, the unions and political and economic policies, relations with workers in other communist countries and an interview with the Chairman of the Trade Unions, B. Luvsantseren. The publication dates from the late 1980s.

121

Employment, Manpower and the Trade Unions

336 **Role of the Mongolian trade unions in the building of socialism.**
Ulaanbaatar: [n.p.], 1976. 47p. (50 years of trade unions in P.R.M.
[MPR]).

A booklet marking the 50th anniversary of the Mongolian trade unions and the
contribution of the Mongolian working class to economic development from 1960, with
some information on the 1974 labour code. See also item no. 333.

337 **Supervision of the Socialist Labor Movement.**
US Joint Publications Research Service: Translations on Mongolia,
no. 80 (23 Aug. 1965), p. 42-50. (JPRS 31,654).

From 1948-90 the Mongolian economy was centrally planned and the labour force was
regularly encouraged to overfulfil target quotas. Labour brigades were set up in most
enterprises to organize initiatives for overfulfilment and to compete for titles and other
awards. This publication is a translation of the 1965 regulations governing such
activities and they provide an insight into Mongolian concepts of the good socialist
working team and the pressures on the worker generally as the economy was widened
from the 1960s onward. The article first appeared in the Mongolian newspaper
Khödölmör, (29 May 1965, p. 3-4). Other informative articles on labour organization
and the unions may be found in the JPRS translation series (see item no. 466).

The wealth of mineral springs in our country.
See item no. 49.

Chinese agent in Mongolia.
See item no. 131.

History of the Mongolian People's Republic.
See item no. 134.

The Mongolian People's Republic, 1924-1928, and the Right Deviation.
See item no. 137.

Women's rights in MPR detailed.
See item no. 157.

Labour organization in livestock breeding.
See item no. 322.

Statistics

338 Development of the People's education in the MPR: a statistical compilation.
Edited by O. Sengee. *US Joint Publications Research Service*: *Translations on Mongolia*, no. 300 (20 Jun. 1978), 165p. (JPRS 71,323).
This is a translation of a selection of statistical tables from a Mongolian Ministry of Education handbook issued in 1976. The compilation includes data on general, specialized, further and higher education for the period 1961-70, with information on the geographical distribution of education, numbers of students and teachers and data on the curriculum.

339 National economy of the MPR for 65 years: anniversary statistical collection.
Ulaanbaatar: Central Statistical Board, 1986. 419p.
A compilation of statistical tables with an introduction, in Mongolian, Russian, English and French. In addition to data on the Mongolian economy there are also statistics on demography, society, culture and geography. Figures for 1960, 1970, 1980 and 1985 are given and in some cases earlier data is also included.

340 National economy of the MPR for 70 years (1921-1991): anniversary statistical yearbook.
Ulaanbaatar: State Statistical Office of the MPR, 1991. p. 153.
The information in this volume is provided both in Mongolian and English. Unlike earlier official collections of statistics, the data in this volume is presented in internationally recognized units and not as a percentage increase on that of previous years. A further innovation is the inclusion of figures on international relations and on Mongolia's import and export trade.

341 **National economy of the MPR in 1967: a compilation of statistics.**
US Joint Publications Research Service: *Translations on Mongolia*,
no. 223 (8 July 1970), 92p. (JPRS 50,896).

A selection of statistical charts, in English translation, concerning the Mongolian
economy, population, society, education and weather which were first published by the
Central Statistical Bureau (Board) in Mongolia in 1968. Other annual compilations
were published in the Joint Publications Research Service translation series in part or
in their entirety as follows: statistics for 1972 in JPRS 65,509 (21 Aug. 1975); 1974 in
JPRS 67,373 (18 June 1976); 1975 in JPRS 69,202 (6 June 1977); 1976 in JPRS 71,991
(5 Oct. 1978); 1977 in JPRS 73,564 (30 May 1979); 1978 in JPRS 75,719 (16 May 1980);
1979 in JPRS 78,299 (16 June 1981); 1980 in JPRS 81,371 (27 July 1982); 1981 in MON-
86-001 (27 Jan. 1986).

Information Mongolia.
See item no. 3.

Mongolia: politics, economics and society.
See item no. 11.

The People's Republic of Mongolia: a general reference guide.
See item no. 20.

**Sovremennaya Mongoliya: otchet Mongol'skoi Ekspeditsii
snaryazhennoi Irkutskoi kontoroi Vserossiiskogo Tsentral'nogo
Soyuza Potrebitel'nykh obshchestvo 'Tsentrosoyuz'.** (Contemporary Mongolia: report of the Mongolian Expedition equipped by the Irkutsk office of
the All-Russian Central Consumer Cooperatives 'Tsentrosoyuz'.)
See item no. 22.

Les langues mongoles. (The Mongolian languages).
See item no. 146.

La R. P. M.: rappel de quelques données. (The MPR: a reminder of some
data).
See item no. 149.

The Mongolian People's Republic: toward a market economy.
See item no. 304.

The Far East and Australasia 1992.
See item no. 481.

Environment

Urban and rural planning

342 **Darkhan city is a symbol of friendship of socialist nations.**
US Joint Publications Research Service: Translations on Mongolia,
no. 79 (5 Aug. 1965), p. 13-15. (JPRS 31,433.)
The new town of Darkhan, was the first large scale urban planning project undertaken
in Mongolia and was constructed with aid from the Soviet Union and countries of
Eastern Europe. The plans for Darkhan are discussed in this article.

343 **From *ger* to *aimag* by leaping the chasm.**
Derek Hall. *Town & Country Planning*, vol. 54 (1985), no. 10
(Oct. 1985), p. 298-300.
A brief account of urban planning and growth in Mongolia from the 1960s with
emphasis on the new towns of Darkhan and Erdenet.

344 **The house of weddings.**
John Lourie. *Journal of the Anglo-Mongolian Society*, vol. 4, no. 1
(July 1978), p. 37-39.
The House of Weddings in the centre of Ulaanbaatar is a large square building which
incorporates architectural features imitating the *ger* (Mongolian tent) and is decorated
with traditional motifs. It houses the registry of births, marriages and deaths, and
marriage ceremonies are conducted there. The author describes the building and its
appointments and remarks on a marriage ceremony he attended there. For another
description of a ceremony at the House of Weddings, see item no. 234.

345 **Various aspects of regional planning clarified.**
    P. Nergui. *US Joint Publications Research Service: Translations on Mongolia*, (17 Jul. 1970), p. 40-45. (JPRS no. 50,971.)

A rare article on regional and town planning carried out by local authorities and local planning commissions. The author explains the indicators used to determine annual and long-term plans. The article first appeared in the Mongolian government journal, *Ardyn Tör* (no. 6 1969, p. 65-69).

The city of friendship.
See item no. 2.

Mongolia today: a traveller's guide: geography, nature, hunting, museums, monuments, customs, tourism.
See item no. 42.

Environmental protection

346 **Conservation and wild life in Mongolia.**
    O. Namnandorj, edited by Henry Field.   Miami, Florida: Field Research Projects, 1970. 26p. map. bibliog.

This pamphlet contains several articles which were originally published in Mongolian in the 1950s and the 1960s and which have been shortened and rewritten. Their subjects cover the physical geography of Mongolia, nature reserves in Mongolia from the Middle Ages to the present, and the Bogd Uul Reserve which is across the river Tuul from Ulaanbaatar and is inhabited by twenty-one protected animal species.

347 **The Mongolian 'Red Book'.**
    Charles Roskelly Bawden.   *Journal of the Anglo-Mongolian Society*, vol. 12, no. 1-2 (1989), p. 73-91.

In the 1980s there was growing concern for environmental issues in Mongolia and a Red Book of endangered species edited by O. Shagdarsüren was published in 1987. The contents of the book are summarized in this article. Twenty-three mammals, six amphibians and reptiles, two fishes and eighty-two plants are identified with brief information on their habitats and the reasons for the decline in their numbers.

348 **Nature conservation, environmental protection discussed.**
    S. Jigj.   *US Joint Publication Research Services: Mongolia Report*, no. 316 (6 Aug. 1979), p. 25-33. (JPRS 73,963).

The Nature Conservation Department of the State Committee of Science and Technology was formed in 1975 and it has cooperated with similar bodies in Comecon countries and with the international environmental protection agencies. In this article the department's director describes what is being done to combat a wide range of environmental problems, most of which are caused by industrial pollution. He also describes the Great Gobi National Park founded in 1974 and thirteen other nature conservation regions. The article first appeared in German in *Internationale Zeitschrift für Landwirtschaft* (vol. 22, no. 6, [1978], p. 562-65.)

Information Mongolia.
See item no. 3.

Mongolia today: a traveller's guide: geography, nature, hunting, museums, monuments, customs, tourism.
See item no. 42.

Observations on some large mammals of the Transaltai, Djungarian and Shargyn Gobi, Mongolia.
See item no. 57.

Education

349 Books and traditions (from the history of Mongol culture).
Byambyn Rinchen.   In: *Analecta Mongolica dedicated to the seventieth birthday of Professor Owen Lattimore*. Edited by John Gombojab Hangin, Urgunge Onon.   Bloomington, Indiana: Mongolia Society, 1972. (Occasional Papers no. 8).

A Mongolian scholar wrote this article to refute charges that before the revolution of 1921 there was almost total illiteracy in Mongolia and that secular education did not exist. He describes local and private secular schools as well as monastic education and provides evidence of the wide distribution of books and the ability to read (though not necessarily to write) during the Manchu period (1691-1911). See also item no. 355.

350 The development of education in Mongolia.
Derrick Pritchatt.   In: *Mongolia today*. Edited by Shirin Akiner. New York, London: Kegan Paul International, 1991, p. 206-15. bibliog.

A concise review of the development of education, schools and the curriculum in Mongolia from 1911 to the 1980s. It updates earlier articles by the same author which are cited as items no. 353 and no. 357 in this bibliography.

351 Education in the Mongolian People's Republic.
Bulletin of the Unesco Regional Office for Education in Asia, vol. 6, no. 2 (Mar. 1972), p. 129-39.

The article describes the planning, structure and development of the Mongolian education system from the period of the second Five Year economic plan (1953-57) when a four-year compulsory education programme was introduced. Teacher training and the seven- and ten-year curricula are also covered, and some statistical tables and charts are provided.

352 Education in the Mongolian People's Republic.
John R. Krueger. *Comparative Education Review*, vol. 4, no. 3
(Feb. 1961), p. 183-87.
A concise but informed article on the development of schools and education at all
levels in the 1940s and 1950s. The author also compares the Mongolian system with the
Soviet system.

353 Education in the Mongol People's Republic.
Derrick Pritchatt. *Asian Affairs*, vol. 61 (1974), p. 32-40.
An article describing in some detail the primary and secondary education, curriculum
and teaching methods in Mongolia as observed by a British specialist during a study
visit to the country in 1971.

354 Mongolian educational venture in western Europe (1926-1929).
Serge M. Wolff. *Zentralasiatische Studien*, vol. 5, (1971), p. 247-320.
A fascinating and detailed account of the experiences of thirty-six Mongolian children
who were sent to school in Germany in the 1920s. The author acted as local agent for
the venture which he first described in 1945 in the *Royal Central Asiatic Journal*
(vol. 32, p. 289-98 and vol. 33, p. 75-93). In 1965 Wolff visited Mongolia for the first
time and met several of the students again. Their life and careers since the 1920s are
also covered in this article. A slightly shortened version was published in *Mongolia
Society Bulletin*, (vol. 9, no. 2 [fall 1970], p. 40-100).

355 Mongolian language education and examinations in Peking and other metropolitan areas during the Manchu dynasty in China (1644-1911).
Mankam Leung. *Canada-Mongolia Review*, vol. 1, no. 1 (1975),
p. 29-44. bibliog.
This article examines the education and examination system set up by the Manchu
government to train official Mongolian translators. This article, like item no. 349, is of
interest because it demonstrates that some Mongols received a secular education
before the revolution, in spite of the denials of communist historians. However, as this
author shows, the official status of the Mongolian language did decline throughout the
Manchu period and the schooling he describes does not appear to have had a marked
influence on Mongolian society and culture.

356 Peoples' education law of the MPR.
US Joint Publications Research Service: *Mongolia Report*, no. 357
(25 Feb. 1983), 23p. (JPRS 82,946.)
The Mongolian Constitution of 1960 guaranteed incomplete secondary education for
all children in Mongolia. Complete secondary education is the necessary qualification
for admission to institutes of higher education. The Mongolian education system, as
prescribed in the education law of 1982, was based on principles of internationalism
and Marxism-Leninism. Its primary purpose was to produce good socialist citizens who
would protect socialist property and defend the socialist homeland. The structure of
the education system from pre-school training to higher education, the training of
teachers and their rights and responsibilities are laid down in the eighty-two articles of
the Education Law which has been translated into English in this publication.

Education

357 **Teacher training in the Mongol People's Republic.**
Derrick Pritchatt. *Asian Affairs*, vol. 61 (1974), p. 267-71.
This article was published after the author visited the Pedagogical Institute in
Ulaanbaatar in 1971. It describes Mongolian methods of training teachers, Mongolian
education and the curriculum. Although some of the information is now dated this is
the only study of teacher training in Mongolia which is available in English.

Area handbook of Mongolia.
See item no. 1.

Information Mongolia.
See item no. 3.

Chinese agent in Mongolia.
See item no. 131.

History of the Mongolian People's Republic.
See item no. 134.

The Mongolian People's Republic, 1924-1928, and the Right Deviation.
See item no. 137.

Mongols of the twentieth century. Part 1.
See item no. 139.

The geography of education and health in the Mongolian People's Republic.
See item no. 240.

Development of the People's education in the MPR: a statistical compilation.
See item no. 338.

The world of learning 1992.
See item no. 482.

Science and Technology

358 Computer requirements of Mongolian handwriting: from bamboo to laser.
Peter Lofting, S. Lodoisamba. In: *Computer processing of Asian languages: proceedings of the second regional workshop March 12-16, 1992, Indian Institute of Technology, Kanpur.* Edited by R. M. K. Sinha.   New Delhi: Tata McGraw-Hill, 1992, p. 93-112. bibliog.

This article outlines the requirements for representing Mongolian script on a visual display unit or a computer printer. These include a script interpreter which alters the shape of a character depending on what other characters occur in a particular word. The article also describes a system for representing Mongolian characters as ASCII values and gives details of other design considerations.

359 Contributions to the geology of northern Mongolia.
Abstracted from the original Russian and annotated by Radcliffe H. Beckwith.   *Bulletin of the American Museum of Natural History*, vol. 67 (1933), p. 311-52.

This is a collection of articles on the geological history of Mongolia which have been abridged, translated and annotated. They report the findings of Soviet specialists in the 1920s and were republished in English to supplement the geological findings of the American Museum of Natural History's Central Asiatic Expeditions of 1921-30 (see item 362). They include studies of the geology of the eastern border of the Kharkhira range by Z. A. Lebedeva, the geology of northeastern Mongolia by B. M. Kupletsky and the geomorphology, soils and biology of the Jargalant Terraces by B. B. Polynov and I. M. Krasheninnikov.

360   A contribution to the anthropology of Khalkh-Mongols. (The
        anthropologists' and physicians' report on the Czechoslovak-Mongolian
        archeological expedition in the year 1958).
        Emanuel Vlĉek.   Bratislava, Czecho-Slovakia: Slovenské pedagogické
        nakladatel'stvo, 1965. 367p. map. (Acta Facultatis Rerum Naturalium
        Universitatis Comenianae Anthropologica, Tome IX, Fasc. VI-VII
        1965).

A scientific report of the physical characteristics of a representative sample of the
Mongolian population. The research team measured and documented height, weight,
the Mongolian spot, finger and palm prints, hair, eyes and other physiological
characteristics. The report is illustrated with twenty-two photographs.

361   Fossils from the Gobi desert.
        Zofia Kielan-Jaworowska.   *Science Journal*, vol. 5a, no. 1 (July 1969),
        p. 32-38.

The Upper Cretaceous layer of the Nemegt basin in the Gobi desert was investigated
by the Joint Mongolian-Polish Palaeontological Expedition from 1963-65. This article
reports the findings of the expedition which included relics of large herbivorous and
carnivorous dinosaurs and also small Cretaceous animals, such as placental mammals
and herbivorous mammals (multituberculates). It is clearly written and suitable for a
non-specialist readership. For an account of the daily life of the expedition see item
no. 364.

362   The geology of Mongolia: a reconnaissance report based on the
        investigations of the years 1922-1923.
        Charles Peter Berkey, Frederick K. Morris.   New York: American
        Museum of Natural History, 1927. 475p. maps. bibliog. (Natural
        History of Central Asia, vol. 2).

Berkey and Morris were the geologists of the American Museum of Natural History's
Third Asiatic Expedition of 1922-23. Their investigations covered an area of 200,000
square miles in Central Mongolia between Kalgan in Inner Mongolia and the present-
day Ulaanbaatar, and from the Khangai to the Altai Mountains. This report is a
monumental and pioneering study of the surface and the underlying geology of the
country. It includes studies of the fossils, rocks and climate of the region and there is
an extensive bibliography. Although much of the content is fairly technical, it is clearly
written and the chapters describing the expedition's intineraries, and many of the
photographs, may be of interest to the general reader.

363   The Gobi-Altai earthquake. (Gobi-Altaiskoe zemletryasenie).
        Edited by N. A. Florensov, V. P. Solonenko.   Jerusalem: Israel
        Program Scientific Translations (distributed by Oldbourne Press), 1965.
        424p. bibliog.

On 4 December 1957 an earthquake measuring 11-12 on the Richter scale occured in
the Gobi-Altai region in southwest Mongolia. Seismic activity had not been registered
there previously. The earthquake produced major faults and completely rearranged the
landscape. It was investigated by Russian and Mongolian scholars in 1957-58 and their
findings are reported in this collection of articles. The book is in two parts, a study of
the geological structure of the region and a descriptive study of the earthquake itself. It

was translated into English because the Gobi-Altai earthquake was the first great earthquake to be studied thoroughly by scientists.

364 **Hunting for dinosaurs.**
Zofia Kielan-Jaworowska, translated from the Polish. Cambridge, Massachusetts; London: MIT Press, 1969. 177p. maps.

An informative and entertaining book for the general reader on the Joint Mongolian-Polish Palaeontological Expeditions to the Gobi, 1963-65. Kielan-Jaworowska was the Polish organizer. She describes the daily life of the expedition and some of the dinosaur and mammal relics discovered, which included some very large dinosaur skeletons. The book is well illustrated with sketches and photographs in black-and-white. See item no. 361 for a more technical account of the discoveries.

365 **Materials on the geology of the Mongolian People's Republic.**
Edited by N. A. Marinov. *US Joint Publications Research Service*: *Translations on Mongolia*, no. 136 (15 June 1957), 194p. bibliog. (JPRS 41,425).

Since the Second World War scientists of the Comecon member states have carried out a number of geological surveys in Mongolia. A collection of articles on Mongolian geology published in Moscow in 1966 reports on the findings of the surveys, a selection of which are published here in English translation. They include studies of the geological formation of various regions of Mongolia, coal and ore deposits and the hydrogeological conditions of water supply in pasture lands.

366 **Mongolian science today (the 15th anniversary of the MPR Academy of Sciences).**
E. Novgorodova. *Far Eastern Affairs*, no. 2 (1976), p. 109-20.

There are two parts to this article. In the first the structure and activities of the twelve institutes of the Mongolian Academy of Sciences, founded in 1961, are described with remarks on specific projects and publications. The second part is a review of the work of the President of the Academy, Bazaryn Shirendev, a historian who has published widely on early 20th century history and on the construction of socialism in Mongolia.

367 **The Permian of Mongolia: a report on the Permian fauna of the Jisu Honguer limestone of Mongolia and its relations to the Permian of other parts of the world.**
Amadaeus William Grabau. New York: American Museum of Natural History, 1931. 665p. maps bibliog. (Natural History of Central Asia, vol. 4).

Marine fossil deposits in limestone are an important feature of the Permian levels of Mongolia. These were investigated by the American Museum of Natural History's Central Asiatic Expeditions of the 1920s and are described in detail in this report. The work includes a chapter on the relations of the Jisu Honguer formation to the general geology by Charles P. Berkey, Ph.D., chief geologist, and Frederick K. Morris, geologist of the Central Asiatic Expeditions, 1922, 1923, and 1925. Specimens are illustrated on thirty-five plates. For other reports of this expedition see items no. 35 and no. 362.

368 **Soils of Outer Mongolia (Mongolian People's Republic).**
N. D. Bespalov. Jerusalem: Israel Program for Scientific
Translations, 1964. 320p. map. bibliog.

This monograph was first published in Russian by the Soviet Academy of Sciences in
1951. It covers the physical geography of Mongolia, including climate and vegetation,
the soils of Mongolia arranged according to type, and the agricultural conditions and
the arable lands of Mongolia. Most of the works cited in the bibliography are in
Russian.

369 **Vertical zonality in the Southern Khangai mountains (Mongolia): result
of the Polish-Mongolian Physico-Geographical Expedition. Vol. 1.**
Edited by Kazimierz Klimek and Leszek Starkel. Polish Academy of
Sciences. Institute of Geography and Spatial Organization.
Wrocław, Warsaw, Kraków, Gdańsk, Poland: Academy of Sciences,
1980. 107p. maps. bibliog. (Geographical Studies no. 136).

A report of the findings of a geographical expedition to the Khangai Mountains in
central Mongolia in 1974-75. The volume comprises a collection of scientific articles by
various authors on soil, hydrology, geomorphology, vegetation and climate, and is
illustrated with photographs and charts. Several of the papers have also been published
separately in the *Bulletin of the Polish Academy of Sciences*.

370 **Written Mongolian from its transliteration to its automatic writing:
analysis and coding of the traditional Mongolian script for computer-
processing.**
Marie-Lise Beffa, Robert Hamayon. *Zentralasiatische Studien*, vol. 21
(1988[1989]), p. 163-75.

A French project for developing a word-processing system for the traditional
Mongolian script is reported in this article. The Mongolian text is keyed in using a
Latin transcription (romanization) and it appears on the screen, and when printed out,
in Mongolian script. The authors point out the special problems of word processing in
Mongolian script and they provide tables of code labels.

**Expedition Mongolia 1990: the first Anglo-Mongolian expedition to Mongolia
in history.**
See item no. 53.

The mammals of China and Mongolia.
See item no. 54.

**Systematic account of a collection of fishes from the Mongolian People's
Republic: with a review of the hydrobiology of the major Mongolian drainage
basins.**
See item no. 62.

Glossary of Mongolian technical terms.
See item no. 180.

Literature

Literary history and criticism

371 **Dictionary of oriental literatures. Volume One: East Asia.**
    Edited by Zbigniew Słupski.   General editor Jaroslav Prušek.
    London: Allen & Unwin, 1974. 226p.

C. R. Bawden has contributed the eighteen entries on Mongolian authors and literary genres in this dictionary. The pieces are brief but informative and together they provide an overview of Mongolian traditional and modern literature. Suggestions for further reading are provided with a few of the entries.

372 **Geschichte der mongolischen Literatur.** (History of Mongolian
    literature.)
    Walther Heissig.   Wiesbaden, Germany: Harrassowitz, 1972. 2 vols.

Only very brief surveys of Mongolian literary history are available in English (see items no. 13, 179 and 375). This study in German is the best and most detailed analysis of Mongolian literary achievement from the 18th to the early 20th century when some outstanding examples of classical literature were produced. The study covers written literature, including historical chronicles, Buddhist prose and verse and early novels. Oral literature such as epic, folktales and verse, and the work of individual writers are also examined.

373 **Mongolian literature.**
Charles Roskelly Bawden. In: *A guide to eastern literatures*. Edited by
David Marshall Lang. London: Weidenfeld & Nicholson, 1971,
p. 343-57. bibliog.

An overview of Mongolian literature comprising a brief historical account and a
description of the main literary trends and writers of modern Mongolia.

374 **Mongolian historical literature of the XVII-XIX centuries written in
Tibetan.**
Sh. Bira, edited by Ts. Damdinsüren, translated from the Russian by
Stanley N. Frye. Bloomington, Indiana: Mongolia Society, 1970. 96p.
(Occasional Papers no. 7).

After the Mongols adopted Tibetan Buddhism in the 16th century many males received
a monastic education in the Tibetan language. As a result, Tibetan became one of the
literary languages of Mongolia. This monograph by a Mongolian historian examines
some of the histories and chronicles written in Tibetan which, he suggests, are a source
of valuable information on Mongolian cultural history.

375 **Skizze der mongolischen Literature.** (An outline of Mongolian
literature.)
Berthold Laufer. *Keleti Szemle* (Budapest), vol. 9, (1907) p. 165-261.

This is a survey in German of classical written Mongolian literature which includes
legal documents and inscriptions from the time of Chinggis Khan, historical, Buddhist
and shamanist literature, and didactic and scientific works. The author also mentions
methods of printing such as blockprinting. The article has been included in this
bibliography because no comparable survey is available in English.

376 **Köke sudur. (The blue chronicle.) A study of the first Mongolian
historical novel by Injannasi.**
John Gombojab Hangin. Wiesbaden, Germany: Harrassowitz, 1973.
188p. bibliog. (Asiatische Forschungen Band 38).

Injannashi was an important literary figure of 19th century Inner Mongolia. He was a
man of strong nationalist sentiments and he was critical of Manchu rule and also of the
Buddhist church. The subject of this monograph is the first long historical novel in
Mongolian, in which Injannashi wrote about the Mongol Empire. It is a critical study
of *The blue chronicle*, with a discussion of the life and work of Injannashi and his
literary position. An annotated translation of the introduction to the chronicle is
included and the work is based on Hangin's Phd thesis at Indiana University, United
States, in 1970.

377 **The heroic epic of the Khalkh Mongols.**
Nicholas Poppe, translated from the Russian by J. Krueger, D.
Montgomery, M. Walter. Bloomington, Indiana: Mongolia Society,
1979. 2nd edition. 192p. (Occasional Papers no. 11).

This monograph, which was first appeared in Russian in 1937, is a scholarly study of
the Mongolian heroic epic as a written form of traditional literature. The roots of this
genre are, however, in oral literature and epics are still performed orally in 20th

century Mongolia. Poppe traces the history of the epic from the *Secret history of the Mongols* (see item no. 84) and other early works about Chinggis Khan. He analyses the themes and heroes of the epic and its structure, which is characterized by alternating passages of verse and prose. For examples of Mongolian epic in English translation see items no. 380, 384-85 and 389.

The history and the life of Chinggis Khan. (The Secret History of the Mongols.)
See item no. 84.

Mongolian language handbook.
See item no. 179.

Notes on the collection of Mongolian books in the Ethnographical Museum of Sweden, Stockholm.
See item no. 460.

A lost civilization: the Mongols rediscovered.
See item no. 461.

Oral literature

378 **An annotated collection of Mongolian riddles.**
Archer Taylor. *Transactions of the American Philosophical Society*, vol. 44, new series no. 3 (1954), 425p. bibliog.
A classified collection of 1,027 riddles with annotations, source and an index of keywords. Some corrections to this work were published in *Folklore Forum*, (vol. 8, 1975, p. 354-56) by J. R. Krueger.

379 **The camel in Mongolian literature and tradition: some examples.**
B. Damdin, Marie-Dominique Even, Michael J. Chapman. *Journal of the Anglo-Mongolian Society*, vol. 13, nos. 1-2, (1991), p. 35-47.
The camel is a valuable animal in the Mongolian economy, especially in the Gobi desert. Therefore it is not surprising to find the camel as the subject of much traditional literature. This publication comprises a short anthology of stories, poems and proverbs about camels in English translation and with brief explanatory notes.

380 **Erintsen Mergen, the most excellent of men: a translation of the Khalkha Mongolian national epic.**
Translated by Ann Louise Şen. *Mongolian Studies*, vol. 7, (1981-1982), p. 93-126.
This article is a good introduction to the Mongolian epic genre. Şen discusses the traditions of epic in Mongolia, its plot, structure, motifs and the customs and practices of epic performance. To illustrate these she retells the verse epic of Erintsen Mergen (Erintsen the Wise) in English prose. The story involves a journey, magic deeds and a

137

talking horse as the hero performs his task of destroying the monster Enkhe Bolot Khan.

381 **Gessar Khan.**
Told by Ida Zeitlin, illustrated by Theodore Nadejen. New Delhi: Asian Publisher, 1978. 200p.

The epic cycle of Geser Khan is Tibetan in origin and its hero is the earthborn son of the god Khormusta. The stories in the cycle are set against a nomadic cultural background which is common both to Tibetans of the Amdo region (now Tsinghai province, China) and to the Mongols and may explain why the epic became so popular in Mongolia. This monograph version of the stories in English translation was first published in 1927. It has been translated in a biblical but pleasant style and has charming illustrations.

382 **The legend of Cuckoo Namjil: folk tales from Mongolia.**
Translated by D. Altangerel, edited by Owen Lattimore. Ulaanbaatar: State Publishing House, [n.d.], 222p.

An anthology of legends, animal fables, magical tales, humorous stories and other traditional tales of the Mongols in English translation.

383 **Mongol: the contemporary tradition.**
Charles Roskelly Bawden. In: *Traditions of heroic and epic poetry*. London: Modern Humanities Research Association, 1980, p.268-99. bibliog.

This excellent and informative study demonstrates that the epic exists as a contemporary literary genre among Mongols inside and outside independent Mongolia. The author presents a critical analysis of epic, the genre, form, content, motifs and the present day performance of the epic illustrated with extended quotations in English in translation.

384 **Mongolian folklore: a representative collection from the oral literary tradition.**
Translated and edited by J. R. Krueger, R. G. Service, Wm. V. Rozycki. *Mongolian Studies*, Part One, vol. 9, (1985-86), p. 13-78; Part Two, vol. 10, (1986-87), p. 107-54; Part Three vol. 11, (1988), p. 47-110; Part Four vol. 12, (1989), p. 7-69. bibliog.

This collection of the oral literature of the Mongols includes descriptions of various genres and their mode of performance with sample translations. Part one covers proverbs and sayings; part two, triads of the universe, songs, raillery and shamanistic invocations; part three, panegyrics, and blessings, and prose tales (ülger); and part four, the heroic epic with a full translation of the *Epic of the Khan Kharangui* (King of Darkness). The Mongolia Society intends to reprint the four parts as a monograph (Mongolia Society Occasional Paper, no. 16).

385 **Mongolian folktales, stories and proverbs in English translation, newly translated from the Mongolian by members and friends of the Mongolia Society.**
Edited by John R. Krueger. Bloomington, Indiana: Mongolia Society, 1967. 86p. bibliog. (Occasional Papers, no. 4).
A selection of folk literature including animal fables, Buddhist tales, 250 proverbs and a short epic about the hero Amar Jargalkhan whose extraordinary cunning and strength enables him to destroy a *mangas* (monster) and its brood. The collection, though limited, gives a good impression of the range of Mongolian folk literature.

386 **Mongolian folktales and stories (in English and Mongolian).**
Translated from the Mongolian by D. Altangerel, edited with an introduction by Owen Lattimore. Ulaanbaatar: State Publishing House, 1979. 261p.
This book is in two parts. In the first are legends, animal fables, magical tales and humorous stories in English translation. The same stories are printed in Mongolian in the second part.

387 **Mongolian heroic literature.**
David C. Montgomery. *Mongolia Society Bulletin*, vol. 9, no. 1 (spring 1970), p. 30-36. bibliog.
This is a concise study of the structure and content of the Mongolian epic. The author identifies two kinds of hero, Chinggis Khan, who is portrayed as a hero and wise teacher, and petty khans or commoners. The Geser Khan epic, which is of Tibetan origin but was absorbed into the heroic canon of the Mongols, is also discussed (see also item no. 381).

388 **A Mongolian picture-tale.**
Translated by Andrea Nixon. *Journal of the Anglo-Mongolian Society*, vol. 6, no. 2 (1980), p. 100-01.
An example of a popular story-telling tradition which is linked to drawing. As the folktale, 'The wolf and the goats', unfolds a drawing of a falcon emerges.

389 **Mongolische Epen X: eight North Mongolian epic poems.**
Translated by Charles Roskelly Bawden. Wiesbaden, Germany: Harrassowitz, 1982. 209p. (Asiatische Forschungen Band 74).
This volume is one of a series of anthologies of the Mongolian epic comprising Cyrillic Mongolian texts and mainly German translations. The eight epics in this volume, however, have English translations and are verse tales of khans, heroes, monsters and talking horses. They are drawn from the repertoire of Tsültemiin Togtool, a blind storyteller who recorded them in Mongolia in 1946. Bawden has also published a study of the repertoire itself in *Fragen der mongolischen Heldendichtung. Teil I, Vortrage des 2. Epensymposiums der Sonderforschungsbereichs 12, Bonn 1979*. (Problems of the Mongolian heroic epic. Part 1: proceedings of the second Epic symposium. Report of a special inquiry Bonn, 1979). Edited by Walther Heissig (Wiesbaden, Germany: Harrassowitz, 1981).

390 **On the Mongolia four-line songs in general.**
Maria Salga. *Canada - Mongolia Review*, vol. 2, no. 2 (1976),
p. 120-26.

This author collected many examples of four-line songs of the 'call and response' type
in Mongolia and in this article she analyses the genre, its vocabulary and its
performance. In songs of this type, the singer expresses his or her longing for a loved
one, a parent or for home, by means of visual imagery such as horse, plants, *ger* (tent)
and colours.

A journey in Southern Siberia: the Mongols, their religion and their myths.
See item no. 163.

The heroic epic of the Khalkh Mongols.
See item no. 377.

The morienhur: a Mongolian fiddle.
See item no. 424.

Protocole manuel. (Manual etiquette.)
See item no. 442.

Literary trends and major writers of 20th-century Mongolia

391 **Dashdorjiin Natsagdorj (1906-1937).**
John Gombojab Hangin. *Mongolia Society Bulletin*, vol. 6, (1967),
p. 15-22.

A biographical sketch of D. Natsagdorj who is regarded as the father of modern
Mongolian literature. A list of his works is included with translations of his most
famous poem 'My homeland' and a prose poem 'Bird Grey'. For other works by
Natsagdorj in English translation see items no. 398-99, 402.

392 **History of modern Mongolian literature (1921-1964).**
Ludmilla K. Gerasimovich, translated from the Russian by members
and friends of the Mongolia Society. Bloomington, Indiana: Mongolia
Society, 1970. 372p. bibliog. (Occasional Papers, no. 6).

This is the only monographic study in English of modern Mongolian literature. It is a
critical socialist appraisal of Mongolian writers and genres, including short stories,
novels and poetry. The role of the Mongolian Writers' Union and the political control
of creative writing are also discussed. The book contains many literary quotations,
biographical information on prominent writers and a detailed index.

393 **Ideological struggle reflected in MPR literature.**
A. Luvsandendev, N. I. Nikulin. *US Joint Publications Research Service: Mongolia Report*, no. 345 (22 Sept. 1982), p. 35-41. (JPRS 81,827).
The purpose of this article is to demonstrate that the development of the literary forms and themes of post-revolutionary Mongolia are entirely typical of a country which is in transition from feudalism to socialism and may therefore serve as a development model for other countries at the same historical stage. The authors note important events in the literary history of 20th century Mongolia, recurring themes, realism in Mongolian literature and the influence of Soviet literature on Mongolian literature. The article was first published in Russian in the the journal *Narody Azii i Afriki* (no. 4 July-Aug 1981, p. 103-08).

394 **Mongolian poetry since the Revolution.**
David B. T. Aikman. *Mongolia Society Bulletin*, vol. 5, (1966), p. 11-21.
A concise study of modern Mongolian poetry from 1921, with remarks on themes, metres and poets.

395 **Proceedings of the Fourth Congress of Mongolian Writers' Union, opened 27 June 1967, in Ulan Bator.**
US Joint Publications Research Service: Translations on Mongolia, no. 145 (13 Sept. 1967), 41p. (JPRS 42,590).
The congress reports translated in this publication first appeared in the Mongolian cultural newspaper *Utga Zokhiol Urlag* (28 June, 1967, 1-6). The main item is the keynote speech by the Chairman of the Committee of the Mongolian Writers' Union, S. Udval, herself a leading poet. She emphasizes the duty of literature to educate the new socialist man and her speech provides a clear illustration of the way all cultural and creative work was controlled by the Mongolian political system during the period of single-party rule. The report also indicates major writers of the period, prescribed literary themes, forms and literary criticism.

History of the Mongolian People's Republic.
See item no. 134.

Dictionary of oriental literatures. Volume One: East Asia.
See item no. 371.

Mongolian short stories.
See item no. 399.

Modern Mongolian literature in English translation

396 Lady Anu.
Byambyn Rinchen, edited by B. Damdin.   Ulaanbaatar: State
Publishing House, 1980. 102p.

A collection of five modern Mongolian short stories and one poem by Rinchen (1905-77), who was one of the founders of modern Mongolian literature. The theme of this collection is the resistance of the Mongols to the Manchus in the 17th century and it includes the title story, 'Letter of betrayal', 'Bunia, a parachutist', 'The hand' and 'When the time comes'. The poem is 'Bride flower'.

397 Modern Far Eastern stories.
Edited by Chong-wha Chung.   Hong Kong: Heinemann Asia, 1978.
356p.

This anthology includes three Mongolian short stories beautifully translated into English by Charles Bawden with brief introductions. The stories are 'What did the tear mean?' by Chadraabalyn Lodoidamba (1917-1970), which criticizes alcoholism, and two love stories 'The Lama's Holy Water', by Tsendiin Damdinsüren, (1908-1986), and 'The Fine' by Sambuugiin Badraa (1923-).

398 Modern Mongolian poetry (1921-1986).
Edited with an introduction by Dojoodyn Tsedev, selected and
translated by D. Altangerel, English translation edited by
L. Khuushaan, N. Enkhbayar, John Gaunt.   Ulaanbaatar: State
Publishing House, 1989. 367p.

The poems in this anthology are representative of modern Mongolian poetry and poets. Nature, love for one's mother, morality, internationalism and Mongol-Soviet friendship are recurring themes and a full translation of one version of D. Natsagdorj's verse libretto for the popular Mongolian opera, 'The three fateful hills,' (see also item no. 430) is included. The quality of the translation is variable but it is the only anthology of modern Mongolian poetry available in English. Biographical notes on the poets are provided.

399 Mongolian short stories.
Edited by Henry Guenter Schwarz.   Bellingham, Washington:
Program in East Asian Studies, Western Washington State College,
1974. 179p. bibliog. (Occasional Paper, no. 8).

Short stories are popular in contemporary Mongolia. This collection comprises twenty-one short stories in English translation and all but three of them were first published after 1955. Writers such as D. Natsagdorj, Ch. Lodoidamba, S. Erdene, L. Tüdev and S. Dashdoorov and several others are represented. Schwarz has taken stories published in the magazines *Mongolia Today* and *Mongolia* (see item no. 467) and re-edited them in contemporary American English. The themes of the stories range from the revolution of 1921, the Second World War, herding cooperatives and the good socialist citizen. There is a good introductory essay on contemporary prose literature, a glossary of Mongolian terms and biographical sketches of the authors.

400 My beloved swallows and other children's stories from Mongolia.
Selected and translated into English by D. Altangerel, edited by Nigel
Bruce, D. Altankhuyag. Ulaanbaatar: State Publishing House, 1986.
160p.
A collection of twelve stories for children by leading Mongolian socialist writers. Many
are set in the countryside.

401 Selected short stories.
Tsendiin Damdinsüren, edited by Owen Lattimore. Ulaanbaatar:
State Publishing House, 1978. 96p.
Tsendiin Damdinsüren (1908-86) was one of the pioneers of modern Mongolian
revolutionary literature together with D. Natsagdorj and B. Rinchen (see items
no. 396 and 391 respectively). This selection of his work comprises four of his most
famous short stories: 'The rejected girl' (1929), 'The two white things' (1945), 'They
are both my sons' (1943) and 'How Sol' was changed' (1944).

402 Six prose poems by Dashdorjiin Natsagdorj (1906-1937).
Translated from Mongolian by Thomas Raff. Naples, Italy: [n.p.],
1978. 16p.
D. Natsagdorj (1906-37) is regarded as the founder of modern Mongolian poetry and
he is honoured with a museum and statue in Ulaanbaatar. He died young, and his
writings were collected in a single volume published in Ulaanbaatar in 1961. This
selection of prose poems in English translation includes 'Yesterday's youngster', 'Bird-
gray' 'The warmth of love', 'A wintry night', 'Spring Sunday' and 'The beauty of the
steppe'. See also items no. 391 and 398-99.

403 Some short stories from Mongolia.
Compiled by Ts. Bold, edited by D. Natsagdorj. Ulaanbaatar: State
Publishing House, 1988. 192p.
An anthology of twenty-one modern short stories in English translation of varying
quality. The heroes are examples of the new socialist man, the worker, the soldier and
the cattle breeder, whose duty it is to defend the homeland and build a new socialist
society in the town and the countryside.

The city of friendship.
See item no. 2.

Dashdorjiin Natsagdorj (1906-1937).
See item no. 391.

The Arts

General

404 **Cultural policy in the Mongolian People's Republic: a study prepared under the auspices of the Mongolian National Commission for Unesco.**
Paris: Unesco, 1982. 49p. (Studies and Documents on Cultural Policies).

Cultural development has been controlled and financed by the Mongolian government since 1921. This pamphlet surveys changes in education, the provision of libraries and museums, the preservation of the cultural heritage, and the development of the media and new forms of art since 1921. A section on international cultural exchange is also included.

405 **Outer Mongolia: from feudal society to socialist culture.**
Sh. Luvsanvandan, translated from the Russian by A. B. Werth.
Cultures, vol. 1, no. 4 (1974), p. 91-102.

In this brief survey of the traditional Mongolian performing arts and the development of contemporary theatre, cinema and opera, Academician Luvsanvandan argues that Mongolia's 20th century culture is socialist in content and national in form.

Area handbook of Mongolia.
See item no. 1.

Information Mongolia.
See item no. 3.

History of the Mongolian People's Republic.
See item no. 134.

Mongolia.
See item no. 467.

Fine art

406 **Lenin in Mongolian art.**
T. Postrelova. *Far Eastern Affairs*, no. 4 (1980), p. 158-62.
Under the socialist system the perceived benign influence of Lenin on the country's development was celebrated in all forms of culture. Lenin was a popular subject for painting, appliqué, sculpture, wood carving, linocuts and fur collage. He was portrayed in an idealized manner with almost religious significance. In this article the author carefully describes a number of works of art which were held in high regard during the period of single-party rule.

407 **Mongolische Malerei: Tradition und Gegenwart mit zwanzig farbigen Tafeln und zweiundvierzig einfarbigen Abbildungen.** (Mongolian painting: traditional and contemporary with twenty colour plates and twenty-two black-and-white reproductions.)
Ingrid Schulze. Berlin: Henschelverlag Kunst und Gesellschaft, 1979. 15p. (+ 51 unpaginated). bibliog. (Welt der Kunst).
A brief introduction in German to Mongolian painting with fifty-eight illustrations, twenty of which are in colour, and brief commentaries. Modern socialist paintings are juxtaposed with pre-revolutionary works to demonstrate the continuity of traditional painting styles in the socialist period. The choice of paintings illustrates the range of styles, materials and subjects of contemporary Mongolian art.

408 **Mongol'skaya natsional'naya zhivopis' 'Mongol zurag'; development of the Mongolian national style of painting 'Mongol zurag' in brief; bref apperçu sur le developpement de la peinture mongole 'mongol zourag'; breve ensayo sobre el desarrollo de la pintura mongola 'mongol zurag'.**
N. Tsültem. Ulaanbaatar: State Publishing House, 1986. 192p.
A volume of 192 coloured photographs of Mongolian paintings, embroidery and appliqué with a brief introduction to the Mongolian national style of painting in Russian, English, French and Spanish. The subjects of the works illustrated are drawn from Buddhism and Mongolian life, and portraits are also included. Many of the pictures are displayed in the Fine Arts Museum and the Bogd Khan Palace Museum in Ulaanbaatar.

409 **Orchin üeiin mongolyn dürslekh urlag.** (Fine arts in contemporary Mongolia).
Ulaanbaatar: State Publishing House, 1971. [n.p.].
Forty-two folios in a paper wrapper illustrating fifty paintings and sculptures which were executed between 1958 and 1968 by modern Mongolian artists. The paintings are in oil, gouache and water colour, in Mongolian and European styles, on a wide variety of subjects, including portraits, aspects of traditional and socialist life and Mongol-Soviet friendship. The quality of reproduction is good and some of the illustrations are in colour.

The Arts. Fine art

410   **Review article: Mongolian art.**
Christopher Atwood.   *Mongolian Studies*, vol. 12 (1989), p. 113-24.
The author reviews three illustrated books on Mongolian art which are cited in this bibliography as items no. 408, 414 and 418. His comments and discussion provide a good, concise introduction to Mongolian styles and schools of art and the various influences on Mongolian art.

411   **The roots.**
A. Barsbold.   *Mongolia*, no. 5 (92) (1986), p. 24-26.
A popular, illustrated account of the artistic work of one of Mongolia's foremost painters, Ü. Yadamsüren, who combined Mongolian styles of painting with European techniques. Among his work is a series of paintings of Mongolian costume (see item no. 435).

412   **The smile of the goddess Tara.**
Byambyn Rinchen, translated by Stanley Frye.   *Mongolia Society Bulletin*, vol. 11, no. 1 (spring 1972), p. 1-4.
A brief account of the artistic achievement of Zanabazar, a Buddhist incarnation who was known as the 1st Javzandamba Khutagt (1635-1723) and also as Öndör Gegeen, (see item no. 222). He was famed as a sculptor in bronze and many works attributed to him may be seen in the museums of Ulaanbaatar. The author of this article also makes reference to other works of art in wood and engraved metal which are attributed to an unknown consort of Zanabazar. For illustrations of the work of Zanabazar see item no. 414.

413   **Some portraits of the First Jebtsundamba Qutugtu.**
Charles Roskelly Bawden.   *Zentralasiatische Studien*, vol. 4 (1970), p. 183-99. bibliog.
A brief description of eight portraits of Zanabazar, the First Javzandamba Khutagt, (1635-23), (see items no. 222 and 412), with comments on ground and technique. Plates are provided, only one of which is in colour. The pictures are preserved at the Völkerkunde Museum, Heidelberg, Germany.

414   **Vydayushchiisya mongol'skii skul'ptor G. Dzanabadzar; the eminent Mongolian sculptor – G. Zanabazar; G. Zanabazar eminent sculpteur mongol; G. Zanabazar, destacado escultor de Mongolia.**
N. Tsültem.   Ulaanbaatar: State Publishing House, 1982. 126p.
This book contains a brief introduction in Russian, English, French and Spanish to the sculpture of Zanabazar, 1st Javzandamba Khutagt, a Mongolian Living Buddha, (1635-1723), (see items 222, 412-13). The main section comprises photographs, many of which are in colour, of bronzes sculpted by Zanabazar and also portraits of him and illustrations of objects associated with him. Many of the works depicted in the book are preserved in the Bogd Khan Palace Museum, the State Central Museum, the Choijin Lama Museum of Religion and the Fine Arts Museum in Ulaanbaatar. For a review of this book see item 410.

Die Mongolen. (The Mongols.)
See item no. 7.

Mongolian journey.
See item no. 16.

Rock 'art galleries' in Mongolia.
See item no. 70.

Life in a Khalkha steppe monastery.
See item no. 223.

Religion and ritual in society: lamaist Buddhism in late 19th-century Mongolia.
See item no. 228.

BNMA Ulsyn ardyn khuvtsas; narodny kostyum MNR; Volksdrachten der MVR; National costumes of the MPR.
See item no. 435.

Applied art and architecture

415   **L'architecture mongole ancienne.** (Old Mongolian architecture.)
Sarah Dars.   *Études Mongoles*, vol. 3 (1972), p. 159-223. map. bibliog.
This article in French describes Mongolian architecture from the 13th to the 15th century and is based on a Russian monograph published in 1958 by N. M. Shchepetil'nikov. The structures described include buildings in Kharkhorin (Karakorum) the imperial capital, *gers* (tents) mounted on carts and monasteries in Tibetan and Chinese styles. The development of a distinct style of Mongolian architecture is also discussed. Many black-and-white illustrations are provided and 750 monasteries in Khalkh Mongolia are located on a map.

416   **Arkhitektura Mongolii; Mongolian architecture; architecture de la Mongolie; la arquitectura de Mongolia.**
N. Tsültem.   Ulaanbaatar: State Publishing House, 1988. [n.p.].
A bound album of 200 photographs with a list of titles and a brief introduction to Mongolian styles of architecture in Russian, English, French and Spanish. The majority of structures illustrated are Buddhist monasteries and temples, but remains of Turkic settlements, tent structures and modern industrial and urban architecture are also included.

417   **The decorative art of Mongolia in relation to other aspects of traditional Mongol culture.**
Krystyna Chabros.   *Zentralasiatische Studien*, vol. 20 (1987),
p. 250-81.
A careful study of the formal characteristics and symbolism of the decoration of textiles, leather, wood and metal in the traditional domestic sphere in Mongolia. Black-and-white illustrations are provided. The author concludes that the character of decorative art is determined by the Mongols' view of the world.

147

The Arts. Applied art and architecture

418 **Dekorativno-prikladnoe iskusstvo Mongolii; Mongolian arts and crafts; arts artisanaux de la Mongolie; arte decorativo aplicado de Mongolia.**
N. Tsültem.   Ulaanbaatar: State Publishing House, 1987. 152p.
This attractively produced book is a collection of high quality coloured photographs of a range of Mongolian craftwork including metalwork, textiles, woodcarving, domestic and religious objects. A brief account of Mongolian arts and crafts is provided in Russian, English, French and Spanish. Many of the objects illustrated are preserved in the State Central and other museums in Ulaanbaatar. For a review of this book see item no. 410.

419 **Erdeni-zuu, un monastère de XVI siècle en Mongolie.** (Erdene Zuu: a sixteenth century monastery in Mongolia.)
Egly Alexandre.   *Études Mongoles*, vol. 10 (1979), p. 7-33.
The monastery of Erdene Zuu was built in 1586 on the site of the Mongol imperial capital Kharkhorin (Karakorum) in Övörkhangai *aimag* and it was the first Buddhist monastery to be built in Khalkh Mongolia. After the destruction of Mongolian Buddhism in the 1930s, Erdene Zuu became a museum in 1941 but it was reopened for religious purposes in 1990. This article in French describes the architecture of the temples of Erdene Zuu and examines the religious and political role of this monastery in the history of the Khalkh Mongols. Twenty-nine photographs are included.

420 **Quilted ornamentation on Mongol felts.**
Krystyna Chabros.   *Central Asiatic Journal*, vol. 33, no. 1-2 (1988), p. 34-60. bibliog.
In Mongolia felt is used as a covering for *gers* (tents), and also for rugs, sleeping mats, socks and camel saddles. For at least 2,000 years the craft of quilting has been practiced in this region to stabilize the felt and also to decorate it. The author of this article examines materials and methods used when making felt and the non-representative designs with which it is decorated. The article is illustrated with thirteen black-and-white photographs and drawings.

Religion and ritual in society: Lamaist Buddhism late 19th-century Mongolia.
See item no. 228.

Mongol jewellery: researches on the silver jewellery collected on the first and second Danish Central Asian expeditions under the leadership of Henning Haslund-Christensen 1936-37 and 1938-39.
See item no. 444.

Music and dance

421 **Lamaistische Tanzmasken: der Erlik-Tsam in der Mongolei.** (Lamaist
dance masks: the Erlik Tsam in Mongolia.)
Werner Forman, Byambyn Rinchen, translated by Olga Kuthanová.
Leipzig, Germany: Koehler & Amelang, 1967. 143p.

Rinchen, a Mongolian scholar, describes the Buddhist *Tsam* dances which were last
performed in their entirety in a monastic context in Ulaanbaatar in 1937. The *Tsam* is a
masked pantomime dance performance and the Erlik *Tsam* portrays the story of Erlik
Khan, the God of Death. The author gives a brief account of the history of the *Tsam* in
general and tells the story of the Erlik *Tsam* in particular, with a description of its
characters, masks and costumes. The text of the book is in German but those who
cannot read this language may still enjoy the book's many coloured illustrations
depicting masks and costumes. The originals are preserved in various museums of
Ulaanbaatar.

422 **The music of the Mongols: an introduction.**
Pentti Aalto. In: *Aspects of altaic civilization: proceedings of the fifth
meeting of the Permanent International Altaistic Conference held at
Indiana University, June 4-9, 1962.* Edited by Denis Sinor.
Bloomington, Indiana: Indiana University Press, 1963, p. 59-65.
Reprinted ed. (Uralic and Altaic Studies vol. 23).

In this paper the author briefly describes the musical instruments used in the religious
rituals and services of shamanism and Buddhism in Mongolia. He also comments on
the characteristics of melodies and on the printed and recorded music of the Mongols,
both instrumental and vocal. The article will appeal to readers who want an overview
of the traditional music of the Mongols.

423 **The music of the Mongols. Part 1 Eastern Mongolia.**
Translations of lyrics by Kaare Grønbech, transcription of music by
Ernst Emsheimer, preface by Sven Hedin, compiled by Henning
Haslund-Christiansen. New York: Da Capo, 1971. 100p. map.
bibliog. (Da Capo Press Music Reprint Series).

This is the only monograph available in English on Mongolian music and it has been
reprinted from the original 1943 edition published in Stockholm. Much of the material
for the study was collected by H. Haslund-Christiansen in Inner Mongolia, 1928-32,
when he was a member of Sven Hedin's Sino-Swedish expedition. Examples of the
music of different groups of Mongols are discussed and there are ninety-seven
additional pages of specimen music for voice, voice and instrument and solo
instrument. Photographs of some of the instruments are included.

424 **The morienhur: a Mongolian fiddle.**
Jean Lynn Jenkins. *Man*, vol. 60, no. 179 (Sept. 1960), p. 129-30.

This article provides a brief description of the *morinkhuur*, the Mongolian horse-
headed fiddle which has a trapezoidal body and two strings. The author comments on
its use as a solo instrument and also for accompanying the voice, and tells the legend of
its origin. A carefully executed painting of the instrument is reproduced.

425 **A propòs de 'Musique populaire mongole' enregistrements de Lajos Vargyas.** (On the traditional music of the Mongols recorded by Lajos Vargyas).
Roberte Hamayon, Mireille Helffer. *Études Mongoles*, vol. 4 (1973), p. 145-80.

A good introduction in French to Mongolian folk music, sung and instrumental, as featured on two gramophone records issued by Hungaroton (LPX 18013-14) in cooperation with Unesco. There are descriptions of the various song genres, vocal techniques and of the *morinkhuur* or horse-headed fiddle (see also item no. 427) which is used to accompany singing and also as a solo instrument. Texts of seven of the songs featured on the recordings are provided in romanization and French translation with explanatory notes.

426 **Performing styles in Mongolian chant.**
Lajos Vargyas. *Journal of the International Folk Music Council*, vol. 20 (1968), p. 70-72.

The author gives a brief description of the techniques of two forms of Mongolian singing. One is the long song which is characterized by rubato, long sustained notes and a wide vocal range. The other is *khöömii* or overtone singing.

Life in a Khalkh steppe monastery.
See item no. 223.

Marriage customs of certain Chahar banners.
See item no. 434.

Theatre, opera and film

427 **Fiftieth anniversary of Mongolian cinema art.**
Mongolia, no. 5 (86) (1985), p. 2-11.

Mongolia's first film documentary was made in 1936 and the first feature film in 1938. This illustrated feature for a popular, English-speaking audience traces the development of film making in Mongolia and also includes articles on the Mongolian film actress Ya. Oyuuntsetseg and actor Ts. Tsegmid.

428 **Long journey of the newlyborn theatre.**
Erdenebatyn Oyuun. *Mongolia*, no. 2(35) (1977), p. 12-19, 30.

The author of this article has had a long and varied career as a writer, actress, critic and director of the State Drama Theatre. Writing here for a popular audience she surveys the Mongolian theatre tradition under socialism, tracing its development from pre-revolutionary forms of performing arts such as storytelling, song and dance. Theatres, performers and repertoire are also featured in the article.

429 **The Mongolian film industry.**
Michael Raymond Underdown. *Canada-Mongolia Review*, vol. 2, no. 1 (1976), p. 47-50.

A Mongolian monograph *Mongolkino delgetsnees* 'From the Mongolian cinema screen' gives details of fifty-five feature films made in Mongolia between 1936 and 1970 and information on film actors and crew. This short survey of film-making in Mongolia is an abstract of that publication. Although many more documentaries than feature films were made in the same period, these are not covered here.

430 **The three sorrowing hills, Mongolia's first opera: an examination of literary and musical genre.**
Winston Wu. In: *Studies on Mongolia: proceedings of the first North American conference on Mongolian studies*. Edited by Henry Guenter Schwarz. Bellingham, Washington: Western Washington University Press, 1979, p. 41-52.

An article on the development of Mongolian opera which uses traditional styles of Mongolian poetry and music. The first Mongolian operatic work was 'The three sorrowing hills' or 'The three fateful hills'. The original libretto was written by the poet D. Natsagdorj (see item no. 391) and the music was composed by B. Damdinsüren and others. The story is set in pre-revolutionary Mongolia. It tells of a wicked prince who tricks a beautiful girl into marrying him, and of the girl and her true love who eventually die. For a translated version of Natsagdorj's text see item no. 398.

History of the Mongolian People's Republic.
See item no. 134.

Outer Mongolia: from feudal society to socialist culture.
See item no. 405.

A lost civilization: the Mongols rediscovered.
See item no. 461.

Folklore and festivals

431 **The feast custom of the Boržigin.**
Sandagsürengiin Badamkhatan, translated by Andrea Nixon. *Journal of the Anglo-Mongolian Society*, vol. 5, no. 1 (July. 1979), p. 31-42.

A Mongolian ethnologist discusses the feasts that mark significant events in the life of a family or the first milking of a mare in spring. He describes the rituals of food, music and song that are still observed in the former Borjigiin banner (administrative district) which straddles parts of the contemporary Dornogov', Dundgov' and Central *aimags* (provinces). The article first appeared in Mongolian in *Studia Mongolica* (*Tom. IV, fasc. 1*).

432 **Fêtes et commémorations en République Populaire de Mongolie: apport à l'étude de la propaganda éducative en pays socialiste.** (Festivals and anniversaries in the Mongolian People's Republic: contributions to the study of educative propaganda in a socialist country.)
Françoise Aubin. *Revue Française de Science Politique*, vol. 23, (1974), p. 33-55.

A critical study in French of the principle and ritual of socialist anniversaries and celebrations in Mongolia, in the context of political propaganda, centralized economic planning and socialist emulation. The author also discusses the cultural and recreational aspects of such events. A list of the national and international socialist anniversaries that are marked in Mongolia is included.

433 **Marriage customs of a Khorchin village.**
Kuo-yi Pao. *Central Asiatic Journal*, vol. 9, no. 1 (March 1964), p. 29-59. map. bibliog.

The author describes marriage and wedding feasts in his native village of Bayin Man in eastern Inner Mongolia. He provides data similar to that given on Chakhar marriage in item no. 434 and he concludes with remarks on how the migration of many young people to the cities during the Japanese occupation of 1931-45 affected marriage customs. For other social studies of Bayin Man village see items no. 154, 230-31.

434 **Marriage customs of certain Chahar banners.**
J. Tömörtseren, translated from Khalkha-Mongolian and annotated by John Gombojab Hangin. *Mongolian Studies*, vol. 2 (1975), p. 41-91.

A detailed account of marriage practices among the Chakhar Mongols of Inner Mongolia which the author believes are derived from ancient Mongolian marriage customs. He describes how marriage partners are selected, the ritual of proposal, the wedding ceremony and its various participants, bridal attire and the aftermath of the wedding. Texts of some of the songs traditionally sung at weddings are given in romanization and many endnotes are provided.

Mongolia's culture and society.
See item no. 13.

Among the Mongols.
See item no. 25.

Mongolia: coming to terms with family legislation.
See item no. 234.

The house of weddings.
See item no. 344.

Tanzmasken: der Erlik-Tsam in der Mongolei. (Lamaist dance masks: the Erlik-Tsam in Mongolia.)
See item no. 421.

Customs and costumes

435 **BNMA Ulsyn ardyn khuvtsas; narodny kostyum MNR; Volksdrachten der MVR; national costumes of the MPR.**
Ulaanbaatar: State Publishing House, 1967. [n.p.].

The 20th century Mongolian artist Ü. Yadamsüren produced a series of watercolour studies illustrating the traditional garments and personal objects which are worn by the Khalkh, Buryat and Oirat Mongols and the Mongols of Inner Mongolia. This collection is available in reproduction on 100 folios in a board wrapper together with an explanatory booklet in Mongolian, Russian, English and German and a list of the items illustrated.

436 **Customary ways of measuring time and time periods in Mongolia.**
Ch. Luvsanjav. *Journal of the Anglo-Mongolian Society*, vol. 1, no. 1 (May 1974), p. 8-16.

A Mongolian scholar explains how the time of day can be measured by the way the sun falls into a *ger* (tent), or out-of-doors from its relation to the landscape. The hours of the night are measured by the moon and the seasons of the year may be defined by the activities of man or beast. Luvsanjav also provides the Mongolian terms for telling time in this way.

437 **Feltmaking in Mongolia.**
András Róna-Tas. *Acta Orientalia (Budapest)*, vol. 16, no. 2 (1963), p. 199-215.

Feltmaking is a traditional activity in herdsmen's camps and much of the finished product is used to cover the *ger* (tent). The author of this article studied the feltmaking methods of Khalkh Mongols. He carefully describes the various stages of the operation and illustrates each one with photographs and sketches. He also compares the Khalkh methods with those of the Khoton, a group of mongolized Turks who live in Uvs *aimag*. For the quilting of felt see item no. 420.

438 **Horse brands of the Mongolians: a system of signs in a nomadic culture.**
Caroline Humphrey. *American Ethnologist*, vol. 1 no. 3 (Aug. 1974), p. 471-88. bibliog.

Horse brands, (*tamga*), indicate ownership of private horse herds and convey information about the owner and his status within the family and society. These concepts are explained in this article with illustrations of seventy different brands and comments on the symbolism and mystical powers of the designs.

439 **Hospitality and customs.**
Byambyn Rinchen. In: *Mongolia today: a traveller's guide: geography, nature, hunting, museums, monuments, customs, tourism.* Edited by
Henry Field. Miami, Florida: Field Research Projects, 1978, p. 59-61.

Academician Rinchen explains how a guest is received in a Mongolia *ger* and the correct way to respond.

440 **Mongol costumes – historical and recent.**
Schuyler Cammann. In: *Aspects of Altaic civilization: proceedings of the fifth meeting of the Permanent International Altaistic Conference held at Indiana University, June 4-9, 1962.* Edited by Denis Sinor.
Bloomington, Indiana: Indiana University Press, 1963, p. 157-66.
(Uralic and Altaic Studies vol. 23).

A concise account of male and female dress during the Mongol Empire (1206-1368) and in the 19th century, with remarks on external influences on Mongolian garments. The author also adds comment and criticisms of some of the statements made on Mongolian costumes and jewellery in items no. 441 and no. 444.

441 **Mongol costumes: researches on the garments collected by the first and second Danish Central Asian expedition under the leadership of Henning Haslund-Christensen, 1936-37 and 1938-39.**
Henny Harald Hansen. Copenhagen: Nordisk Forlag, 1950. 199p.
(Nationalmuseets skrifter Etnografiskrække, no. 3).

Henning Haslund-Christensen collected many items of clothing which are now in the National Museum in Copenhagen. They were carefully examined and analysed and their structure, materials, style and ornamentation are described in this book. Among the costumes are male and female body garments, hats and footwear, the attire of lamas and shamans, and wrestlers' costumes. The author has drawn on statements of earlier European writers in his analysis and some of his conclusions are criticized by S. Cammann in item no. 440.

442 **Protocole manuel.** (Manual etiquette.)
Roberte Hamayon. *Études mongoles et sibériennes*, vol. 2 (1971),
p. 145-205. bibliog.

The author of this article has analysed forty-one manual gestures which she observed in common use among the Mongols. She discusses the contexts in which they are performed, accompanying words and meanings, and popular attitudes towards the gestures. A collection of thirty-five proverbs and eleven riddles which refer to arms and hands is appended.

443 **Some notes on the role of dogs in the life of the Mongolian herdsman.**
Caroline Humphrey. *Journal of the Anglo-Mongolian Society*, vol. 3,
no. 2 (Dec. 1976), p. 14-23.

Mongolian herdsmen recognize three types of dogs, those which protect the herds, hunting dogs and pet dogs. This article describes the distinguishing features of each type, their treatment and training, popular attitudes to dogs and beliefs about dogs.

154

The author has also collected a number of expressions referring to dogs, for example, an unreliable person is called *nokhoi khün* 'a dog-like man'.

444   **Mongol jewellery: researches on the silver jewellery collected on the first and second Danish Central Asian expeditions under the leadership of Henning Haslund-Christensen 1936-37 and 1938-39.**
Martha Boyer.   Copenhagen: Gyldendalske Boghandel, Nordisk Forlag, 1952. 223p. map. bibliog.
Many pieces of Mongolian jewellery were collected by the expeditions of the Danish Royal Geographical Society to Central Asia in the 1930s. Among them were neck, breast and ear ornaments, bracelets, rings, chatelaines and other decorated silver objects which were traditionally worn or carried by various groups of Mongols. This study examines the craftmanship and motifs of the objects and attempts to fit them into a cultural and historical context. Methods of hairdressing are also mentioned. The book is well illustrated with drawings and black-and-white photographs. For some criticisms of this study see item no. 440.

Larson, Duke of Mongolia.
See item no. 5.

Mongolia's culture and society.
See item no. 13.

Among the Mongols.
See item no. 25.

More about the Mongols.
See item no. 34.

Inside a Mongolian tent.
See item no. 232.

Mongolia.
See item no. 467.

Sports and Recreation

445   **Analys formelle et classification des jeux de calculs mongols.** (Formal
       analysis and classification of Mongolian board games.)
       Assia Popova. *Études Mongoles*, vol. 5, (1974), p. 7-60. bibliog.

This is a scholarly study of the many board games played in Mongolia and is based on
information given in a Mongolian publication of 1963-66 by Namjildorj. Popova
describes some of the games, the techniques of play, and the boards and counters, in
the context of traditional Mongolian society and economy. Strategies of play are drawn
from activities such as herding, hunting and from the structure of the Mongolian *ger*
(tent).

446   **Hsia.**
       Steffan Skallsjö. *Ethnos*, vol. 17, nos. 1-4 (1952), p. 15-23.

This article explains how a number of games may be played with the knucklebones of
sheep. Some of these are similar to English jacks or five stones and others resemble
dice games. The author explains the techniques of play and says which games are
traditionally played out-of-doors and which indoors. See also item no. 447.

447   **Games with bones: a note on nomenclature.**
       Michael J. Chapman. *Journal of the Anglo-Mongolian Society*, vol. 7,
       no. 1 (Dec. 1981), p. 85-91.

The author discusses the games Mongols play with various small bones of animals,
especially the knucklebones. He describes some of the bones used, gives the
Mongolian anatomical terms and suggests which surfaces are most likely to land
uppermost when the bones are thrown. See also item no. 446.

448   **Les jeux de calculs des Mongols.** (Board games of the Mongols.)
Namtcha Bassanoff.   *Études Mongoles*, vol. 5, (1974), p. 61-66.
bibliog.

Like item no. 445 this study of board games is based on the Mongolian study by
Namjildorj (1963-66). The games are based on aspects of the nomadic life such as
herding, hunting and the *ger* (tent). The author also discusses the role of such games in
Mongolian traditional society.

449   **The Mongolian game of Norobo or Cindi.**
Georg Söderbom.   *Ethnos*, vol. 15, nos. 1-2 (1950), p. 95-100.

This author learned the game of Norobo in Inner Mongolia where it is enjoyed by
young and old people. This game is a variety of checkers or draughts, played with
fifteen sets of counters with four to a set. Instructions on how to play, illustrations of
the checkers and their names in Mongolian are given in this article.

450   **Mongolian national games.**
R. Galindev, translated from the Russian by Aline B. Werth.
Cultures, vol. 6, no. 4 (1979), p. 165-69.

This brief but informative article describes the 'three manly sports' of archery,
horseracing and wrestling which are performed at traditional Mongolian festivals,
especially the Naadam which marks Mongolian independence each July. The author
gives details of the rituals, costumes, equipment and numbers of contestants taking
part in the three sports.

451   **National sports.**
O. Namnandorj, G. Amar.   Ulaanbaatar: Mongolian Committee of
Physical Culture and Sports, 1971. 16p.

This information booklet for English readers describes the Mongolian 'three manly
sports' of wrestling, horseracing and archery, with details of their history, equipment,
techniques and contests. There is also brief mention of the various modern games and
sports that are popular in Mongolia, including field, team and winter sports, and chess.

Information Mongolia.
See item no. 3.

Mongolia's culture and society.
See item no. 13.

Libraries, Art
Galleries and
Museums

452 **Catalogue of Mongol books, manuscripts and xylographs in the Royal Library Copenhagen.**
Walther Heissig, assisted by Charles Roskelly Bawden.   Copenhagen: Royal Library, 1977. 305p.

The 568 Mongolian manuscripts, xylographs (block prints) and other documents in the Royal Library, Copenhagen, make up the most important collection of Mongolian materials in Europe. They were collected by the Second Central Asia Expedition of the Danish Royal Geographical Society led by Henning Haslund-Christensen as described in item no. 461. The documents are listed in twenty-six subject categories with a brief description.

453 **Catalogue of the Mongol-Manchu section of the Toyo Bunko.**
Nicholas Poppe, Leon Hurvitz, Hidehiro Okada.   Tokyo: Toyo Bunko; Washington, DC: University of Washington Press, 1964. 387p. bibliog.

This catalogue lists works written wholly or in part in Mongolian and held in the Toyo Bunko library in Tokyo. The citations are arranged according to subject and identified as manuscript or xylograph (blockprint). Titles and colophons are given in Mongolian with English translation together with other pertinent information. An index of titles in romanization and an index of Chinese and Japanese titles in characters are provided.

454 **A description of the Mongolian manuscripts and xylographs in Washington, D.C.**
David M. Farquhar. *Central Asiatic Journal*, vol. 1, no. 3, (1955), p. 161-218.
The collection described in this article comprises seventy-three items most of which are xylographs (blockprints). They have been acquired from a variety of sources and include Buddhist canonical works, philosophy, history, biography, literature and didactic texts. This article was also issued as an offprint in London in 1955.

455 **A first description of a collection of Mongol manuscripts in the University Library, Cambridge.**
Charles Roskelly Bawden. *Journal of the Royal Asiatic Society*, nos. 3-4, (1957), p. 150-60
A catalogue of thirty-four texts in 389 folios giving the title of each text, a brief description of the manuscript and the colophon. Most of the texts cited contain descriptions of Buddhist rituals and were once the property of a son of the Manchu emperor Kangxi (r. 1661-1727). A further ten texts belonging to the same prince are housed in Aberdeen University Library, Scotland, and have been described by Bawden in the *Journal of the Royal Asiatic Society* (no. 1 (1973), p. 43-45).

456 **Mongolian publications at Western Washington University.**
Henry Guenter Schwarz. Bellingham, Washington: Western Washington University Press, 1984. 371p.
The Wilson Library of Western Washington University has been collecting publications in Mongolian since 1978 when the University's Center for East Asian Studies established a Mongolian studies programme. This catalogue lists 2,123 items published in Mongolia, the USSR and Inner Mongolia, most of which are articles from serial publications. The citations are listed alphabetically by author and coded to indicate the subject of each publication.

457 **The Mongol manuscripts and xylographs of the Belgian Scheut Mission.**
Walther Heissig. *Central Asiatic Journal*, vol. 3, no. 3 (1957), p. 161-89.
The Catholic Fathers of the Immaculate Heart Mission (CICM) opened a mission among the Chakhar Mongols of Inner Mongolia in 1865. The fifty-one Mongolian manuscripts they acquired are now preserved in the library of the University of Louvain, Belgium. This catalogue lists the title and date of each item with a brief description. The texts include Buddhist canonical and ritual works, stories, epics and works of Catholic instruction.

458 **Günjiin süm: the monastery of the princess.**
Tsendiin Damdinsüren, translated by Larry Moses. *Mongolia Society Bulletin*, vol. 9, no. 2 (fall 1970), p. 15-30.
Günjiin süm, 100 km. from Ulaanbaatar, is the tomb of an 18th century Manchu princess who married a Mongolian prince. The site was excavated in 1949 by the Mongolian Committee of Sciences and then reconstructed. The author gives an account of these activities and describes the building and the objects found. The tomb has a Manchu inscription which is reproduced in the article.

Libraries, Art Galleries and Museums

459 **Museums of Mongolia.**
Yondongiin Dorjsüren. In: *Mongolia today: a traveller's guide*:
geography, nature, hunting, museums, monuments, customs, tourism.
Edited by Henry Field. Miami, Florida: Field Research Projects,
1978, p. 35-50.

A survey of the national museums of Mongolia and their holdings. These include the Museum of Revolution (now closed), the Fine Arts Museum, the Palace of the Bogd Khan (the Eighth Javzandamba Khutagt who ruled Mongolia from 1911 to 1924) and the State Library all of which are in Ulaanbaatar; the Museum of Revolution in Altan Bulag and the 17th century monastery of Erdene Zuu (see item no. 419) in Övörkhangai *aimag* (province). This article has been translated from Mongolian.

460 **Notes on the collection of Mongolian books in the Ethnographical Museum of Sweden, Stockholm.**
Pentti Aalto. *Ethnos*, vol. 15, nos. 1-2 (1950), p. 1-14.

The Ethnographical Museum in Stockholm holds 121 Mongolian books which were collected by expeditions to Central Asia led by Sven Hedin in 1893-97 and 1927-35. Many are Buddhist works of a religious, scientific or literary nature which have been translated into Mongolian from Sanskrit or Tibetan. This article gives a short account of the collection.

The new Mongolia.
See item no. 36.

Petitions of grievances submitted by the people (18th-beginning of 20th century).
See item no. 117.

Mongol'skaya natsional'naya zhivopis' 'Mongol zurag'; development of the Mongolian style of painting 'Mongol zurag'; bref apperçu sur le developpement de la peinture mongole 'mongol zourag'; breve ensayo sobre el desarrollo de la pintura mongola 'mongol zurag'.
See item no. 408.

Vydayushchiisya mongol'skii skul'ptor G. Dzanabadzar; the eminent Mongolian sculptor – G. Zanabazar; G. Zanabazar eminent sculpteur mongol; G. Zanabazar, destacado escultor de Mongolia.
See item no. 414.

Dekorativno-prikladnoe iskusstvo Mongolii; mongolian arts and crafts; arts artisanaux de la Mongolie; arte decorativo aplicado de Mongolia.
See item no. 418.

Erdeni-zuu, un monastère de XVI siècle en Mongolie. (Erdene Zuu: a 16th century monastery in Mongolia.)
See item no. 419.

Lamaistische Tanzmasken: der Erlik-Tsam in der Mongolei. (Lamaist dance masks: the Erlik Tsam in Mongolia).
See item no. 421.

The Mongolian documents in the Musée de Teheran.
See item no. 463.

The world of learning 1992.
See item no. 482.

Books

461 **A lost civilization: the Mongols rediscovered.**
Walther Heissig, translated from the German by D. J. S. Thomson.
London: Thames & Hudson, 1966. 271p. map. bibliog.

A German Mongolist has written this very entertaining book for a general audience. It tells how he and others, including members of some of the European Asiatic expeditions undertaken before the Second World War, searched for rare Mongolian written records. Among the finds were inscribed stele, historical and religious chronicles, 19th century novels, maps and a copy of the early 20th century Mongolian drama, the *Moon cuckoo*. As the author describes how these records were discovered the history, life and culture of the Mongols also unfold. This book was first published in German in 1964.

462 **The Mongol chronicles of the seventeenth century.**
Tseveen Zhamtsarano, translated by Rudolf Loewenthal. Wiesbaden, Germany: Harrassowitz, 1955. 93p. (Göttinger Asiatische Forschungen Band 3).

The Oriental Institute of St. Petersburg, Russia, holds about 200 Mongolian manuscripts, several of which are copies of chronicles and legends of the Mongol khans. In this monograph a Buryat Mongol scholar, who was himself an avid literary collector, discusses the provenance of copies of four texts preserved by the Institute with remarks on the physical appearance, linguistic features and content. The *Erdeniyin Tobchi* 'Precious Summary' composed in 1662, *Altan Tobchi* 'Golden Summary' (see item no. 74) of ca. 1655 preserve the history and legends of the Mongol khans. The *Chagan Teüke* 'White History' is a 13th century work of history and political thought, and the *Shara Tuguji* 'Yellow Narrative' a history with genealogies. This monograph was first published in Russian in 1936.

463   **The Mongolian documents in the Musée de Teheran.**
      Francis Woodman Cleaves.   *Harvard Journal of Asiatic Studies*,
      vol. 16 (1953), p. 1-107.

This is a detailed study of eight Mongolian chancery documents from the Middle Ages
which are preserved in the Teheran Museum, Iran. Three of the texts concern
domestic affairs and five foreign affairs. The author discusses the physical condition of
the documents, their material disposition, spelling and punctuation. He also provides
transcripts in romanization with English translations.

Mongolian historical literature of the XVII-XIX centuries written in Tibetan.
See item no. 374.

Skizze der mongolischen Literatur. (An outline of Mongolian literature).
See item no. 375.

Mass Media

464   Bibliographical survey of Mongolian periodical publications.
   John R. Krueger.   *Ural-Altaische Jahrbücher*, vol. 35, fasc. B (1963),
   p. 220-28.

A brief introduction to the Mongolian press and printing shops in the 1920s and 1930s
and a list of approximately seventy-five titles of periodicals with dates of publication if
known. Buryat and Inner Mongolian publications are included on the list.

465   Far Eastern Economic Review.
   Hong Kong: Far Eastern Economic Review, 1946-. weekly.

This publication carries articles on Mongolian current affairs and the economy from
time to time, with occasional larger features. From 1972 many of the contributions on
Mongolia were written by A. J. K. Sanders. Such articles are easily located in the
annual index.

466   US Joint Publications Research Service: East Asia: Mongolia.
   Washington, DC: Foreign Broadcasting Information Service, 1961-.
   irregular.

This publication was first subtitled *Translations on Mongolia*, (1961-79) and then
Mongolia Report (1979-88). It contains English translations of articles mainly from the
Mongolian newspaper and periodical press and occasionally from other sources. These
are valuable sources of information on Mongolia especially for the 1960s and 1970s
when other materials in English were not plentiful. A wide range of subjects is covered
including administration, party work, society, economic development, relations with
the Comecon countries, law, education, science and society. Lists of officials with brief
biographical information are a recurring feature. In the 1980s fewer articles from
professional periodicals were published and more attention was given to shorter news
reports, especially on foreign relations and the Sino-Soviet dispute. Few issues of this
publication have appeared since 1988.

467 **Mongolia.**
Ulaanbaatar: Montsame News Agency, 1971-1990. bimonthly.
An illustrated magazine for English speakers which superseded *Mongolia Today* (published from New Delhi from 1959-70). It carried brief articles on all aspects of contemporary Mongolian life, culture and society, including interviews with prominent figures and ordinary people, features on different regions and towns, translations of contemporary literature and features on the political issues of the day and economic development. Although the magazine was published for propaganda purposes it can be a useful source of information on contemporary Mongolian life if read with caution.

468 **Mongol Messenger.**
Ulaanbaatar: Montsame News Agency, 1991-. weekly.
An English language newspaper published by the official Mongolian news agency for foreign residents in Mongolia and English speakers abroad. It carries articles on all aspects of current affairs and presents a much more balanced view of the contemporary state and society than *Mongolia* (see item no. 470) to which it is effectively a successor. The *Mongol Messenger* is essential reading for anyone who wishes to keep up-to-date on events and trends in Mongolia.

469 **Mongolian People's Republic.**
D. Urjinbadam.   In: *Newspapers in Asia: contemporary trends and problems*. Edited by John A. Lent.   Hong Kong: Heinemann Asia, 1982. 597p.
Under the single-party system the Mongolian press was expected to popularize the policies and decisions of the Mongolian People's Revolutionary Party and the government. Here the Chairman of the Mongolian Union of Journalists provides a brief survey of the Mongolian socialist press from 1920. The editor of the book adds notes on circulation and frequency of publications where available.

470 **Summary of World Broadcasts Part Three: the Far East.**
Reading, England: British Broadcasting Corporation, Monitoring Service, 2nd series, 1967-. daily.
A 'listening service' reporting items of current affairs and economic, political and demographic data as broadcast on foreign radio services. Mongolia is covered frequently although not every day. Because the quality of reception varies there are sometimes gaps in the reports. A similar service is provided by the US government's *Foreign Broadcasting Information Service* (FBIS) and Mongolia is covered in its publication *Daily Report: East Asia*.

Area handbook for Mongolia.
See item no. 1.

Information Mongolia.
See item no. 3.

Mongolia: a country study.
See item no. 9.

Mass Media

History of the Mongolian People's Republic.
See item no. 134.

The Mongolian People's Republic, 1924-1928, and the Right Deviation.
See item no. 137.

Cultural policy in the Mongolian People's Republic: a study prepared under the Mongolian National Commission for Unesco.
See item no. 404.

Mongols of the Twentieth Century. Part Two: bibliography.
See item no. 487.

Professional
Periodicals

471 **Asian Survey.**
Berkeley, California: University of California Press, 1960-. monthly.
The January issue of this journal carries a review of the previous years' political events and economic trends in Mongolia. Other articles on Mongolia are published occasionally.

472 **Bulletin of the International Association of Mongolian Studies.**
Ulaanbaatar: International Association for Mongolian Studies, 1988-.
irregular.
This serial reviews international scholarship in Mongolian studies by publishing reports of conferences, bibliographical information and articles on the work of individual scholars and centres of Mongolian studies. Articles of scholarship are also accepted.

473 **Canada-Mongolia Review-La revue Canada-Mongolie.**
Saskatoon, Canada: University of Saskatchewan, Canada-Mongolia Society-Association Canada-Mongolie, 1975-80. irregular.
A short-lived society journal which published a range of articles on Mongolian studies for the general reader as well as the specialist. It also carried bibliographical information on Mongolia and Mongolian studies.

474 Central Asiatic Journal.
Wiesbaden, Germany; The Hague: Harrassowitz, 1955-. annual.

A scholarly publication which has frequently published articles on Mongolian history, linguistics and culture, in English, German and other European languages.

475 Études Mongoles et Sibériennes.
Nanterre, France: Centre de Documentation et d'Études Mongoles, University of Paris, 1970-. annual.

This journal was called *Études Mongoles* until 1976 (vol. 7) when it acquired its present title. It publishes articles on all aspects of Mongolian studies with particular emphasis on anthropology and ethnology. Many of its contributors have carried out fieldwork in Mongolia and speak Mongolian. Most of the articles are written in French but pieces in English and other languages have appeared from time to time.

476 Journal of the Anglo-Mongolian Society.
Cambridge, England: Anglo-Mongolian Society, 1974-1991. semi-annual.

This society journal published articles on Mongolian history, culture and society for the scholar, student or the general reader. From 1981 the two issues of each volume appeared under a single cover.

477 Mongolian Studies.
Bloomington, Indiana: Mongolia Society, 1974-. annual.

This journal has superseded *Mongolia Society Newsletter* (1962-64) and *Mongolia Society Bulletin* (1965-73). It publishes articles on a wide range of subjects aimed at scholars, students and the general reader. The Mongolia Society also publishes the *Mongolia Society Newsletter* containing news items, short, general articles on Mongolia, Inner Mongolia, and Mongol-US relations, and bibliographical information.

478 Mongolica: an international annual of Mongol studies.
Ulaanbaatar: International Association for Mongol Studies, 1990-. annual.

An international publication carrying scholarly articles in Mongolian, English and Russian. The first issue was devoted to articles on the *Secret History of the Mongols* (see item no. 84) to mark the 750th anniversary of this chronicle.

479 Zentralasiatische Studien.
Wiesbaden, Germany: Harrassowitz, 1967-. annual.

Articles on Mongolia in German, English, French and occasionally Russian and Mongolian appear frequently in this journal. The subjects covered include history, linguistics, textual studies and socio-political topics. The journal is intended primarily for the specialist scholar but many of the articles would appeal to a wider audience too.

Bibliographical survey of Mongolian periodical publications.
See item no. 464.

Bibliography of Asian Studies.
See item no. 484.

Bibliotheca Mongolica.
See item no. 485.

Mongols of the twentieth century. Part II: bibliography.
See item no. 487.

Encyclopaedias and Directories

480 **Asia 1992 yearbook.**
Hong Kong: Far Eastern Economic Review, 1991. 216p.
The most recent issue of a yearbook which provides an annual survey of major events and trends in Mongolia together with a map and economic indicators. The information is updated annually.

481 **The Far East and Australasia 1992.**
London: Europa, 1991. 23rd ed. 1161p. bibliog.
This annual, formerly published under the title *The Europa yearbook: the Far East and Australasia*, contains a concise annual survey of events and trends in Mongolia. Also included are social and economic statistics abstracted from international agency sources, a directory of Mongolian state and public organizations with addresses and telephone numbers, and a bibliography. The information is updated annually.

482 **The world of learning 1992.**
London: Europa, 1991. 42nd ed. 2021p.
The higher educational institutes, libraries and museums with addresses and telephone numbers, if known, and other brief information are given in this yearbook. The institutions are listed by country and a section on Mongolia is included.

483 **Yearbook on international communist affairs 1991: parties and revolutionary movements.**
Edited by Richard F. Staar.   Stanford, California: Hoover Institution Press, 1991. 25th ed. 1991p.
An annual publication supplying data and information on ruling political parties of the communist world with a profile of the political trends in each country for the year in question and biographical sketches of party, state and government heads. W. R. Heaton contributed the section on the Mongolian People's Revolutionary Party in the 25th edition and R. A. Rupen was also a contributor for several years.

Bibliographies

484 **Bibliography of Asian Studies.**
New York: Association for Asian Studies, 1969-. annual.
This serial publication has a section devoted to Mongolia. It lists both monographs and articles from collections and serials in a range of languages, including Russian and Mongolian, although coverage is not comprehensive. Citations are arranged under broad subject classifications. Unfortunately there is considerable delay between the publication of a work and its appearance in the bibliography. The most recent issue, containing works with a 1986 imprint, appeared in 1991. Before 1969, this bibliography was issued as an annual supplement to the *Journal of Asian Studies*.

485 **Bibliotheca Mongolica Part 1: works in English, French, and German.**
Henry Guenter Schwarz. Bellingham, Washington: Western Washington University, 1978. 355p. (Occasional Papers, no. 12).
An extensive bibliography on Mongolia and the Mongols listing 2,987 publications in western European languages, chiefly English. The citations are arranged according to subject, some with brief annotations, and there is an index of authors. A list of periodicals that have published articles on Mongolia and the Mongols is also provided. Plans to publish two additional volumes citing works in Russian and in Chinese have been abandoned.

486 **La Mongolie intérieure et les Mongols de Chine: élements de bibliographie.** (Inner Mongolia and the Mongols of China: a selected bibliography.)
Françoise Aubin. *Études Mongoles*, vol. 3, (1972), p. 1-158.
This publication in French is the only bibliography on the Mongols and Mongol territories of China in a western language. It is classified and annotated and cites articles and monographs in European languages, Chinese and Japanese. It is selective and excludes, in particular, a large number of Chinese and Japanese works on the archaeology of Inner Mongolia. These may, however, be traced in the bibliographies listed.

171

487 **Mongols of the twentieth century. Part II: bibliography.**
Robert Arthur Rupen. Bloomington, Indiana: Indiana University
Press, 1964. 167p. map. bibliog. (Uralic and Altaic Series, vol. 37
Part II).

An alphabetical listing of 2,839 monographs, articles and periodicals on the Mongols of
Mongolia, Russia and China published between the late 19th century and the mid- 20th
century. Most of the works cited are in English or Russian but a few publications in
other western languages and in Mongolian, Chinese and Japanese are also included. A
list of Mongolian periodicals and a subject index are also provided. The companion
volume (Part I) is a history of the Mongols in the 20th century by the same author
which is cited as item no. 139.

488 **Outer Mongolia, 1911-1940: a bibliographical review.**
Thomas Esson Ewing. *Zentralasiatische Studien*, vol. 14, no. 2 (1980),
p. 205-19.

An evaluation of primary and secondary contemporary sources and modern studies on
Mongolia from 1911-40. The works referred to are in Mongolian, Russian and western
European languages.

489 **Works by Mongolian historians (1960-1974); trudy mongol'skikh
istorikov (1960-1974).**
Compiled by Ts. Ishdorj, D. Dorj, translated by Ts. Tsendsüren, edited
by Sh. Bira. Ulaanbaatar: MPR Academy of Sciences, 1975. 254p.

An annotated bibliography in English and Russian of books and articles by Mongolian
historians. Most of the works cited are written in Mongolian but a few are in Russian.

Area handbook for Mongolia.
See item no. 1.

Mongolia: a country study.
See item no. 9.

Mongolia: politics, economics and society.
See item no. 11.

Khubilai Khan: his life and times.
See item no. 87.

The Mongols.
See item no. 91.

The Daurs of China: an outline.
See item no. 161.

Some notes on the Mongols of Yunnan.
See item no. 170.

**How Mongolia is really ruled: a political history of the Mongolian People's
Republic, 1900-1978.**
See item no. 245.

Mongolian publications at Western Washington University.
See item no. 456.

Bibliographical survey of Mongolian periodical publications.
See item no. 464.

Bulletin of the International Association for Mongolian Studies.
See item no. 472.

Canada-Mongolia Review-La revue Canada-Mongolie.
See item no. 473.

Mongolian studies.
See item no. 477.

Index

The index is a single alphabetical sequence of authors (personal and corporate), titles of publications and subjects. Index entries refer to both the main items and to other works mentioned in the note to each item. Title entries are in italics. Numbers refer to bibliographic entries.

17, 72, 75, 137, 205, 209, 213, 218-229
after Second World War 12, 135, 218, 221, 229
destruction of 75, 134, 139, 219, 227
music 223, 422
Qing regulations 75, 111, 224-25,
see also Monasteries
Buell, P. D. 182
Bügd Nairamdakh Mongol Ard Uls: üdesnii atlas. (The Mongolian People's Republic: national atlas) 51
Bulletin of the International Association of Mongolian Studies (Ulaanbaatar) 472
Bulletin of the Museum of Natural History (New York) 35
Bulstrode, B. 38
Buriat grammar 191
Buriat reader 192
Buryat Mongols 149, 159, 163, 212, 237, 256
language 146, 191-92
religion 163, 211-12, 229
Butler, W. E. 186, 234, 267, 270, 273

C

Calender 207, 436
Cambridge history of early Inner Asia 76
Cambridge University Library 455
Camels 34
in literature 379
wild 57, 63, 64
Canada-Mongolia review-La revue Canada-Mongolie 473
Canada-Mongolia society-Association Canada-Mongolie 473
Carsow, M. 238
Case studies on human rights and fundamental
freedoms: a world survey 165
Catalogue of Mongol books, manuscripts and xylographs in the Royal Library Copenhagen 452
Catalogue of the Mongol-Manchu section of the Toyo Bunko 453
Catholic Fathers of the Immaculate Heart Mission 457
CEDAW 152
Census
see Population, Livestock
Central Asiatic Journal 474
Central Statistical Board 339, 341
see also State Statistical Office of the MPR
Chabros, K. 417, 420
Chagan Teüke 462
Chakhar Mongols 110, 233
see also History
Chambers, J. 81
Chaney, R. W. 35
Chang, C. H. 160
Chang, N. J. 160
Chapman, M. J. 379
Chen, J. X. 106
Cheney, G. A. 21
Chiang, K. S. 290
Child, G. S. 57
Children 143, 169, 230, 239
girls 155
literature for 400
Children's Fund of the MPR 239
Chimidtseren, E. 153
China and Inner Asia from 1368 to the present day 289
China's Inner Mongolia 160
Chinese agent in Mongolia 131
Ch'ing administration of Mongolia up to the nineteenth century 111
Chinggis Khan
biographies 72, 74, 82-84, 86, 89, 94, 96, 151
contemporary attitudes to 294
cult of 30, 205, 209
in literature 377, 387
Chingunjav 116
Choibalsan, Kh. 14, 132
Choijil, L. 157
Choijin Lama Museum 414
Christian missions 5, 25, 39, 88, 206, 210
Bible translation 210
Chuluun, O. 296
Chumichev, D. C. 297
CICM
see Catholic Fathers of the Immaculate Heart Mission
Cinema 405, 427, 429
Cleaves, F. W. 84, 207, 463
Climate
see Geography
CMEA
see Comecon
Coal 2, 309
Collectives
in the 1930s 134, 141
after Second World War 32, 134, 141, 315, 322-27
Comecon 9, 278, 299, 313-14, 466
coordinated planning 297
Comintern
see Communist International
Committee of Sciences MPR 15, 134, 458
Communist agriculture: farming in the Far East and Cuba 316
Communist armies in politics 283
Communist International 137
Communist strategies in Asia 293
Comparative study of postpositions in Mongolian dialects and the written language 172

Turks in Mongolia 66, 71, 76
Tuul river 66
Tuva
see Uriankhai

U

Udbal
see Udval
Udval, S. 150, 395
Uigurs 76
Ulaanbaatar
before 1921 33, 40, 113
after 1921 41-43, 129
map 41, 43
see also History
Ulaangom 31
Ulanfu
see Inner Mongolia
Uliastai 40, 48
Underdown, M. R. 114, 276, 429
Ünensechen, B.
see Pao, K. Y.
Unesco 156, 404
Unesco Mongolian National Commission 404
Ungern Sternberg, Baron 128
Unicef 143
United Nations 135
United Nations Committee of the Elimination of Discrimination Against Women 152
United Nations Permanent Commission of the Mongolian People's Republic 268, 279
Uriankhai (people)
see Darkhad
Uriankhai (region) 131
Urjinbadam, D. 469
US Foreign Broadcasting Information Service 470
Us Joint Publications Research Service, East Asia: Mongolia 466
Uvs *aimag* 208

V

Valliant, R. B. 263-64
Vargyas, L. 425-26
Vaurie, C. 61
Veenhoven, W. A. 165
Veit, V. 117, 126
Vernadsky, G. 92
Vertical zonality in the southern Khangai mountains (Mongolia) 369
Vietze, H.-P. 188-89, 199
Vladimircov
see Vladimirtsov
Vladimirtsov, B. Ya. 238
Vlček, E. 360
Völkekunde Museum (Heidelberg) 413
Von Cinggis Khan zur Sowjetrepublik: eine kurze Geschichte der Mongolei unter besonderer Berücksichtigung der neuesten Zeit (From Chinggis Khan to Soviet republic: a short history of Mongolia with special attention to the contemporary period 130
Vreeland, H. H. 3r 233
Vydayushchiisya mongol'skii skulp'tor G. Dzanabadzar; the eminent Mongolian sculptor – G. Zanabazar; G. Zanabazar eminent sculpteur mongol; G. Zanabazar, destacado escultor de Mongolia 414

W

Waddington, C. H.
see Humphrey, C.
Wädekin, K.-E. 316
Walford, N. 71

Walter, M. 377
Wapiti 44
Weideplätze der Mongolen im Reich der Chalcha (Mongol pastures in Khalkh) 40
Welch, H. 221
Werth, A. B. 405, 450
Western Washington University Library
see Wilson Library, Western Washington University
Wildmen
see Almas
Wilson Library, Western Washington University 456
With the Russians in Mongolia 129
Wolff, S. M. 354
Women 103, 137, 143, 150-58, 232
'Motherhood Glory' title 157
status 152-53, 156-57
traditional role of 154
see also History
Women's Committee 150, 156
Worden, R. L. 9
Works by Mongolian historians (1960-1975); trudy mongol'skikh istorikov (1960-1974) 489
World of learning 1992 482
Wörterbuch deutsch mongolisch (German Mongolian dictionary) 189
Wörterbuch mongolisch-deutsch (Mongolian-German dictionary) 188
Wu, W. 430

X

Xiang R. 166
Xiongnu 69, 71, 76
Xue, W. L.

Map of Mongolia

This map shows the more important towns and other features.

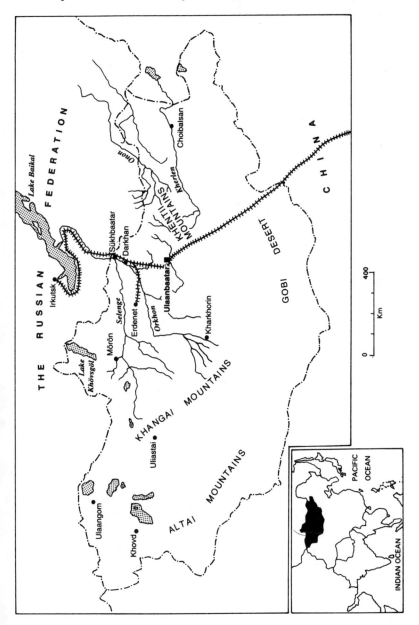